MCSE Test Success:
NT Server 4 in the
Enterprise

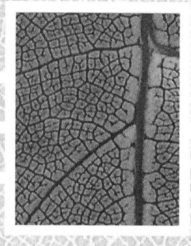

MCSE Test Success™: NT® Server 4 in the Enterprise

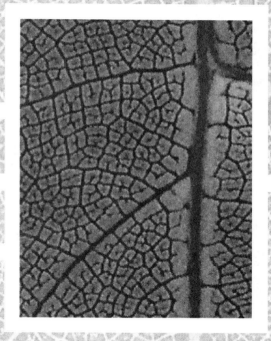

Lisa Donald

San Francisco • Paris • Düsseldorf • Soest

Associate Publisher: Guy Hart-Davis
Contracts and Licensing Manager: Kristine Plachy
Acquisitions & Developmental Editor: Bonnie Bills
Editor: Kathy Grider-Carlyle
Project Editor: Michael Tom
Technical Editor: Ron Reimann
Book Designers: Bill Gibson and Pat Dintino
Graphic Illustrator: Andrew Benzie
Electronic Publishing Specialist: Bill Gibson
Production Coordinator: Amy Eoff
Production Assistants: Beth Moynihan and Rebecca Rider
Indexer: Ted Laux
Cover Designer: Archer Design
Cover Illustrator/Photographer: FPG International

Screen reproductions produced with Collage Complete.

Collage Complete is a trademark of Inner Media Inc.

SYBEX, Network Press, and the Network Press logo are registered trademarks of SYBEX Inc.

Test Success is a trademark of SYBEX Inc.

TRADEMARKS: SYBEX has attempted throughout this book to distinguish proprietary trademarks from descriptive terms by following the capitalization style used by the manufacturer.

Microsoft® Internet Explorer ©1996 Microsoft Corporation. All rights reserved. Microsoft, the Microsoft Internet Explorer logo, Windows, Windows NT, and the Windows logo are either registered trademarks or trademarks of Microsoft Corporation in the United States and/or other countries.

The author and publisher have made their best efforts to prepare this book, and the content is based upon final release software whenever possible. Portions of the manuscript may be based upon pre-release versions supplied by software manufacturer(s). The author and the publisher make no representation or warranties of any kind with regard to the completeness or accuracy of the contents herein and accept no liability of any kind including but not limited to performance, merchantability, fitness for any particular purpose, or any losses or damages of any kind caused or alleged to be caused directly or indirectly from this book.

SYBEX is an independent entity from Microsoft Corporation, and not affiliated with Microsoft Corporation in any manner. This publication may be used in assisting students to prepare for a Microsoft Certified Professional Exam. Neither Microsoft Corporation, its designated review company, nor SYBEX warrants that use of this publication will ensure passing the relevant exam. Microsoft is either a registered trademark or trademark of Microsoft Corporation in the United States and/or other countries.

Library of Congress Card Number: 97-61722
ISBN: 0-7821-2147-0

Manufactured in the United States of America

10 9 8 7 6 5 4 3 2 1

For Terry Whinery and Lars Phillips.
Thanks for teaching me that I could do anything.

Acknowledgments

Working on this Test Success Guide has been great. I want to start by thanking Bonnie Bills of Sybex for involving me in this project. Between the Sybex *Study Guides* and the *Test Success* books, I am feeling very intimate with the MCSE exams. It's great to have a chance to share this information through these projects. Bonnie was great to work with and allowed me to do the job to the best of my ability.

I also want to thank Michael Tom, the project editor. Michael was amazingly organized, professional, and very easy to work with. Special thanks to Kathy Grider-Carlyle. She did a great job of editing this book and was a real pleasure to work with. Ron Reimann worked on this book as the technical editor. Thanks to Ron for his hard work and technical savvy. Ron surely impressed me with the thoroughness that he brought to the job.

The Sybex production team of Bill Gibson, Amy Eoff, and Andrew Benzie all did a great job. Thanks to everyone for their hard work.

Contents at a Glance

Table of Contents

Introduction

One of the greatest challenges facing corporate America is finding people who are qualified to manage corporate computer networks. One of the most common operating systems is Windows NT. As you already know, Windows NT is not a trivial operating system. It requires skill and knowledge to manage. Microsoft's certification program demonstrates to employers that someone with Microsoft certification is capable of managing complex NT networks. The most highly coveted certification is MCSE or Microsoft Certified Systems Engineer.

Why become an MCSE? The main benefit is to have much greater earning potential. MCSE carries high industry recognition. Certification can be your key to a new job, or a higher salary—or both.

So what's stopping you? If you're hesitating because you don't know what to expect from the tests or you are worried that you might not pass, then this book is for you.

Your Key to Passing Exam 70-068

This book provides you with the key to passing Exam 70-068, Implementing and Supporting Windows NT Server 4.0 in the Enterprise. Inside, you'll find all the information relevant to this exam, including information on some of the "picky" questions on less frequently used options, and hundreds of practice questions.

Understand the Exam Objectives

This book is structured according to the MCSE NT Server exam objectives. At-a-glance review sections and more than 400 review questions bolster your knowledge of the information relevant to each objective and the exam itself. You'll learn exactly what you need to know without wasting time on tangents not covered by the exam. This book prepares you for the *exam* in the shortest amount of time possible (although to be ready for the real world, you need to study the subject in greater depth and get a lot of hands-on practice).

Get Ready for the Real Thing

More than 200 sample test questions prepare you for the test-taking experience. These multiple-choice questions resemble actual exam questions—some are even more difficult than what you'll find on the exam. If you can pass the Sample Tests at the end of each unit and the Final Exam at the end of the book, you'll know you're ready.

Is This Book for You?

This book is intended for certification candidates who already have some experience with NT Server. It is especially well-suited for:

- Students using courseware or taking a course to prepare for the exam, and who need to supplement their study material with test-based practice questions.

- Network engineers who have worked with the product, but who still need to fill in some holes.

- Anyone who has studied for the exams—using self-study guides, computer-based training, on-the-job training, or classes—and wants to make sure that he or she is adequately prepared.

Understanding Microsoft Certification

Microsoft offers several levels of certification for anyone who has or is pursuing a career as a network professional working with Microsoft products:

- Microsoft Certified Professional (MCP)

- Microsoft Certified Systems Engineer (MCSE)

- Microsoft Certified Professional + Internet

- Microsoft Certified Systems Engineer + Internet

- Microsoft Certified Trainer (MCT)

The one you choose depends on your area of expertise and your career goals.

Microsoft Certified Professional (MCP)

This certification is for individuals with expertise in one specific area. MCP certification is often a stepping stone to MCSE certification. It allows you some benefits of Microsoft certification after just one exam.

By passing one core exam (meaning an operating system exam), you become an MCP.

Microsoft Certified Systems Engineer (MCSE)

This is the certification for network professionals. By becoming an MCSE you differentiate yourself from an MCP. This certification is similar to a college degree in that it shows that you can make a commitment to complete all of the steps required for certification and that you meet high standards in being able to successfully complete all of the required exams.

To become an MCSE, you must pass a series of six exams:

1. Networking Essentials (waived for Novell CNEs)

2. Implementing and Supporting Microsoft Windows NT Workstation 4.0 (or Windows 95)

3. Implementing and Supporting Microsoft Windows NT Server 4.0

4. Implementing and Supporting Microsoft Windows NT Server 4.0 in the Enterprise

5. Elective

6. Elective

The following list applies to the NT 4.0 track. Microsoft still supports a track for 3.51, but 4.0 certification is more desirable because it is the current operating system.

Some of the electives include:

- Internetworking with Microsoft TCP/IP on Microsoft Windows NT 4.0

- Implementing and Supporting Microsoft Internet Information Server 4.0

- Implementing and Supporting Microsoft Exchange Server 5.5

- Implementing and Supporting Microsoft SNA Server 4.0

- Implementing and Supporting Microsoft Systems Management Server 1.2

- Implementing a Database Design on Microsoft SQL Server 6.5

- System Administration for Microsoft SQL Server 6.5

Microsoft Certified Trainer (MCT)

As an MCT, you can deliver Microsoft certified courseware through official Microsoft channels.

The MCT certification is more costly, because in addition to passing the exams, it requires that you sit through the official Microsoft courses. You also have to submit an application that must be approved by Microsoft. The number of exams you must pass depends on the number of courses you want to teach.

For the most up-to-date certification information, visit Microsoft's Web site at www.microsoft.com/train_cert.

Understanding Microsoft's Exam Objectives

In order to help you prepare for certification exams, Microsoft specifies a list of exam objectives for each test. This book is based on the objectives.

For this exam, the objectives were designed to measure your ability to design, administer, and troubleshoot NT Server 4.0 when it is part of an enterprise network. In this case, an enterprise network is a network that spans a wide area network and consists of multiple domains.

Scheduling and Taking an Exam

Once you think you are ready to take an exam, call Prometric Testing Centers at (800) 755-EXAM (755-3926). They'll tell you where to find the closest testing center. Before you call, get out your credit card because each exam costs $100. (If you've used this book to prepare yourself thoroughly, chances are you'll only have to shell out that $100 once!)

You can schedule the exams for your convenience. The exams are downloaded from Prometric to the testing center, and you show up at your scheduled time and take the exam on a computer. Once you complete the exam, you will know right away whether you have passed or not. If you pass the exam, you don't need to do anything else—Prometric uploads the test results to Microsoft. If you don't pass, it's another $100 to schedule the exam again.

At the end of the exam, you will receive a score report. It will list the six areas you were tested on and how you performed. Each unit in this book corresponds to one of the six main objectives. If you do not pass the exam, you will know from the score report where you did poorly, so you can study that particular unit in the Test Success book more carefully.

Test-Taking Hints

Get there early and be prepared   This is your last chance to review. Bring your *Test Success* book and review any areas you feel you need to reinforce. Be prepared to show two forms of ID. If you need a quick drink of water or a visit to the restroom, take the time before the exam. Once your exam starts, it won't be paused for these needs.

What you can and can't take in with you   These are closed-book exams. You may use only the scratch paper provided by the testing center. Use this paper as much as possible to diagram the questions. Diagramming the questions will help you clarify the answer. You will need to give this paper back to the test administrator at the end of the exam.

Many testing centers are very strict about what you may take into the testing room. Some testing centers won't even allow zipped-up purses. If you feel tempted to take in any outside material, beware! Many testing centers use monitoring devices such as video and audio equipment (so don't swear, even if you are alone in the room!).

Prometric Testing Centers take the test-taking process and the test validation very seriously.

What to expect   When you arrive for your exam, you'll be asked to present your ID. You'll also be asked to sign a piece of paper signifying that you understand the testing rules (for example, that you will not cheat on the exam).

Before you start the exam, you'll have an opportunity to take a practice exam. It isn't related to NT and it used to give you a feel for the exam process.

Then you will take the exam. When you are done with the exam, you will receive your score report. You will also have an opportunity to evaluate the exam and the testing center.

Test approach   This really depends on what type of test taker you are. If you know the answer, answer the question and move on. If you aren't sure of the answer, mark your best guess, then "flag" the question. At the end of the exam, you can view all of your answers or only the questions you have marked. Depending on the amount of time remaining, you can review all of the questions again, or you can review only the questions you were unsure of. Double-check all of your answers if time allows, you may have misread a question on the first pass. A related question might provide the answer for a question you have been unsure of.

Answer every question. Unanswered questions are scored as incorrect and will count against you. Make sure you keep an eye on the remaining time so that you can pace yourself accordingly.

One piece of advice: If you have narrowed down the answers to two options, always go with your gut reaction, it is usually correct.

If you do not pass the exam, note everything that you can remember while the exam is still fresh in your mind. This will help you prepare for your next exam. The questions frequently overlap, and you don't want to miss the same questions again.

After You Become Certified

Once you become an MCSE, Microsoft kicks in some goodies, including:

- A one-year subscription to Microsoft Technet, a valuable CD collection that contains Microsoft support information.

- A one-year subscription to the Microsoft Beta Evaluation program, which is a great way to get your hands on new software. Be the first kid on the block to play with new and upcoming software.

- Access to a secured area of the Microsoft Web site that provides technical support and product information. This certification benefit is also available for MCP certification.

- Permission to use the Microsoft Certified Professional logos, which look great on letterhead and business cards. (Each certification has its own logo.)

- An MCP certificate suitable for framing or sending to Mom. (You'll get a certificate for each level of certification you reach.)

- A one-year subscription to *Microsoft Certified Professional Magazine,* which provides information on professional and career development.

Preparing for the MCSE Exams

To prepare for the MCSE certification exams, try to work with the product as much as possible. There are a variety of resources from which you can learn about the products and exams.

Courses

Instructor-led Be very careful when choosing instructor-led courses. The Microsoft training materials do not always have a high correlation with the exam objectives. If your primary goal is to pass the certification exams, this book is an excellent resource because it will fill in the holes left by the Microsoft courseware.

Online Online training is an alternative to instructor-led training. This is a useful option for people who are prohibited geographically from attending instructor-led training.

Self-Study Guides

If you prefer to use a book to help you prepare for the MCSE tests, you'll find a wide variety available. They range from complete study guides (such as the Network Press MCSE Study Guide series, which covers the core MCSE exams and key electives) through test-preparedness books similar to this one.

For more MCSE information, point your browser to the Sybex Web site, where you'll find information about the MCP program, job links, and descriptions of other quality titles in the Network Press line of MCSE-related books. Go to http://www.sybex.com and click the MCSE logo.

How to Use This Book

This book is designed to help you prepare for the MCSE exam. It reviews each objective and relevant test-taking information. It gives you the chance to test your knowledge through Study Questions and a Sample Test.

For each unit:

1. Review the exam objectives list at the beginning of the unit. (You may want to check the Microsoft Train_Cert Web site to make sure the objectives haven't changed recently.) There are six main objectives. They include:

    A. Planning

    B. Installation and Configuration

    C. Managing Resources

    D. Connectivity

    E. Monitoring and Optimization

    F. Troubleshooting

2. Depending on your level of expertise, read through or scan the reference material following the objectives list. Broken down according to the objectives, this section helps you brush up on the information you need to know for the exam.

3. Review your knowledge in the Study Questions section. These straightforward questions are designed to test your knowledge of the specified topic. The answers to the Study Questions are listed in the Appendix at the back of the book.

4. Once you are confident of your knowledge of the area, take the Sample Test. The Sample Test is formatted in content and style to match the real exam. Instead of asking the "cut-and-dried" questions, you are presented with scenario-based questions. These questions will help prepare you for the real exam. Sometimes, half of the battle is trying to figure out exactly what the question is asking you. Set a time limit based on the number of questions. A general rule of thumb is that you should be able to answer 20 questions in 30 minutes. When you're finished, check your answers with the Appendix in the back of the book. If you answer at least 85% of the questions correctly within the time limit (the first time you take the Sample Test), you're in good shape. To really prepare, you should note the questions you miss and be able to score 95-100% correctly on subsequent tries.

5. After you successfully complete Units 1–6, you're ready for the Final Exam in Unit 7. Allow 90 minutes to complete the 55-question test. If you answer 85% of the questions correctly on the first try, you're well prepared. If not, review the areas you struggled with, and take the test again.

6. Right before you take the test, scan the reference material at the beginning of each unit to refresh your memory.

At this point, you are well on your way to becoming certified!
Good Luck!

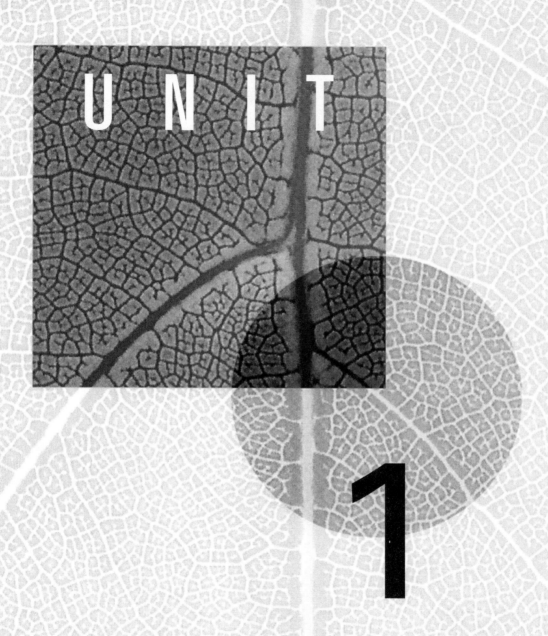

UNIT

1

Planning

Test Objectives: Planning

- Plan the implementation of a directory services architecture. Considerations include:
  - Selecting the appropriate domain model
  - Supporting a single logon account
  - Allowing users to access resources in different domains

- Plan the disk drive configuration for various requirements. Requirements include choosing a fault tolerance method.

- Choose a protocol for various situations. Protocols include:
  - TCP/IP
  - TCP/IP with DHCP and WINS
  - NWLink IPX/SPX Compatible Transport Protocol
  - Data Link Control (DLC)
  - AppleTalk

Exam objectives are subject to change at any time without prior notice and at Microsoft's sole discretion. Please visit Microsoft's Training & Certification website (www.microsoft.com/Train_Cert) for the most current exam objectives listing.

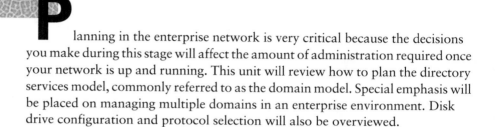

Planning in the enterprise network is very critical because the decisions you make during this stage will affect the amount of administration required once your network is up and running. This unit will review how to plan the directory services model, commonly referred to as the domain model. Special emphasis will be placed on managing multiple domains in an enterprise environment. Disk drive configuration and protocol selection will also be overviewed.

Planning Directory Services

NT 4 does not use true directory services. Instead it uses a domain model. A domain is a logical collection of accounts and resources. In this section, you will study:

- NT domain models
- NT trust relationships
- The four domain models
- Domain access across WAN links

Domain Models

An NT domain is a collection of computers and user accounts that have been logically organized and share the same accounts database known as the Security Accounts Manager (SAM) database.

By default, the domain contains an NT Server that has been installed as a Primary Domain Controller (PDC). This computer is responsible for maintaining the read-write master copy of the SAM database. Unit 2 covers server roles in more detail.

Conceptually, a domain looks like Figure 1.1. All domain users log on to the domain through a domain controller. Once a user is authenticated, an access token is generated. When a user tries to access network resources, the access token is checked against the objects Access Control List (ACL). If the user, through user or group membership has permission, he or she can then access the network resource.

FIGURE 1.1

The NT Domain Model

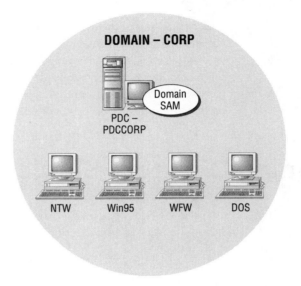

The domain model provides the following benefits:

- Allows users to have a single logon account and enables them to access resources from within their domain or other trusting domains

- Allows administrators to manage user accounts and resources from a central location

- Supports user accounts, passwords, and NT services in diverse environments

- Network information and account information are automatically updated through network services

NT Trust Relationships

In Windows NT, multiple domains can be managed as a single administrative unit through a transitive link called a *trust*. A trust allows a user in the trusted domain to access a resource in a trusting domain.

Consider the example in Figure 1.2.

FIGURE 1.2

Trust Example

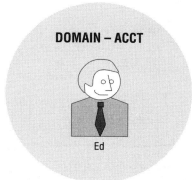

DOMAIN – ACCT   DOMAIN – SALES

Ed

\\SALES\SALESDB

Ed is a user in the ACCT domain. He needs to access the \\SALES\SALESDB share that exists in the SALES domain. In order for Ed to access this resource, Ed must have an account in the SALES domain or a trust relationship must exist between the two domains.

Because one goal of the NT domain model architecture is to allow a user to access resources in any domain with a single logon, we'll use a trust relationship.

The domain that contains the user account is called the *trusted domain*. The account that contains the resource is called the *trusting domain*.

If you always think of the user as Ed, then it's easy to remember that the domain with the account is Trust-Ed. Get it?

A trust relationship is represented by an arrow. In a trust relationship, the trusting domain points to the domains that it trusts. For our example, the trust relationship would be represented as shown in Figure 1.3.

FIGURE 1.3

Trust Example Arrow
Representation

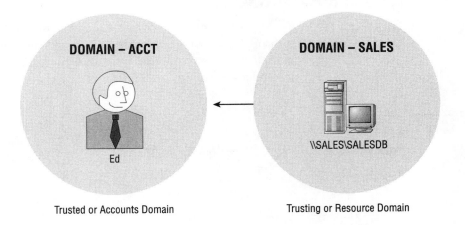

Trusted or Accounts Domain   Trusting or Resource Domain

To establish a trust relationship, both domains must configure the trust
through the User Manager for Domains utility.

If you also want to allow users in the SALES domain to access resources in
the ACCT domain, implement a two-way trust where ACCT trusts SALES in
addition to the one-way trust that has already been established.

The number of trusts you will configure is based on the domain model you
choose. The next subsection defines the four domain models.

The Four NT Domain Models

Microsoft specifies four main domain models from which administrators can
choose. They include:

- The single domain model
- The master domain model
- The multiple master domain model
- The complete trust domain model

These models are defined in the following subsections.

The Single Domain Model

The *single domain model* assumes that your entire network's needs can be configured and managed using a single domain. With this domain model, all account and resource administration is centralized within the single domain. Figure 1.4 illustrates the single domain model.

F I G U R E 1.4

The Single Domain Model

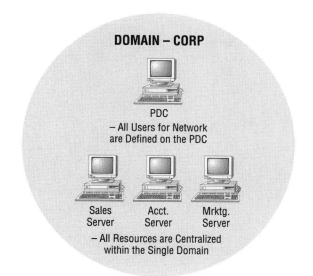

Advantages

- The single domain model allows all accounts and resource management to be centralized.

- One advantage of the single domain model is that there are no trust relationships to manage.

- This is the easiest model to manage for a small company.

Disadvantage

- If you have over 40,000 user, group, and computer accounts, this model will not work due to inherent limitations of the size of the SAM database.

Trust Relationships

This model requires no trust relationships because you have only one domain.

The Master Domain Model

The *master domain model* contains a single accounts domain that contains all of the user accounts. All resources are contained in resource domains. This model is used to centralize accounts management and decentralize resource management.

Figure 1.5 illustrates an example of the master domain model. In this case, the CORP domain contains all of the user accounts for the entire organization and accounts management is centralized. The SALES, ACCT, and LEGAL domains are only used to logically organize the resources of the respective departments. This allows each resource domain to have its own administrator who has complete control over the departmental resources. Resource management is decentralized.

F I G U R E   1.5

The Master Domain
Model

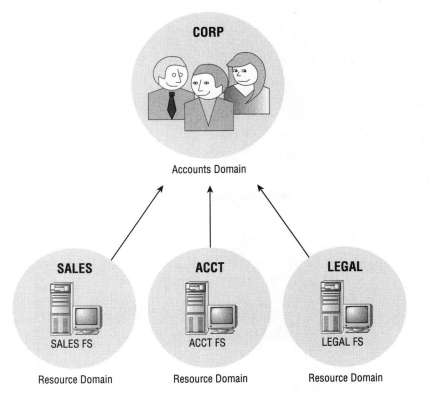

Advantages

- All user account management is centralized to one domain.
- The option of decentralized management of resource domains is allowed.
- Only one-way trust relationships are needed because users access resources from one account domain to all resource domains.

Disadvantages

- Due to inherent limitations of the size of the SAM database, this model will not work if there are more than 40,000 user, group, and computer accounts.
- This model requires more administrative overhead than the single domain model.

Trust Relationships

In this model, all of the resource domains trust the accounts domain; therefore, trust relationships are minimized. Figure 1.5 shows how the trust relationships should be established.

The Multiple Master Domain Model

The *multiple master domain model* is similar to the master domain model, but it assumes that the users can't be centralized into a single domain. A large number of accounts (over 40,000 users, groups, and computers) or the need to centralize accounts for major functional or geographic purposes (for example, domains in the United States and Asia) are possible reasons to use a multiple master domain model. Resource domains are created as needed.

Figure 1.6 illustrates the multiple master domain model.

Advantages

- All account management is retained in multiple account domains.
- The option of decentralized management of resource domains is allowed.
- This model is scaleable to any size organization.

FIGURE 1.6

The Multiple Master
Domain Model

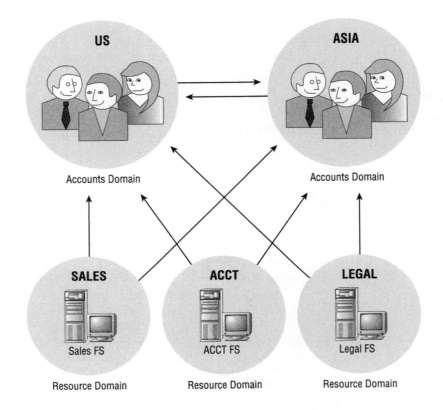

Disadvantage

- This model requires more administration to set up and manage the trust relationships.

Trust Relationships

In this model, there is a two-way trust between all accounts domains. The resource domains trust each of the accounts domains. The trust relationships are illustrated in Figure 1.6.

The Complete Trust Domain Model

The *complete trust domain model* assumes that each domain contains accounts (users) and resources. If users require access to resources in other domains, you must create two-way trust relationships between all domains.

The complete trust domain model is illustrated in Figure 1.7.

FIGURE 1.7

The Complete Trust
Domain Model

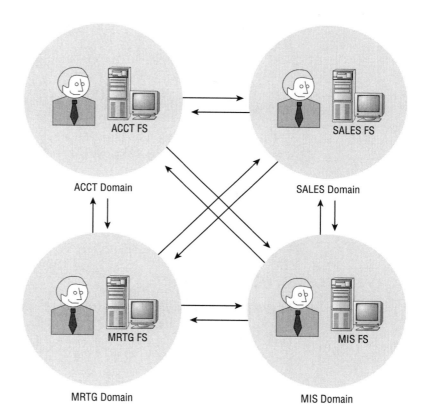

ACCT FS

SALES FS

ACCT Domain

SALES Domain

MRTG FS

MIS FS

MRTG Domain

MIS Domain

Advantages

- Each domain has full control over its accounts and resources.

- This model works well for companies that don't have central planning, because each business unit or geographic location can manage its own accounts and resources. However, some central planning will be required in order to manage the trust relationships that will need to be established and managed.

- This model is also suited to companies that have localized small operations linked by WAN technology. This allows each location to manage its own accounts and resources.

Disadvantage

- This model requires the most trust relationships to set up and maintain.

Trust Relationships

To determine the number of trust relationships, the following formula is used:

$N*(N-1)$

N is the number of domains.

For example, with four domains you would need $4*(4-1)$ or 12 trust relationships. Figure 1.7 illustrates what the trust relationships would look like.

Domain Access across WAN Links

Sometimes an NT domain may span WAN (Wide Area Network) links. In this case, domain controller placement impacts network traffic. The two issues you must consider are logon validation traffic and SAM synchronization traffic.

Logon Validation Traffic

Logon validation traffic is generated whenever a client authenticates to a domain controller. Clients can authenticate to the PDC or to a BDC (Backup Domain Controller). If the domain spans a WAN link as shown in Figure 1.8, the planner must be aware of the following issues:

- By placing a BDC on the LA link, the LA clients will be able to authenticate on their side of the WAN link, reducing WAN logon validation traffic.

- By placing a BDC on the LA link, the LA clients have some fault tolerance, meaning if the WAN link goes down, they will still be able to authenticate to the domain via the BDC.

- By placing a BDC on the LA link, the WAN traffic will include SAM database synchronization and browsing service data. It may involve directory replication.

FIGURE 1.8

Domain Controller
Placement

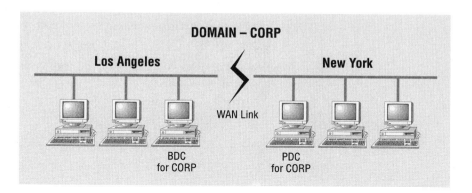

SAM Synchronization Traffic

The flip side of placing BDCs on remote sides of WAN links is that the SAM synchronization will now occur across the WAN link. Depending on the number of changes that are made to the PDC's SAM database, the synchronization could negatively impact network traffic.

So, the rules are:

- If you want quick client authentication, place domain controllers on each end of the WAN link.

- If you don't want SAM synchronization over the WAN link, place all domain controllers on the same side of the WAN link.

These issues also apply to Dynamic Host Configuration Protocol (DHCP), Windows Internet Name Server (WINS), and Domain Name Service (DNS) traffic.

The next section will address planning your disk drive configurations.

Planning Disk Drive Configurations

Before you install your NT Server, you should choose a disk drive configuration. The main considerations in choosing a disk drive configuration are:

- Does the drive contain the system or boot partition or data only?

- Does the disk drive configuration support fault tolerance?
- What kind of performance can you expect from the disk drive configuration?

Some of the options you can select are presented in the following subsections.

Disk Mirroring

Disk mirroring or RAID 1 is used to mirror one physical partition to another physical partition. With disk mirroring (see Figure 1.9), one physical controller and two physical hard drives are used. *Disk duplexing* (see Figure 1.10) is a variation of disk mirroring , providing further redundancy by having individual controllers for each of the hard drives.

Disk mirroring and duplexing require both partitions to be the same logical size.

FIGURE 1.9

Disk Mirroring

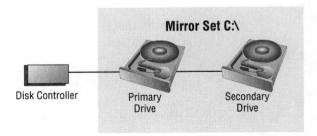

FIGURE 1.10

Disk Duplexing

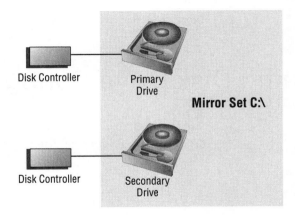

Requirements

- Disk mirroring requires one controller and two hard drives.
- Disk duplexing requires two controllers and a hard drive attached to each controller.

Advantages

- If one of your drives fails, the other drive will continue to function without an interruption to service.
- This is the only fault-tolerant configuration that can be used on system and boot partitions.
- Read operations can be faster on a mirror set than on a single drive.

Disadvantages

- There is 50% disk overhead on disk mirroring, meaning if you are using two 2GB drives in your mirror set, only 2GB is available for data, the other 2GB is an exact duplicate of the data.
- Write operations are slower on a mirror set than on a single drive because the data must be written twice. Duplexing helps improve write performance because it provides a second I/O channel.

Disk Striping

Disk striping or RAID 0 uses between 2 and 32 drives in a stripe set (see Figure 1.11). All drive partitions in the stripe set must be the same logical size.

F I G U R E 1.11

Disk Striping

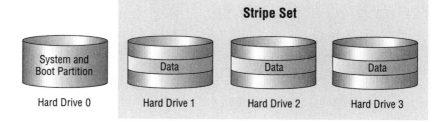

Requirements

- Disk striping requires between 2 and 32 drives with logical space of the same size that will be combined into the stripe set. You could have one or many disk controllers.

Advantage

- Striping data over multiple disk channels improves performance on disk reads and writes as compared to typical disk configurations.

Disadvantages

- Striping has no fault tolerance. No parity information is stored.
- If any drive in the stripe set fails, you lose all access to the stripe set data.
- The system and boot partition can't be part of a stripe set.

Disk Striping with Parity

Disk striping with parity or RAID 5 is similar to disk striping, except that mathematical calculations are performed and stored as parity information striped across the drives in the array. Figure 1.12 illustrates disk striping with parity.

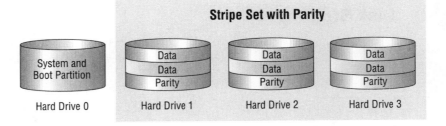

FIGURE 1.12

Disk Striping with Parity

Requirements

- Disk striping with parity requires between 3 and 32 drives with logical space of the same size that will be combined into the stripe set. You could have one or many disk controllers.

Advantages

- If one drive fails, the data can be reconstructed from the parity on the surviving drives in the array.

- You can use the NT implementation of RAID 5 on an array of 3 to 32 drives.

- RAID 5 provides an improved, usable data capacity over RAID 1, which uses the same size partition for data as it does for mirroring. With RAID 5, you basically lose the sum of one logical partition of the stripe set. For example, an array with four 100MB drives would allow 300MB for data and 100MB for parity. The more drives in the stripe set, the greater the percentage of effective data capacity.

Disadvantages

- Until the failed drive is replaced, system performance will be very slow as the data is reconstructed through parity information.

- The system and boot partition can't be a part of a stripe set.

- If two or more drives fail, all the data from the stripe set is lost.

 In Unit 6 you will learn how to recover from disk failure when a fault-tolerant disk configuration has been used.

The next section will cover how to select your network protocols.

Protocol Selection

NT supports a variety of transport protocols. You can select from:

- TCP/IP
- TCP/IP with DHCP and WINS
- NWLink IPX/SPX Compatible Transport
- DLC

- AppleTalk
- NetBEUI

These protocols are all covered in the following subsections. Unit 2 will contain more complete information on configuring these protocols.

TCP/IP

Transmission Control Protocol/Internet Protocol (TCP/IP) is the industry standard for transport protocols. It is widely used and is supported by many networking platforms. TCP/IP is one of the two default network protocols installed on NT Server.

The following list summarizes TCP/IP:

- Suite of related protocols developed by DARPA (Department of Defense Advanced Research Projects Agency)
- Slightly slower than NWLink and much slower than NetBEUI
- Relatively high overhead to support seamless connectivity and routing
- Supports features like DHCP and WINS
- Used in most networks, especially if Internet connectivity is required
- Requires the most configuration data (you must specify an IP address, subnet mask, and default gateway) unless you have installed and configured a DHCP server

The DHCP and WINS services are defined in the next subsection.

TCP/IP with DHCP and WINS

The Microsoft implementation of TCP/IP allows you to take advantage of DHCP and WINS. These services are described in the following subsections.

DHCP

DHCP stands for Dynamic Host Configuration Protocol and is used to automate IP configuration. NT Server can have the DHCP service installed so that it becomes a DHCP server. The DHCP server then provides DHCP clients with IP configuration information.

Advantages

- DHCP reduces client configuration errors.

- DHCP makes it easier to support users with mobile computers who attach to more than one subnet.

- DHCP makes IP configuration less administrator intensive.

- DHCP allows better use of limited IP addresses for clients that are not permanently attached to the network.

Disadvantage

- DHCP slightly increases network traffic as it assigns and renews IP configuration information.

WINS

WINS stands for Windows Internet Name Server. The main purpose of WINS is to resolve NetBIOS names to IP addresses in routed networks. By using WINS you greatly reduce broadcast traffic. When used with Domain Name Servers, WINS allows clients to resolve NetBIOS names to fully qualified domain names (FQDN) or Internet names.

NWLink IPX/SPX Compatible Transport

The NWLink IPX/SPX (Internetwork Packet Exchange/Sequenced Packet Exchange) Compatible Transport is a commonly used network transport protocol. This protocol is routable and can be used to access NetWare client-server applications that use sockets-based APIs to communicate with other IPX/SPX-based applications.

The following list summarizes the NWLink IPX/SPX Compatible Transport protocol properties:

- Based on Novell's proprietary IPX/SPX transport protocol

- Microsoft implementation supports NetBIOS

- Faster than current NT implementation of TCP/IP, but much slower than NetBEUI

- Slightly lower overhead than TCP/IP, but it does not offer all of the features of TCP/IP

- Supports routing
- Used when compatibility or interoperability with NetWare networks is required
- Requires configuration of frame type (supports auto-detection of a single frame type)

NWLink IPX/SPX by itself does not provide access to NetWare file and print resources. For this access, you need GSNW (Gateway Services for NetWare), which is covered in Unit 4.

DLC

The Data Link Control (DLC) protocol does not offer the support that TCP/IP and NWLink IPX/SPX Compatible Transport offer. The following list summarizes the characteristics of DLC.

- DLC is not designed to transport data between personal computers.
- DLC is used to provide applications with direct access to the data-link layer, but it is not supported by the Microsoft redirector.
- DLC is mainly used to provide access to IBM mainframes running 3, 270 applications and HP network printers.

You only need to install DLC on the network computers that will use DLC services (for example, a print server on which an HP network printer is configured). Clients that access the network printer do not need to have DLC installed. Install DLC through Control Panel ➤ Network ➤ Protocols.

AppleTalk

AppleTalk is the protocol transport that Apple Macintosh computers use. Install AppleTalk when you install the Services for Macintosh service. This service will be covered in more detail in Unit 2.

NetBEUI

You can also choose to install NetBEUI as your NT server's transport protocol. It is a simple protocol and it provides the best performance on a local network. The greatest drawback of NetBEUI is that it is nonroutable, so it is not commonly used in enterprise networks.

Planning Directory Services

1. List the four domain models.

_____

_____

_____

_____

2. Your company uses the master domain model. All users are in the CORP domain and all of the resources are in the EAST and WEST domains. Draw the appropriate trust relationship arrows that would support this configuration.

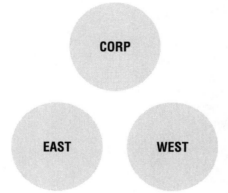

3. Your company has two domains: MIS and SALES. The users in the SALES domain need to access resources in the MIS domain. Users in MIS do not need to access resources in the SALES domain. Draw the appropriate trust relationship for the scenario and indicate which domain is trusted and which domain is trusting.

Questions 4-7 are based on the following graphic.

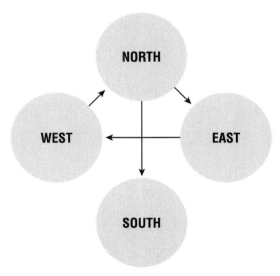

4. True or False. A user in domain NORTH can access resources in domain WEST.

5. True or False. A user in domain WEST can access resources in domain NORTH.

6. True or False. A user in domain EAST can access resources in domain WEST.

7. True or False. A user in domain SOUTH can access resources in domain NORTH.

8. Domain SALES trusts domain MARKETING. Complete the diagram to show which way the trust relationship should be represented. In this case, users in domain _____
_____ can access resources in domain _____.

SALES   MARKETING

9. Your company is using the complete trust model. You are using five domains. How many one-way trust relationships must be configured?

_____

10. You have decided to use the master domain model. US and ASIA are the accounts domains. SALES, MARKETING, and ACCT are the resource domains. Draw the trust relationship arrows this model would require.

US   ASIA

SALES   MARKETING   ACCT

11. Michelle is a user in domain SF and she wants to access a resource in domain LA. The following diagram illustrates the trust relationship. Based on this diagram, can Michelle access the resource?

12. You have two domains, WEST and EAST. The WEST domain is trusted and the EAST domain is trusting. Based on this description, show the appropriate trust relationship arrow and the location of the user and group accounts.

Questions 13-15 are based on the following scenario.

You have three domains, domain ONE, domain TWO, and domain THREE. Based on the trust relationships defined in the diagram, what access do users in each domain have to resources in other domains?

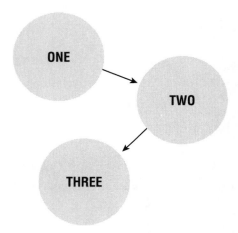

13. Users in domain ONE can access resources in domain(s):

_____

14. Users in domain TWO can access resources in domains(s):

_____

15. Users in domain THREE can access resources in domain(s):

_____

Questions 16-19 are based on the following scenario.

You have four domains, domain ONE, domain TWO, domain THREE, and domain FOUR. Based on the trust relationships defined in the diagram, what access do users in each domain have to resources in other domains?

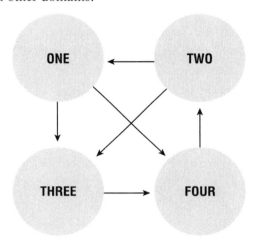

16.   Users in domain ONE can access resources in domain(s):

_____

17.   Users in domain TWO can access resources in domains(s):

_____

18.   Users in domain THREE can access resources in domain(s):

_____

19.   Users in domain FOUR can access resources in domain(s):

_____

20.   True or False. You are using the domain model shown in the figure. EAST and WEST are the accounts domains. MIS, SALES, and ACCT are the resource domains. Based on this scenario, the trust relationships have been established correctly.

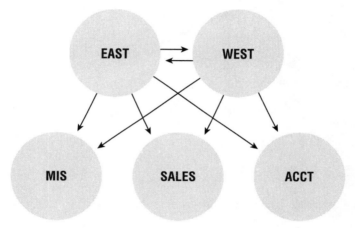

21.   Your domain spans WAN links as shown in the following diagram. The SF office has 100 users and the PDC is placed on its local segment. The LA, NY, and CHIC segments all support 150 users each. You want to minimize the WAN traffic that is caused by logon validation requests. Where should the BDCs for your domain be placed?

22. Your domain spans WAN links as shown in the following diagram. The SF office has 100 users and the PDC is placed on its local segment. The LA, NY, and CHIC segments all support 150 users each. You want to minimize the WAN traffic that is caused by SAM synchronization. Where should the BDCs for your domain be placed?

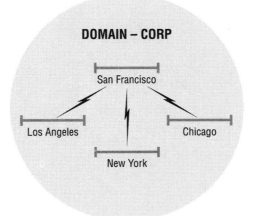

Planning Disk Drive Configurations

23. With disk _____ you use a redundant data channel through two disk controllers and two hard drives.

24. With disk _____ you use a redundant data channel through a single disk controller and two hard drives.

25. _____ is the only disk drive configuration that can be used to provide fault tolerance for the system and boot partition.

26. Assume that you are using five drives in a stripe set with parity. Each drive consists of 500MB. How much disk space will be used for data and how much disk space will be used to store parity information?

disk space _____

parity information _____

27. Disk mirroring is considered RAID _____.

28. Disk striping with parity is considered RAID _____.

29. You can have a minimum of _____ drives in a stripe set and a maximum of _____ drives.

30. You can have a minimum of _____ drives in a stripe set with parity and a maximum of _____ drives.

Protocol Selection

31.   Assume you want to use TCP/IP as your transport protocol and you want to use automatic configuration for your clients instead of using manual configuration. What service do you install?

_____

32.   What are the two common scenarios when DLC would be used?

_____

_____

33.   The _____ protocol can be used to connect to NetWare servers that are using Sockets-based APIs.

34.   How do you install the AppleTalk protocol?

_____

35.   The _____ protocol supports features such as DHCP and WINS.

36.   You are trying to provide connectivity to the Internet. What transport protocol must you use?

_____

37.   The _____ service is used with TCP/IP to minimize broadcast traffic by mapping NetBIOS names to IP addresses.

38. What two protocols that support internetwork routing can be installed during the installation of NT server?

_____

_____

SAMPLE TEST

1-1   Your company has five main departments. Each department has about 100 users and maintains a server for departmental use. You are in charge of planning a domain model. Your main goal is to centralize accounts management and resource management. Which domain model will best suit your needs?

    A. Single domain

    B. Master domain

    C. Multiple master domain

    D. Complete trust domain

1-2   Your company uses the TCP/IP transport protocol. Some of your users use laptop computers to travel between your Houston and Dallas offices. The users have been complaining that each time they plug into a different subnet, they must reconfigure their IP settings. What service would alleviate the problem?

    A. WINS

    B. DNS

    C. DHCP

    D. TCPCONFIG

1-3   You are in the process of purchasing the equipment that will be used for your NT server. You know that the first hard drive in the computer will be used to store the system and boot partition. The rest of the server storage will be used to house a database your sales group uses. You want to implement a stripe set with parity on the drives on which the database will be stored and disk mirroring for the drive that will contain the system and boot partition. What is the minimum number of additional drives you will need, excluding the existing first drive that currently stores the system and boot partition?

    A. 3

    B. 4

    C. 5

    D. 6

SAMPLE TEST

1-4 Your company has five main departments. Each department has about 100 users and maintains three servers for departmental use. You are in charge of planning a domain model. Your main goal is to centralize accounts, but each department wants to retain full control over its departmental resources. Which domain model will best suit your needs?

    A. Single domain model

    B. Master domain model

    C. Multiple master domain model

    D. Complete trust domain model

1-5 Your company has four domains, MIS, SALES, ACCT, and RESEARCH. The MIS domain contains a member server that users in all domains need to access. In addition, users in the ACCT domain need to access resources in the SALES domain. Other than these two requirements, no inter-domain access is required. What are the minimum trust relationships that need to be configured?

    A. Create a one-way trust where MIS trusts SALES, ACCT, and RESEARCH. Then, create a one-way trust where SALES trusts ACCT.

    B. Create a one-way trust where MIS trusts SALES, ACCT, and RESEARCH. Then, create a one-way trust where ACCT trusts SALES.

    C. Create a one-way trust where SALES, ACCT, and RESEARCH trusts MIS. Then, create a one-way trust where SALES trusts ACCT.

    D. Create a one-way trust where SALES, ACCT, and RESEARCH trusts MIS.

1-6 Your company is in the process of selecting a disk configuration for a server that will be used as the company's applications server. You have been given the following criteria:

Required Element: The disk configuration must be fault tolerant.

Optional Elements: The disk configuration must provide high performance.

The disk configuration should support the system and boot partition.

Solution: Use disk striping.

What does the stated solution provide?

    A. It meets the required element and both of the optional elements.

    B. It meets the required element and one optional element.

    C. It doesn't meet the required element, but it meets both optional elements.

    D. It doesn't meet the required element, but it meets one optional element.

    E. It doesn't meet the required element or the optional elements.

1-7   Which of the following statements are true of the DLC protocol. Choose all that apply.

    A. It is designed to support communications between two computers.

    B. It is fully supported by the Microsoft redirector.

    C. It is mainly used by IBM mainframes running 3270 applications and HP network printers.

    D. Network clients who send print jobs to network printers that use DLC must have the DLC protocol installed on their client computers.

1-8   Your company is using the master domain model. The CORP domain contains all of the user accounts and the resource domains are SALES, RESEARCH, and MIS. Based on the master domain model, how should the trust relationships be defined?

    A. Configure a one-way trust where CORP trusts SALES, RESEARCH, and MIS.

    B. Configure one-way trusts where SALES, RESEARCH, and MIS trust CORP.

    C. Set up two-way trust relationships between CORP and SALES, CORP and RESEARCH, and CORP and MIS.

    D. Set up two-way trust relationships between all of the domains.

1-9   Your company is in the process of selecting a disk configuration for a server that will be used as the company's applications server. You have been given the following criteria:

Required Element: The disk configuration must be fault tolerant.

Optional Elements: The disk configuration must provide improved performance.

The disk configuration should support the system and boot partition.

Solution: Use disk mirroring.

What does the stated solution provide?

A. It meets the required element and both of the optional elements.

B. It meets the required element and one optional element.

C. It doesn't meet the required element, but it meets both optional elements.

D. It doesn't meet the required element, but it meets one optional element.

E. It doesn't meet the required element or the optional elements.

1-10   The _____ utility is used to configure trust relationships.

A. Server Manager

B. User Manager for Domains

C. Control Panel, Network

D. Control Panel, Server

1-11   Which of the following statements best describes the WINS service?

A. It maps IP addresses to domain names.

B. It maps IP addresses to MAC addresses.

C. It maps MAC addresses to domain names.

D. It maps IP addresses to NetBIOS names.

1-12   Your company has three domains. They are NY, LA, and HOUSTON. The LA domain trusts the NY domain and NY trusts HOUSTON. Based on these trust relationships, what access is possible?

    A. Users in LA can access resources in NY, and users in NY can access resources in HOUSTON.

    B. Users in HOUSTON can access resources in NY, and users in NY can access resources in LA.

    C. Users is LA can access resources in NY and HOUSTON, and users in NY can access resources in HOUSTON.

    D. Users in HOUSTON can access resources in NY and LA, and users in NY can access resources in LA.

1-13   Your company has 50,000 users. The decision has been made to use NT. Now you must plan the domain model. You are required to centralize accounts management, yet leave each division with the ability to manage its own resources. Which domain model will be your best option?

    A. Single domain model

    B. Master domain model

    C. Multiple master domain model

    D. Complete trust domain model

1-14   Your company is in the process of selecting a disk configuration for a server that will be used as the company's applications server. You have been given the following criteria:

Required Element: The disk configuration must be fault tolerant.

Optional Elements: The disk configuration must provide improved performance.

The disk configuration should support the system and boot partition.

Solution: Use disk striping with parity.

What does the stated solution provide?

A. It meets the required element and both of the optional elements.

B. It meets the required element and one optional element.

C. It doesn't meet the required element, but it meets both optional elements.

D. It doesn't meet the required element, but it meets one optional element.

E. It doesn't meet the required element or the optional elements.

1-15   Which options provide fault tolerance for the system and boot partition? Choose all that apply.

A. Disk striping

B. Disk mirroring

C. Disk duplexing

D. Disk striping with parity

1-16   What is the minimum disk configuration required for disk striping with parity?

A. Two drives, both with equal-sized logical partitions

B. Three drives, all with equal-sized logical partitions

C. Two drives, one is reserved as a parity drive

D. Three drives, one is reserved as a parity drive

1-17   Which fault-tolerance option would provide the highest level of fault tolerance on a system and boot partition?

    A. Disk striping

    B. Disk mirroring

    C. Disk duplexing

    D. Disk striping with parity

1-18   Your company is very decentralized and didn't have a way to coordinate and use central planning when NT was originally installed. In the current setup, SALES, ACCT, and RESEARCH each have their own domains. Each domain has user accounts and resources. Now each domain wants to share resources with the other domains. Which domain model do you choose?

    A. Single domain

    B. Master domain

    C. Multiple master domain

    D. Complete trust domain

1-19   Tom is a user in the ACCT domain and needs to access resources in the SALES and MARKETING domains. In addition, the SALES and MARKETING domains need to be able to share information across domains. However, the ACCT department wants to retain full control over its resources and wants no one outside of ACCT to have any kind of access. What do you do?

    A. Set up a one-way trust where SALES and MARKETING trust ACCT, then set up a two-way trust between SALES and MARKETING.

    B. Set up a one-way trust where ACCT trusts SALES and MARKETING, then set up a two-way trust between SALES and MARKETING.

    C. Create two-way trusts between all domains.

    D. Add a user account for Tom in the SALES and MARKETING domains, don't configure any trust with ACCT, then set up a two-way trust between SALES and MARKETING.

1-20 You have four drives in your stripe set with parity, each drive is 1GB in size. How much space will be available to store data?

  A. 4GB

  B. 3.5GB

  C. 3GB

  D. 2.5GB

1-21 You have four drives in your stripe set, each drive is 1GB in size. How much space will be available to store data?

  A. 4GB

  B. 3.5GB

  C. 3GB

  D. 2.5GB

1-22 Your company consists of four offices: Seattle, Boise, Houston, and Orlando. The Seattle office is the company's corporate headquarters and has WAN links to each office as shown in the following diagram.

You are designing the network and have been given the following criteria:

Required Element: User administration must be centralized to the corporate headquarters.

Optional Elements: Resource management should be decentralized to each branch office. There should be no logon traffic over the WAN link.

Solution: Use the single domain model, place the PDC is Seattle and BDCs in each branch office.

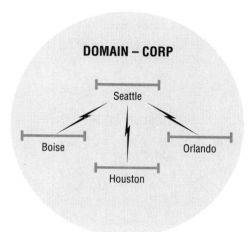

What does the stated solution provide?

A. It meets the required element and both of the optional elements.

B. It meets the required element and one optional element.

C. It doesn't meet the required element, but it meets both optional elements.

D. It doesn't meet the required element, but it meets one optional element.

E. It doesn't meet the required element or the optional elements.

1-23   Your company consists of four offices: Seattle, Boise, Houston, and Orlando. The Seattle office is the company's corporate headquarters and has WAN links to each office as shown in the following diagram.

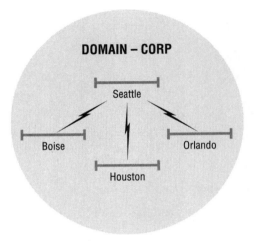

You are designing the network and have been given the following criteria:

Required Element: User administration must be centralized to the corporate headquarters.

Optional Elements: Resource management should be decentralized to each branch office. There should be no logon traffic over the WAN link.

Solution: Use the master domain model with the user account domain being in Seattle. Each location will contain a PDC and BDC for their own domain.

What does the stated solution provide?

A. It meets the required element and both of the optional elements.

B. It meets the required element and one optional element.

C. It doesn't meet the required element, but it meets both optional elements.

D. It doesn't meet the required element, but it meets one optional element.

E. It doesn't meet the required element or the optional elements.

1-24   You are in the process of designing your network. Your company consists of four locations: Seattle, Boise, Houston, and Dallas as shown in the following diagram.

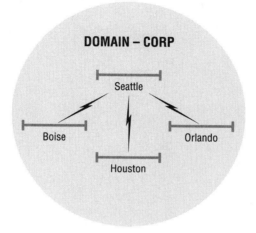

Each remote location connects to the corporate headquarters in Seattle though WAN links. You decide to use the single domain model. How do you eliminate SAM replication traffic across the WAN links?

A. Install all domain controllers on the Seattle segment.

B. Install a PDC on the Seattle segment and BDCs on the remote segments.

C. Install a PDC on each LAN segment.

D. Install a BDC on each WAN segment, but configure the ReplicationGovernor value in the registry of the BDCs to eliminate synchronization traffic.

UNIT

2

Installation and Configuration

Test Objectives: Installation and Configuration

- Install Windows NT Server to perform various roles. Server roles include:
  - Primary domain controller
  - Backup domain controller
  - Member server

- Configure protocol and protocol bindings. Protocols include:
  - TCP/IP
  - TCP/IP with DHCP and WINS
  - NWLink IPX/SPX Compatible Transport Protocol
  - DLC
  - AppleTalk

- Configure Windows NT Server core services. Services include:
  - Directory Replicator
  - Computer Browser

- Configure hard disks to meet various requirements. Requirements include:
  - Providing redundancy
  - Improving performance

- Configure printers. Tasks include:
  - Adding and configuring a printer
  - Implementing a printer pool
  - Setting print priorities

- Configure a Windows NT Server computer for various types of client computers. Client computer types include:
  - Windows NT Workstation
  - Windows 95
  - Macintosh

 Exam objectives are subject to change at any time without prior notice and at Microsoft's sole discretion. Please visit Microsoft's Training & Certification website (www.microsoft.com/Train_Cert) for the most current exam objectives listing.

This unit will cover the NT server roles, configuration of network protocols, the NT server core services, server hard drive configuration, printer configuration, and server configuration required to support different client platforms.

NT Server Roles

NT Servers can be installed in three types of roles within an NT domain:

- Primary Domain Controller (PDC)
- Backup Domain Controller (BDC)
- Member Server

The server roles are illustrated in Figure 2.1.

Primary Domain Controller

Each domain must have one, and only one, PDC. The PDC contains the user accounts database known as the Security Accounts Manager (SAM) for the domain. It is the only computer that contains a read-write database of the SAM, which is then copied to any servers that act as BDCs.

Backup Domain Controller

A BDC offloads logon authentication from the PDC and provides fault tolerance in the event that the PDC becomes unavailable. The BDCs receive automatic updates of the SAM from the PDC every five minutes, or they can be manually updated at any time through the Server Manager.

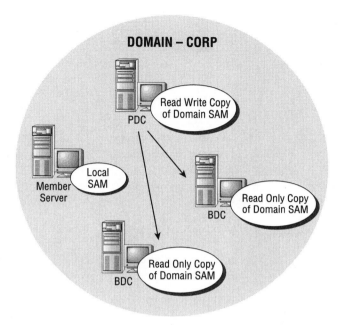

FIGURE 2.1
NT Server Roles

Some important things to keep in mind about BDCs:

- A BDC can't be installed into a domain if the PDC for the domain is unavailable.

- Once installed into a domain, a BDC can't change domains without reinstallation.

- A BDC can't become a member server without reinstallation.

Member Server

A member server is a server that does not contain the SAM database. This allows the server to act in a specialized capacity without the overhead of logon authentication and SAM synchronization. The member server may be moved from any NT domain to any other NT domain.

The server roles are compared in Table 2.1.

T A B L E 2.1: Domain Controller Synchronization

	PDC	BDC	Member Server
Number in Domain	One	None required, but normally you would want at least one—you can have as many as you need.	None required; you can have an unlimted number for domain services.
Primary Purpose	Controls the NT Domain. Assumes role of Domain Master Browser. Contains the read-write SAM database.	Contains a read-only copy of the SAM database, used to offload logon authentication and provide fault tolerance.	Acts as a dedicated file, print, or applications server.
Switchable Roles	A PDC can become a BDC if a BDC is promoted, but the PDC can't become a member server without reinstallation.	A BDC can become a PDC, but the BDC can't become a member server without reinstallation.	A member server can't become a PDC or BDC without reinstallation.
Domain Hopping	A PDC can't switch domains without reinstallation.	A BDC can't switch domains without reinstallation.	A member server can change domains.

Domain synchronization can occur automatically, or you can manually force domain synchronization.

Automatic Domain Synchronization

As noted, changes to the domain SAM database are announced by the PDC to BDCs every five minutes. When the BDC receives the synchronization announcement, it responds and requests the changes (Figure 2.2). This is called a partial synchronization, and it is the type that is usually performed between the domain controllers.

Through the registry, you can configure how frequently:

- The PDC sends out change announcements
- The BDC responds to change announcements if changes have occurred since the last synchronization

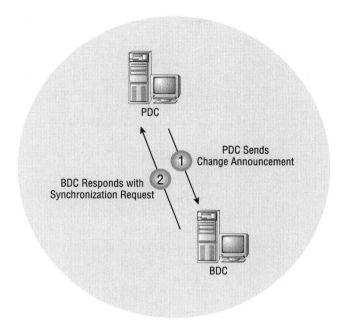

FIGURE 2.2

Domain
Synchronization

PDC Configuration

The PDC registry values that pertain to domain synchronization are found in:

```
HKEY_LOCAL_MACHINE\System\CurrentControlSet\Services\
NetLogon\Parameters
```

The two entries you should be aware of are listed in Table 2.2.

T A B L E 2.2: PDC Synchronization Registry Entries

PDC Synchronization Entry	Description	Default	Range of Settings
Pulse	Pulse is used to define how frequently the PDC will send change announcements to the BDCs.	300 seconds (five minutes)	60–3,600 seconds (one minute– one hour)

T A B L E 2.2: PDC Synchronization Registry Entries *(continued)*

PDC Synchronization Entry	Description	Default	Range of Settings
Pulse Concurrency	This number specifies the maximum number of BDCs to which a change announcement will be sent concurrently.	20	1–500

BDC Configuration

You can also specify how often BDCs respond to a PDC's change announcement.

Assume that your network is configured as shown in Figure 2.3. In this case, you have three physical network segments that are all a part of the CORP domain. San Jose's BDC is local to the PDC, and the Houston and Chicago segments are separated through WAN links.

F I G U R E 2.3

BDC through WAN Links Example

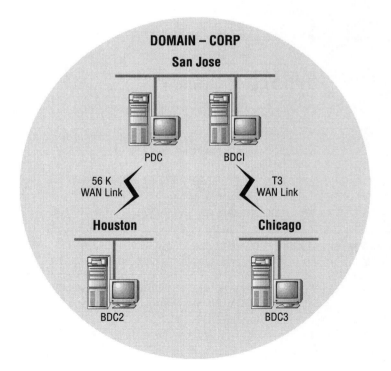

DOMAIN – CORP

San Jose

PDC   BDCI

56 K WAN Link   T3 WAN Link

Houston   Chicago

BDC2   BDC3

In this case, BDC2 in Houston connects through a 56K WAN link. If the WAN link is already overloaded with network traffic, you can adjust the registry of this specific BDC to control the amount of traffic generated through domain synchronization.

To control how often the BDC responds to the PDC change announcements, adjust the ReplicationGovernor value. Do this through the registry in:

```
HKEY_LOCAL_MACHINE\System\CurrentControlSet\Services\
NetLogon\Parameters
```

You can adjust this number from 1–100. The default value assumes that the BDC will respond to synchronization requests 100% of the time and will use a 128K buffer. By manipulating this value, you specify how often the BDC will respond to synchronization requests and how much of the buffer will be used. For example, if you set this number to 50, the BDC would respond 50% of the time and use 50% or a 64K buffer.

Domain synchronization should include only the changes to the domain SAM. Full synchronization should occur only when a new BDC is brought on-line or when the change log has overwritten changes that have not yet been replicated.

Manual Domain Synchronization

You can also manually synchronize a domain. Assume that you have just made changes to the PDC SAM. You could wait for automatic synchronization to occur, or you could force synchronization through Server Manager.

You have two options for this:

- From the PDC, you can choose to synchronize the entire domain.

- From a specific BDC, you can synchronize with the PDC (other BDCs will be updated during the automatic synchronization process).

In the next section, you will learn about network protocols and protocol bindings.

Network Protocols and Bindings

This section will cover NT Server protocols and the process of binding. The protocols included are:

- TCP/IP
- TCP/IP with DHCP and WINS
- NWLink IPX/SPX Compatible Transport Protocol
- DLC
- AppleTalk

NOTE

Selection of the main protocols and protocol selection is covered in Unit 1. This section focuses on protocol configuration.

TCP/IP

The TCP/IP protocol requires the most configuration of the three protocols. The TCP/IP configuration can be manual or automatic (see Figure 2.4). Table 2.3 compares the two installation types.

FIGURE 2.4

TCP/IP Configuration Screen

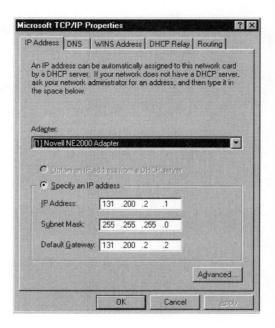

T A B L E 2.3	Manual Configuration	Automatic Configuration
TCP/IP Manual and Automatic Configurations	Does not require that a DHCP server be up and running.	Requires that a functional DHCP server be available.
	Requires you to configure an IP address, subnet mask, and default gateway (gateway is required only if routing outside subnet is needed).	Only requires you to select the Obtain An IP Address from A DHCP Server radio button.
	Must be changed manually every time the computer changes subnets.	Automatically assigns the correct IP configuration information when a computer changes subnets.
	Humans are more likely to make configuration errors that result in problems.	Assuming that the DHCP server is set up correctly, many configuration problems are avoided.
	More labor intensive for an administrator.	Low administrative overhead for an administrator.

The next subsection will cover how TCP/IP offers enhanced features through DHCP and WINS.

TCP/IP with DHCP and WINS

If you install the TCP/IP protocol on your NT server, you can also install DHCP server and WINS server. These services are covered in the following subsections.

DHCP

DHCP stands for Dynamic Host Configuration Protocol. DHCP is used to automatically configure DHCP clients with at least IP addresses and subnet masks, and optionally other configuration data.

Install DHCP as a service through Control Panel ➤ Network ➤ Services. Once you install DHCP, configure it through the DHCP Manager.

DHCP can have basic or advanced configuration. The following is a basic DHCP configuration.

1. From DHCP Manager, first create a *scope*. Scope is a range of IP addresses that can be leased by DHCP clients.

2. Edit the properties of the scope to reflect your configuration (see Figure 2.5).

FIGURE 2.5

DHCP Scope Properties
Dialog Screen

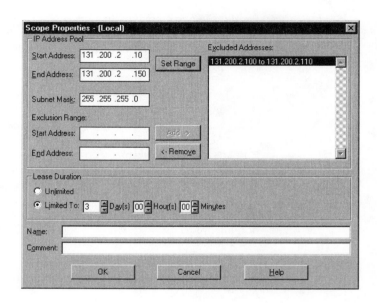

The DHCP scope properties are defined in Table 2.4.

TABLE 2.4

DHCP Scope Properties
Defined

DHCP Scope Property	Description
IP Address Pool	The IP address pool is used to specify the range of IP addresses that are available to the DHCP clients. You also specify the subnet mask the clients will use. This field also allows you to specify exclusion ranges and addresses for IP addresses that are already in use.

	DHCP Scope Property	Description
T A B L E 2.4 *(cont.)* DHCP Scope Properties Defined	Lease Duration	Lease duration defines how long DHCP clients will keep their assigned addresses. By default, leases are set to three days. When a lease is 50% over, the DHCP clients will attempt to contact the DHCP server to renew their leases.
	Name and Comment	Used for informational purposes.

The next subsection will overview WINS.

WINS

WINS stands for Windows Internet Name Service. The primary function of WINS is to resolve NetBIOS computer names to IP addresses in routed networks.

Install WINS through Control Panel ➤ Network ➤ Services.

WINS offers the following benefits:

- Dynamic database creation and maintenance that is used to support computer name registration and name resolution

- Centralized management of IP to NetBIOS computer name mapping, which eliminates the need to manually manage lmhosts files

- Reduction of IP broadcast traffic generated by computers that broadcast to NetBIOS names in an effort to determine IP addresses

By default, a WINS server will create a database of all the WINS clients' name registrations (NetBIOS names and IP addresses). Any Microsoft client using TCP/IP can be configured as a WINS client. To become a WINS client, simply specify the IP address of the primary (and optional secondary) WINS server the client will use. In NT, this is accomplished through Control Panel ➤ Network ➤ Protocols tab ➤ TCP/IP Protocol ➤ Properties ➤ WINS Addresses tab. For non-WINS clients, you must configure an lmhosts file that is used for name resolution.

DHCP and WINS are covered in much greater detail in the *MCSE: TCP/IP for NT Server 4 Study Guide.*

The next subsection covers the NWLink Compatible Transport protocol.

NWLink IPX/SPX Compatible Transport

The NWLink IPX/SPX Compatible Transport protocol requires minimal configuration. As seen in Figure 2.6, the only configuration parameters are for Internal Network Number and Frame Type.

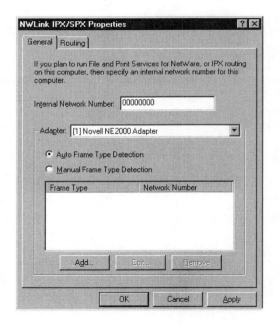

Internal Network Number

The Internal Network Number identifies a unique address that is used by NetWare. This is an optional configuration.

Use this option if:

- You are running File and Print Services for NetWare.

- You are using your NT Server as an IPX router.

If you won't be using the previous configurations, you should leave this field at its default of eight zeros (00000000).

Frame Type

In order to communicate through NWLink, you must configure frame type. The Frame Type is associated with Ethernet transport protocols. You can choose from four Ethernet frame types, which are not compatible with each other. If the computers are not configured consistently, they will not communicate with each other.

Instead of manually picking frame types, you can choose the Auto-detect option, which will prefer the Ethernet_802.2 frame type. If this frame type is not available, it will auto-detect the next frame type it detects.

If you are going to connect to resources that have more than one frame type, then all frame types must be entered manually during configuration.

DLC

As mentioned in Unit 1, the DLC protocol is used to connect to an IBM mainframe running 3270 applications or HP network printers.

To install the DLC protocol, use Control Panel ➤ Network ➤ Protocols tab, and add the DLC protocol. Once this protocol is added, it requires no configuration and the Properties button is grayed out.

AppleTalk

Macintosh computers use the AppleTalk protocol. This protocol differs from the other protocols that NT uses in that it is not installed through Control Panel ➤ Network ➤ Protocols tab. Instead, install the AppleTalk protocol when you install Services for Macintosh.

During the installation of Services for Macintosh, you can configure the AppleTalk protocol by specifying:

- Default adapter

- Default zone

- Routing information

The next section will cover the binding process.

Binding Protocols

Binding is the linking of the physical adapter and NDIS driver to the network protocols and services you are running. To access the bindings configuration and enable and disable bindings:

1. Choose Control Panel ➤ Network, then choose the Binding tab. The Binding tab first lists all of the services that require network interaction.

2. Click on a service to see what protocols are bound to the service.

Because protocol selection is based on the order in which protocols are listed, the most frequently used protocols should be at the top of the binding list for better performance.

You can enable and disable bindings through this tab. You will have better network performance if you disable unnecessary bindings.

The next section will cover NT servers core services.

NT Server Core Services

In this section, you will learn about the directory replicator and computer browser core services.

Directory Replicator

Directory replication is used to maintain exact directory structures on multiple computers. This is done by designating a computer as an export server (the one from which you're copying and another computer or computers as import servers (the one to which you're copying). Directory replication is usually used to replicate read-only data (like logon scripts and system policies) to domain controllers within a domain.

For example, assume that your domain has a PDC and three BDCs. Any of the domain controllers could potentially authenticate a user. You create and maintain logon scripts and system policy files on the PDC and then export the data to the BDCs, as shown in Figure 2.7.

FIGURE 2.7

Directory Replication

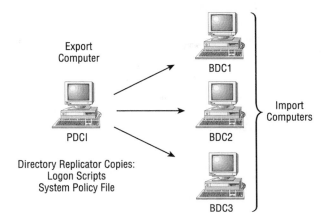

Export
Computer

BDC1

Import
Computers

PDCI

BDC2

Directory Replicator Copies:
Logon Scripts
System Policy File

BDC3

The directory replicator service will only replicate directories and files on the export computer in the WINNT\SYSTEM32\REPL\EXPORT directory (this directory is shared as NETLOGON by default). Files are replicated to the WINNT\SYSTEM32\ REPL\IMPORT directory on import computers. Directory replication will not replicate files in the directory that are currently in use or opened by an application.

Requirements

- The export computer must be NT Server.

- The import computer can be NT Server or NT Workstation.

- The import and export computers must be running the directory replicator service.

- A user account must be created in the NT domain to allow the directory replicator service to run. The user account must be a part of the Replicator and Backup Operators group. This account allows the replicator service to run while satisfying the NT security models.

- Directory replication must be configured on the export and import computers through Server Manager.

Next, you will learn about the computer browser service.

Computer Browser

The browser service is used to display the available domains and computers and their associated resources that are available to the local computer. Users can see the results of the browser list through utilities like Network Neighborhood.

In this section, you will learn about browser roles and how browser computers are chosen.

Browser Roles

The NT browser system consists of:

- Domain Master Browser
- Master Browsers (including Preferred Master Browsers)
- Backup Browsers
- Potential Browsers
- Nonbrowsers
- Client Systems

Figure 2.8 illustrates how browsing services work. All computers in the network will have a browser status.

In this example, our network consists of two segments, Segment #1 and Segment # 2, which are using TCP/IP connected through a router. Notice that the first segment contains the PDC and Segment #2 contains a BDC. In this example:

- The PDC is always the domain master browser. This computer is responsible for maintaining the browser list for the entire domain.

- Each computer on Segment #1 will announce its presence to the domain master browser and this computer will maintain the browse list.

- Each segment will also contain a master browser. The master browser on Segment #2 will be the BDC. The master browser is responsible for keeping track of all of the computers on their local segment.

- The domain master browser swaps browse lists with all of the master browsers. This allows each segment to have a complete list of the resources for the domain.

- If the network contains more than one domain, the domain master browsers will swap browse lists with each other so that all domains have complete browse lists for the entire network.

FIGURE 2.8

Browser Example

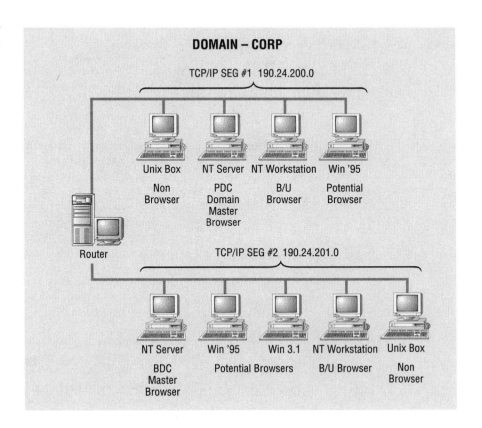

The roles that computer browsers can play are defined in Table 2.5.

TABLE 2.5

Browser Roles

Browser Role	Description
Domain Master Browser	The domain master browser keeps track of all resources on the domain. The domain master browser is always the PDC. This computer is responsible for coordinating the browse lists from all of the master browsers which are located on remote subnets. In addition, the domain master browser collects browse lists from other domain master browsers that manage the browse lists for other domains that are connected on the same network. The Domain Master Browser can act as the Master Browser for its subnetwork.

T A B L E 2.5 (cont.) Browser Roles	Browser Role	Description
	Master Browser	In a TCP/IP network, browser broadcasts are filtered by routers. This necessitates that each segment specify a master browser to coordinate a browse list that can then be swapped with the domain master browser.
	Backup Browser	In addition to domain master browsers and master browsers, each network segment also uses backup browsers. This offloads network traffic from master browsers.
	Preferred Master Browser	This is a computer with the registry configured so that it is always the master browser for the segment. This circumvents the election process that is covered in the next subsection.
	Potential Browser	A potential browser is a computer that can participate in the browser election. This is covered in more detail in the next subsection.
	Nonbrowser	A nonbrowser can be a browser client, but it does not provide browser services.
	Browser Client	A browser client accesses and uses browser services (for example, from a master browser or backup browser).

Browser Computer Selection

Browser computers are selected by an election process. The following criteria are used in selecting a master browser (in the order which they are used to evaluate the election):

- Operating system platform
    - NT Server domain controller (PDC wins over BDC)
    - NT member server

- NT Workstation

- Windows 95

- Windows for Workgroups

- Operating system version (if two or more computers tie after operating system evaluation)

  - NT 4.0

  - NT 3.51

  - NT 3.5

  - NT 3.1

- Computer that has been running the longest amount of time (if two or more computers tie after operating system version evaluation)

If two computers are still in the election process and are in a tie, the final determining factor is which computer has the highest alphanumeric name. The next section will overview hard disk configurations.

Hard Disk Configuration

You can configure your NT Server hard disks in many different ways. Some of the options you can choose from include: volume sets, stripe sets, mirror sets, and stripe sets with parity. Each of these hard-disk configurations will determine the amount of disk space available, redundancy of data, and performance.

Allocating Disk Space Capacity

You can allocate disk space in many ways. NT Server supports volume sets, stripe sets, mirror sets, and stripe sets with parity. These configurations are compared in Table 2.6.

T A B L E 2.6: NT Disk Drive Configurations and Capacities

	Volume Set	Stripe Set	Mirror Set	Stripe Set with Parity
Description	A volume set is disk space that spans more than one partition; however, it is recognized as a single volume, and has a single drive letter assigned to it.	A stripe set combines disk space from multiple drives into a single logical drive. Data is written evenly across the stripe set.	A mirror set consists of two partitions of equal size that mirror each other for redundancy. (Called duplexing when partitions are controlled by separate controllers.)	A stripe set with parity is similar to a stripe set, except that it contains parity information which is used for fault tolerance.
Requirements	2–32 drives. Partitions can be any size.	2–32 drives. Partitions must be the same size.	2 partitions. They must be the same size.	3–32 drives. Partitions must be the same size.
Setup	A volume set can be initially created from free space through Disk Administrator. Volume sets can also be extended after initial creation through Disk Administrator. Extended volume sets must be NTFS.	Stripe sets are created through Disk Administrator by selecting free space that is of equal size on multiple physical partitions. Once a stripe set has been created, it can be deleted, but not extended.	To create a mirror set, create a partition first, then select an area of free space on another partition that is equal to the first partition. From Disk Administrator, then choose Establish Mirror.	Stripe sets with parity are created by using Disk Administrator and selecting free space on three or more drives, and then choosing Create Stripe Set with Parity.
Advantages	Volume sets allow you to extend available disk space when your drive is reaching capacity. You also have the advantage of combing partitions that are not the same size.	Stripe sets increase performance by writing data evenly over two or more drives in a set. This also allows you to take advantage of multiple I/O channels.	Mirror sets provide fault tolerance. If either drive fails, your system will continue to function. Mirror sets are the only method of fault tolerance available for system and boot partitions.	Stripe sets with parity provide fault tolerance and maximize storage space utilization by adding a parity stripe to each drive in the set.

T A B L E 2.6: NT Disk Drive Configurations and Capacities *(continued)*

	Volume Set	Stripe Set	Mirror Set	Stripe Set with Parity
Disadvantages	If any drive in a volume set fails, the entire volume is unavailable.	Stripe sets provide no fault tolerance, and if any drive fails, the entire set is unavailable.	Only 50% of the space in a mirror set is available for data.	If a drive fails, you can still access the data, but it is very slow. If two drives fail, you must rely on your backup.
Usable Space for Data	All space is available for data.	All space is available for data.	Only 50% of the space in the mirror set is available for data.	You lose the space of one drive partition in the stripe set that is used to store parity information.

Providing Redundancy

NT Server has two disk configurations for providing redundancy: disk mirroring (and disk duplexing) and disk striping with parity. See Table 2.6 for an explanation of these two options.

Improving Performance

Read/write performance can be increased through two disk drive configurations: disk striping and disk striping with parity. Performance is also affected by the number of controllers used for the storage partitions. These options are covered in Table 2.6.

Providing Security

Security is provided through the New Technology File System (NTFS). Once a partition has been formatted as NTFS, you can assign file level permissions, audit usage, and specify ownership. This will be covered in greater detail in Unit 3.

Creation of NTFS Partition

You can create an NTFS partition through:

- The Disk Administrator utility
- The FORMAT command by using the following command line syntax:

  FORMAT *drive letter*: /fs:NTFS

CONVERT Utility

You can convert a File Allocation Table (FAT) partition to an NTFS partition through the CONVERT command line utility. The syntax is:

CONVERT *drive letter*: /fs:NTFS

Note that the CONVERT command line utility is one-way. To go from NTFS back to FAT, you'd need to back up or copy the data to another location, reformat the drive as FAT, create a new partition, and then restore the data from backup tape. Remember that storage volumes can be converted to NTFS during the NT Server installation.

Formatting

In this section, we'll cover how disks are organized and formatted and how ARC naming conventions are established.

Organization and Formatting

Hard drives are organized into usable space through the creation of volumes. Once a volume has been created, it must be formatted with a file system, such as FAT or NTFS.

ARC Naming Conventions

ARC stands for Advanced RISC Computing. ARC names are used in the BOOT.INI file to point to the location of the NT operating system. If you use default values, this is the \WINNT directory, and this partition is referred to as the boot partition. The ARC naming convention is as follows:

[multi(w) or scsi(w)]disk(x)rdisk(y)partition(z)

These options are described in Table 2.7.

TABLE 2.7	Option	Description
ARC Naming Options Defined	Multi(w) or SCSI(w)	The ARC name begins with either Multi or SCSI. Multi is used for any disk other than a Small Computer Systems Interface (SCSI) controlled drive or when a disk using an SCSI adapter that has its BIOS enabled. SCSI is used with SCSI controllers that have their BIOS disabled.
	Disk(x)	Used with the SCSI option. This number will always be 0 if you used Multi. If you use SCSI, this number will be the SCSI bus number or target ID and will begin with 0.
	Rdisk(y)	Used with the Multi option. If you used SCSI, this number will always be 0. For Multi, this number is the ordinal number of the disk and begins with 0.
	Partition(z)	Used with multi or SCSI. This number is the ordinal number of the hard drive partition and always starts with 1.

In the next section, you will learn about printer configuration.

Printer Configuration

This section will cover printer configuration. Specifically, you should know how to:

- Add and configure a printer

- Implement a printer pool

- Set print priorities

- Manage printer permissions

- Support printing in a TCP/IP environment

- Configure printers using the DLC protocol

Adding and Configuring a Printer

This section will address how to add a printer, then how to configure a printer. Configuring most printers attached to a domain computer running a DOS or Windows NT operating system is simple. Interfacing to network printers can be more complex initially. However, users can easily connect to shared network devices after the initial setup is performed.

Remember the differences between a *printer* and a *print device* in the Windows NT print model. A printer refers to a logical object within NT. A print device is the actual hardware device. Additionally, NT can map a printer to more than one print device (printer pool) or more than one printer to a single print device (printer priorities).

Adding a Printer

To add a printer:

1. Select Start ➤ Settings ➤ Printers.

2. NT uses a Printer Wizard that walks you through the process of installing a printer. The Printer Wizard will ask you to specify the options shown in Table 2.8.

	Configuration Option	Description
T A B L E 2.8 Printer Wizard Configuration Selections	My Computer or Network Print Server	My Computer assumes that you are configuring the printer for local access. You may then elect to share the printer for network access. The computer upon which you are defining the printer automatically becomes that printer's print server. If you choose Network Print Server, it is assumed that you are attaching to an existing network printer.
	Port	This defines the port to which the printer is attached. The port can be local or a network printer port.
	Manufacturer and Printer	This option is used to specify your specific printer so that the correct driver can be selected.
	Printer Name	Defines the printer's name. Through this screen, you can also specify if this printer should be the user's default printer.

TABLE 2.8 *(cont.)* Printer Wizard Configuration Selections	**Configuration Option**	**Description**
	Shared or Not Shared	Shared implies that the printer is available for network access. Not shared means that it is available only to users of the local computer. If you choose shared, you can also configure the printer to support drivers for Windows 95 and all Windows NT client versions, including non-Intel platforms. Print Drivers for other clients must be loaded separately. You also specify a share name.

Configuring a Printer

Once a printer has been created under NT, you can configure it through the Printer Properties option. The six printer configuration tabs are defined in Table 2.9.

TABLE 2.9 Printer Tab Configuration Options	**Tab**	**Configuration Options**
	General	The General tab allows you to configure a comment, a location, a driver (can be used to update), a separator page file, and a print processor. It also allows you to print a test page.
	Ports	This tab is used to specify to which port (local or network) the printer is attached. You can also add, delete, and configure ports through this tab.
	Scheduling	Scheduling allows you to specify when a printer is available, the printer's priority, and how print jobs should be spooled.
	Sharing	This tab specifies whether or not a printer is shared. If the printer is shared, you can also specify a share name here, and which alternate drivers should automatically be available to remote users.
	Security	Security is used to configure permissions, ownership, and auditing.
	Device Settings	This tab is used to configure printer-specific settings such as tray assignment printer memory and font cartridges.

One of the benefits of NT printing is that you can load print drivers for Windows NT 3.5x, Windows NT 4.0, and Windows 95 platforms on the print server, not the clients. When users attach to the print server, the print driver is automatically downloaded to the client. This means that updates to print drivers only need to be installed on the print server for the operating systems that were listed.

Implementing a Printer Pool

Printer pools are used to logically group print devices together, yet they only define a single printer. Conceptually, a printer pool looks like Figure 2.9. The benefit of a printer pool is that you can send your job to the logically defined printer, and the job will be sent to the first available print device.

FIGURE 2.9

Printer Pool

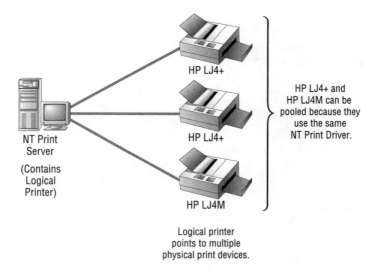

In order to create a printer pool, you must meet the following criteria:

- The print devices should be in close proximity because the print job could go to any print device in the pool.

- The print devices must be able to use the same print driver.

Setting Print Priorities

Print priorities specify when a printer is available and specify its priority. The concept is the opposite of a printer pool. This concept assumes that you will have multiple logical printers that point to the same print device. Conceptually, this looks like Figure 2.10.

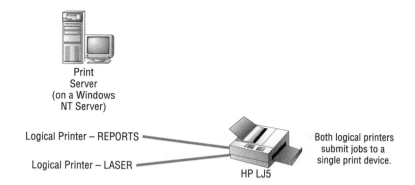

FIGURE 2.10

Multiple Logical Printers Pointing to a Single Print Device

The following subsections define availability and priority.

Availability

Printers can be configured so that they are available only during a single, specified time period of the day.

Example:

You define two printers, REPORTS and LASER, that point to the same laser printer. The REPORTS printer could be configured to print only between 12:00 and 6:00 A.M., while the LASER printer is available 24 hours a day. Users could then be directed to send jobs that are over 30 pages to the REPORTS printer so that the printer is not tied up with long jobs during the day.

Priority

Printers can be assigned priority between 1 and 99. The highest priority is 99 and the lowest priority is 1 (default).

Example:

Assume that you have a printer called EXECS and a printer called ACCT that points to the same physical print device. You could assign permissions so that the EXECS group can use the EXECS printer and the ACCT group can use the ACCT printer. By giving the EXECS printer a priority of 99 and the ACCT printer a priority of 1, the EXECS printer will always submit its jobs first to the physical print device.

Managing Printer Permissions

When a printer is created, by default group EVERYONE has Print permissions to that printer. However, as with NTFS file objects, you can specify permissions to printers. Table 2.9 lists the NT printer permissions.

	Printer Permission	Description
TABLE 2.10 NT Printer Permissions	No Access	Denies all access to the printer, even if the user has other permissions through a user account or other group memberships.
	Print	Allows a user to submit jobs to the print queue.
	Manage Documents	Allows a user to manage documents within the print queue (spooler) for the associated printer. By default users can manage documents they submit, but a user who has the Manage Documents permission is able to manage documents submitted by any user.
	Full Control	Allows you to manage documents, as well as manage all properties of a printer. A user with the Full Control permission can also take ownership of a printer.

Printing in a TCP/IP Environment

You can support TCP/IP printers through the Add Printer Wizard. The following list summarizes important facts relevant to TCP/IP printing.

- You must first install the TCP/IP protocol and the Microsoft TCP/IP Printing service on the computer that will act as the print server for the TCP/IP printer.

- You must know the IP address of the print device. This will be one of the following:

  - The IP address of the network printer

  - The IP address of the computer to which the TCP/IP printer is directly attached

- You must specify the DNS (domain name) for the printer you are installing.

The print server that defines the TCP/IP printer becomes an LPD (line printer daemon) print server.

To print to printers that have been configured as LPD print servers, use the LPR command.

To obtain the status of an LPD server queue, use the LPQ diagnostic utility.

Configuring Printers to Use the DLC Protocol

As noted previously, you can use the DLC protocol to connect an HP print device to the network. When configuring a network printer that will use DLC, you should take the following steps:

- Install the DLC protocol on the computer that will act as the print server with which the printer is associated.

- Use the self-test on the network printer to identify the MAC address of the network card.

- Select a logical name that will be used by the printer.

- Through the Add Printers Wizard, add a printer that is configured to use the Hewlett-Packard Network Port and specify the MAC address of the printer when prompted.

Now that you know how to configure NT printers, the next section will show you how to configure NT server for different clients.

NT Server Configuration for Client Support

NT Server supports a variety of clients, including NT Workstation, Windows 95, and Macintosh clients.

Windows NT Workstation

NT Workstations must be configured to be part of the NT domain. To add a workstation to the domain, you must be logged on as a user who is a member of the Administrators group, Account Operators group, or as a user who has the "add workstations to the domain" user right (which is assigned through User Manager for Domains ➤ Policies ➤ User Rights).

To add a workstation to the domain, take the following steps:

1. Create a computer account using the NetBIOS name for the workstation through Server Manager.

2. At the NT workstation, go to Control Panel ➤ Network ➤ Identification tab. Enter the domain to which the workstation should belong.

You can also create a computer account through Control Panel ➤ Network ➤ Identification tab, by checking the Add Computer to the Domain box. If you use this option, you must supply a user name and the password of an administrative user or a user who has the "add workstation to the domain" system-policy user right.

Microsoft Windows 95

Windows 95 computers are not objects within an NT domain. Because Windows 95 computers are not part of the domain, they are not added through the Server Manager as are NT Workstations. To configure the Windows 95 client to be a part of an NT domain, take the following steps on the Windows 95 client:

1. From Control Panel ➤ Network, choose the Configuration tab.

2. Add the Client Software for Microsoft Networks software.

3. After the software is installed, highlight Client Software for Microsoft Networks and click on the Properties button.

4. In the Properties dialog box, check Log on to Windows NT domain. Specify the domain to which you will log on as a client.

Macintosh Clients

In order to support Macintosh clients, you must install Services for Macintosh on the NT Server to which the Macintosh clients will attach. Installing Services for Macintosh allows Macintosh clients to access NT file and print resources.

The Macintosh clients can connect to an NT server without any additional software if Services for Macintosh is configured to allow guest logons or cleartext (unencrypted) passwords. If you specify that encrypted passwords will be used, the Macintosh clients will require that the UAM (User Authentication Module) be installed. When you install Services for Macintosh, the UAM is installed on the NTFS partition with the most free space.

If you will support a Macintosh network that uses LocalTalk as its connection media, you must upgrade the Macintosh clients to EtherTalk (or some other common media with the PC network), install a third-party router that connects Ethernet (or whatever you are using) with LocalTalk, or install a LocalTalk into your NT server so that it functions as a router.

NT Server Roles

1.　List the three roles for which NT Server can be configured.

_____

_____

_____

2.　True or False. When you install an NT Server as a member server, you can upgrade it to a BDC without reinstalling the computer.

3.　True or False. When you install an NT Server as a BDC, it can be promoted to a PDC even if the PDC is off-line.

4.　You have a slow WAN link that connects your domain which spans San Antonio and your Detroit offices. You have the PDC and two BDCs on the San Antonio network segment and a BDC on the Detroit segment. You want to control the traffic that is generated across the WAN link from SAM synchronization. You do not want to affect synchronization on the local BDCs.

Do you configure the PDC or BDC? _____

What registry option do you configure? _____

5.　What utility do you use to manually force the BDCs to synchronize to the SAM database on the PDC?

_____

6. True or False. You can install a BDC into a domain as long as another BDC is on-line.

7. True or False. You can change a BDC's domain by specifying the domain it belongs to through the Control Panel ➤ Network ➤ Identification tab.

8. True or False. You can change the domain of a member server by specifying the domain it belongs to through the Control Panel ➤ Network ➤ Identification tab.

9. True or False. A BDC is automatically promoted to PDC if the PDC becomes unavailable through an election process.

10. True or False. NT 4.0 requires at least one BDC per domain.

11. A BDC contains a _____ (domain or local) SAM database.

12. A member server contains a _____ (domain or local) SAM.

13. By default, the PDC SAM is copied to member servers every _____ minutes.

14. True or False. You can make changes to the SAM database located on a BDC.

15. True or False. By default the entire SAM database is copied from the PDC to the BDCs during SAM synchronization.

Network Protocols and Bindings

16. How do you install the AppleTalk protocol?

_____

17. If you want to configure TCP/IP addresses automatically, you should use the _____ _____service on an NT server.

18. The primary function of the _____ service is to resolve NetBIOS computer names to IP addresses dynamically.

19. True or False. The DLC protocol requires that you specify the DLC address and default gateway.

20. If you are using the NWLink IPX/SPX Compatible Transport protocol, the most common configuration error is associated with incorrect _____.

21. The range of IP addresses defined on a DHCP server is referred to as _____ _____.

22. True or False. You must enter static mappings of all of the IP addresses and NetBIOS computer names for your WINS clients through the WINS Manager of a WINS server for WINS to be fully functional.

23. You must configure the _____ option in TCP/IP if you will require routing services.

24. The _____ utility is used to manage DHCP configuration.

25. The _____ file can be used as an alternative to WINS. This file must be manually configured and placed on each host computer.

26. Should heavily used protocols be at the top or bottom of the binding order?

_____

NT Server Core Services

27. Which computers can be used as export computers for directory replication?

_____

28. Which computers can be used as import computers for directory replication?

_____

29. By default, the domain master browser is located on this computer.

_____

30. _____ computers are used to offload browser-request traffic from the master browsers on each network segment.

31. During a browser election, which computer would win: an NT Workstation version 3.5 or a Windows 95 computer?

_____

32. The directory replicator service account must be a part of which two groups?

_____

_____

33. What is the default export directory used by directory replication?

_____

34. List two common uses for directory replication.

_____

_____

Hard Disk Configuration

35. Which two NT hardware configurations provide redundancy for disk drive configurations?

_____

_____

36. The _____ hard disk configuration provides the only fault tolerance for the NT server system and boot partition.

37. In order to configure disk striping with parity, you must have at least _____ drives. The maximum number of drives that can be used in a stripe set with parity is _____ _____.

38. True or False. Disk mirroring offers better performance than disk striping for read and write access.

_____

39. The _____ utility is used to manage NT disk configurations.

40. If you want fault tolerance and you also want to maximize disk space on your data drives, you should use the _____ disk configuration.

41. True or False. To establish disk duplexing, choose the Establish Disk Duplex option from Tools within Disk Administrator.

42. The _____ utility is used to change a FAT partition to NTFS while still preserving the data on the partition.

Printer Configuration

43. What requirement must be met for print devices that will be configured as a print pool?

_____

44. The _____ service must be installed on the computer that will act as the print server for an LPD printer.

45. The _____ command is used to send print jobs to LPD print servers.

46. The _____command is a diagnostic utility used to view the status of an LPD print server queue.

47. You are installing a network printer that uses the DLC protocol. What information must be provided regarding the DLC printer?

_____

48. You have a single print device that is shared by the Managers group and the Sales group. What can you do to ensure that jobs from the Managers group always print before jobs from the Sales group?

_____

49. You are installing a printer that uses TCP/IP and will function as an LPD server. What two pieces of identifying information do you need to specify for the LPD server to be functional?

_____

_____

50. By default the group EVERYONE gets _____ permission to newly created printers.

51. You have users who share the same print device. The printer services jobs that average 1–10 pages in length and jobs that average 250 pages (the reports for the department). How do you configure the print environment so that the 1–10 job pages are sent any time and the 250 page jobs can print only between 10:00 P.M. and 6:00 A.M.?

52. NT print servers can store print drivers for the following operating systems.

53. You have a secretarial pool that has five identical printers. What printing feature should be implemented so that print jobs are sent to the first available print device?

NT Server Configuration for Client Support

54. A user must have what group memberships or must have what rights in order to add NT computers to the domain?

55. What utility is used to add NT computers to the domain from the PDC?

_____

56. What software must be installed in order to support Macintosh clients?

_____

57. You have a Macintosh network that uses LocalTalk as its connection to the network. Your PC network uses Ethernet to connect to the network. What three options can you use that would allow the Macintosh clients to access the NT server running Services for Macintosh?

_____

_____

_____

58. True or False. You can add Windows NT Workstations and Windows 95 computers through the Server Manager utility.

SAMPLE TEST

2-1 You have a network that spans a WAN link as shown in the following diagram:

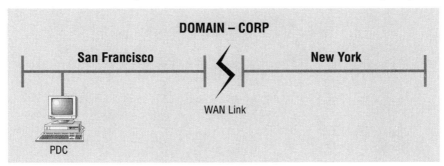

The WAN link connects the CORP domain. You are in the NY office and are in the process of installing a BDC. During the installation process, you receive an error message indicating the PDC for domain CORP can't be located. You investigate and realize that the WAN link has failed. What course of action do you take?

A. Install the computer as a PDC, specifying the domain CORP. When the WAN link is functional again, use the Server Manager utility and demote the computer to a BDC.

B. When you receive the error message, choose the Ignore option and specify that the computer is a BDC in the CORP domain.

C. Install the server as a member server. Specify that the computer is part of a workgroup. When the WAN link becomes available, use Control Panel ➤ Network ➤ Identification tab, and specify that you will be a part of the CORP domain. Use the Server Manager utility to specify that the computer should be configured as a BDC.

D. Do nothing. You can't install the BDC until the WAN link is available again because the BDC must be able to contact the PDC during the installation process.

2-2   You have a network that spans a WAN link as shown in the following diagram:

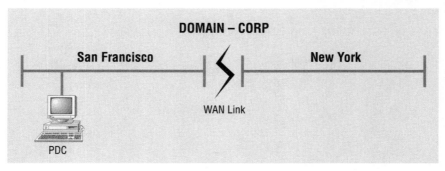

The WAN link connects the CORP domain. You are in the NY office and are in the process of installing a member server. During the installation process, you receive an error message indicating the PDC for domain CORP can't be located. You investigate and realize that the WAN link has failed. What course of action do you take?

A. Install the computer as a member server, specifying the domain CORP. When the WAN link is functional again, the server already is configured and no further work is required.

B. When you receive the error message, choose the Ignore option and specify that the computer is a member server in the CORP domain.

C. Install the server as a member server. Specify that the computer is part of a work-group. When the WAN link becomes available, use Control Panel ➤ Network ➤ Identification tab, and specify that you will be a part of the CORP domain.

D. Do nothing. You can't install the member server until the WAN link is available again because the BDC must be able to contact the PDC during the installation process.

2-3 The Sales department has recently decided to move from the workgroup model to the domain model. You have 150 Windows NT workstations and 100 Windows 95 computers that need to be configured. Which of the following steps must you take? Choose all that apply.

    A. Use Server Manager on the domain PDC to add the NT Workstations to the domain.

    B. Use Server Manager on the domain PDC to add the Windows 95 computers to the domain.

    C. At each Windows NT Workstation use Control Panel ➤ Network ➤ Identification tab to specify that the computer is part of the domain.

    D. Install the Client Software for Microsoft Networks on the Windows 95 clients. Within the Client Software for Microsoft Networks property box, check the Log on to Windows NT domain option and specify the domain to which you will log on.

2-4 Your domain spans WAN links as shown in the following figure:

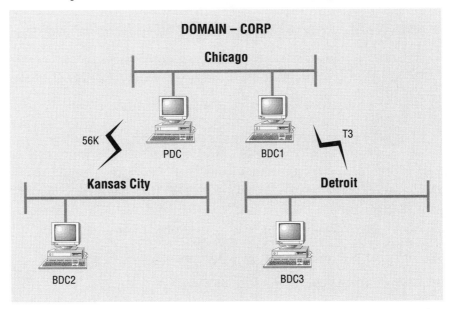

```
S A M P L E   T E S T
```

Your company has offices in Chicago, Kansas City, and Detroit. The three locations are connected through WAN links and are all part of the CORP domain. You are concerned that SAM synchronization is using too much bandwidth on the link between Chicago and Kansas City because it uses a 56K link and is already overloaded. What do you do?

   A. Adjust the ReplicationGovernor registry value on BDC2.

   B. Adjust the ReplicationGovernor registry value on PDC.

   C. Adjust the BDCSynch registry value on BDC2.

   D. Adjust the BDCSynch registry value on PDC.

2-5 Your network consists of a PDC, a BDC, and three member servers. You have a large number of users and they are complaining that when they attempt to log on in the morning, they experience a significant delay. What can you do to speed up logon response time?

   A. Install another BDC for your domain or reinstall NT Server on an existing member server so that it is configured as a BDC.

   B. Configure the NetLogon service on your PDC and BDC with high priority.

   C. Install the NetLogon service on one of your member servers. Configure the NetLogon service to point to the PDC. The member server will act as a Logon Relay Agent.

   D. Use the Server Manager utility to promote one of your member servers to a BDC.

2-6 Your domain consists of a PDC, a BDC, and 100 Windows 95 computers. You have decided to upgrade the Windows 95 clients to Windows NT Workstation. John is a network technician who will upgrade the computers. You want the NT Workstations to be added to the domain. John's user account will be used to add the workstations to the domain. Which of the following options would allow John the appropriate permission? Choose all that apply.

   A. Make him a member of the Server Operators group.

   B. Make him a member of the Account Operators group.

C. Make him a member of the Administrators group.

D. Assign him the Add Workstations to the Domain User Right.

2-7 Your company supports a mixture of NT and UNIX computers. You have been asked to install a printer on the NT Server that will act as an LPD server. Which of the following options must be met to support this printer? Choose all that apply.

A. You must install the LPD service on the server.

B. You must install the TCP/IP Printing service on the server.

C. You must specify an IP address for the printer or a domain name for the printer.

D. You need to specify the subnet mask that will be used by the printer.

E. You need to specify a default router for the printer.

2-8 You are in the process of installing an HP network print device. The network printer is being configured to use the DLC protocol. Which of the following options apply to this scenario? Choose all that apply.

A. You must specify the NetBIOS name that will be used by the printer.

B. You must specify the DLC network address that will be used by the printer.

C. You must specify the MAC address of the DLC printer network interface.

D. You must install the DLC protocol on the print server that will host the network print device.

E. Each client that will connect to the network print device must have the DLC protocol installed.

```
SAMPLE TEST
```

2-9   You have been asked to select the disk drive configuration that will be used on a computer that will be installed as NT Server. The computer contains three SCSI hard drives that are each 4GB. You have been asked to select a method that will utilize the maximum amount of disk storage space, while still providing some form of fault tolerance. You decide to use disk striping with parity. What do you do?

    A. During installation, specify that all of the disk space will be combined into a stripe set with parity.

    B. Create a small partition on the first hard drive and install NT to this partition. Use the remaining free space on the first drive, and combine it with equal free space on the second and third drives that will become the stripe set with parity through the Disk Administrator utility.

    C. Install Windows NT on the first physical disk. On the remaining disks, create a stripe set with parity through the Disk Administrator utility.

    D. This scenario does not have the minimum hardware requirements to support disk striping with parity.

2-10   Your domain consists of a PDC, two BDCs, and 500 assorted Microsoft clients. The network is configured to use the TCP/IP protocol. While using the Network Monitor, you realize that network traffic is high due to broadcasts being generated through name-resolution requests. Which of the following options will help eliminate this traffic?

    A. Install a WINS server on each network segment, and manually add the clients' IP addresses.

    B. Install a WINS server on each network segment, and configure each client as a WINS client. The WINS servers will automatically create a database that will be used for name resolution.

    C. Install one WINS server, it will automatically register each client's NetBIOS and IP information.

    D. Configure each client as a WINS server.

2-11 Your network has a network print device that is used by 20 people in the Accounting Department. Most of the jobs that are printed are between 1–10 pages. However, at the end of the month several print jobs are sent that average 300 pages. When these long jobs are generated, you receive many complaints about how long the print device takes to print the long jobs. What do you do?

A. Specify two groups, ACCOUNTANTS and REPORTS. Create two printers that will point to the same print device called AcctPrinter and ReportPrinter. Assign the Acct-Printer priority 99 and the ReportPrinter priority 1. Specify that jobs that are greater than 50 pages are sent to the print device, and they should be submitted through the ReportPrinter printer.

B. Create two printers that will point to the same print device called AcctPrinter and ReportPrinter. Configure the AcctPrinter so that it is available 24 hours a day and the ReportPrinter so that it is available only during nonproduction hours. Instruct users to send print jobs that are greater than 50 pages to the ReportPrinter.

C. Specify that users should only submit long print jobs when they are ready to leave for the day, so they will print during off-peak hours.

D. Specify that long print jobs be submitted, then place them on hold until you leave for the day at which time they can be released.

2-12 Your network consists of the SALES domain and the CORP domain. NTSERVER is a BDC in the CORP domain. You want to move this computer to the SALES domain. What do you do?

A. Use the Server Manager utility to move the computer from one domain to another.

B. On NTSERVER, use Control Panel ➤ Network ➤ Identification tab to specify that the computer will now be a part of the SALES domain. When adding the computer to the domain, you will need to specify an administrative name and password.

C. Use the Domain Manager utility to move the computer from one domain to another.

D. This task can't be completed without reinstallation.

2-13 Your network consists of the SALES domain and the CORP domain. NTSERVER is a member server in the CORP domain. You want to move this computer to the SALES domain. What do you do?

    A. Use the Server Manager utility to move the computer from one domain to another.

    B. On NTSERVER, use Control Panel ➤ Network ➤ Identification tab to specify that the computer will now be part of the SALES domain. When adding the computer to the domain, you will need to specify an administrative name and password.

    C. Use the Domain Manager utility to move the computer from one domain to another.

    D. This task can't be completed without reinstallation.

2-14 Your domain consists of a PDC and three BDCs. Your PDC has been having problems and will need to be taken down for maintenance. What utility or procedure do you do to promote one of your BDCs to PDC?

    A. Server Manager

    B. Domain Manager

    C. Control Panel ➤ Network

    D. This can only be accomplished by editing the registry on the PDC and the BDC that will be promoted to PDC.

2-15 Your domain consists of a PDC and three BDCs. You make changes to the SAM database on a regular basis and are frustrated because of delays in SAM synchronization. What registry value can be edited to decrease the time it takes for the SAM database to be updated to the BDCs on an automatic basis?

    A. The ReplicationGovernor value on the PDC

    B. The ReplicationGovernor value on the BDCs

    C. The Pulse value on the PDC

    D. The Pulse value on the BDCs

2-16 What option can be used to reduce broadcast traffic generated by resolving IP to NetBIOS names in the event that the WINS service is not used?

    A. Place an `lmhosts` file on each host.

    B. Place a `hosts` file on each host.

    C. Place an `lmhosts` file on each server and router.

    D. Place a `hosts` file on each server and router.

2-17 Your network consists of a PDC and three BDCs. Sometimes users receive their logon scripts when they log on, and at other times the logon scripts do not execute. What is the best course of action to correct this problem?

    A. When specifying the logon script name, use a UNC name.

    B. Place the logon scripts on the PDC, use directory replication with the PDC as an export computer and the BDCs as import computers.

    C. Place the logon scripts on the PDC, use file replication with the PDC as an export computer and the BDCs as import computers.

    D. For each computer, specify a preferred logon server. Store each user's logon script on his or her preferred server.

2-18 Your network has a network print device that is used by 20 people in the Accounting Department. The Accounting Department has two managers, and the rest of the department is staff level. The managers have complained to you that sometimes there is a long wait before their print jobs print. They want their print jobs to be submitted from the print queue first. What is the best solution for this case?

    A. Specify two groups, MANAGERS and ACCOUNTANTS. Create two printers that will point to the same print device called ManagerPrinter and AcctPrinter. Assign the ManagerPrinter priority 99 and the AcctPrinter priority 1. Tell the users to send their jobs to the AcctPrinter and the managers to send their jobs to the ManagerPrinter.

B. Specify two groups, MANAGERS and ACCOUNTANTS. Create one printer called AcctPrinter. Assign Print permissions to the MANAGERS group with a priority of 99. Assign Print permissions to the ACCOUNTANTS group with a priority of 1.

C. Specify two groups, MANAGERS and ACCOUNTANTS. Create two printers that will point to the same print device called ManagerPrinter and AcctPrinter. Assign the ManagerPrinter priority 99, and assign the AcctPrinter priority 1. Remove the Print permission from group EVERYONE on the ManagersPrinter and only allow the MANAGERS group to have Print permissions. Tell the staff to send their jobs to the AcctPrinter and the managers to send their jobs to the ManagerPrinter.

D. Specify two groups, MANAGERS and ACCOUNTANTS. Create one printer called AcctPrinter. Assign Manage Documents permissions to the MANAGERS group and leave group EVERYONE with Print permission. Instruct the managers to place their print jobs at the top of the print queue because they have permission through the Manage Documents print permission.

2-19 Your network consists of a mixture of NT and UNIX clients. You install a TCP/IP printer on your NT print server. What command will be used by the UNIX clients to submit jobs to your NT TCP/IP printer?

A. lp*d*

B. lpr

C. lpq

D. NET SEND

UNIT

3

Managing Resources

Test Objectives: Managing Resources

■ **Manage users and group accounts. Considerations include:**

- Managing Windows NT users accounts
- Managing Windows NT user rights
- Managing Windows NT groups
- Administering account policies
- Auditing changes to the user account database

■ **Create and manage policies and profiles for various situations. Policies and profiles include:**

- Local user profiles
- Roaming user profiles
- System policies

■ **Administer remote servers from various types of client computers. Client computer types include:**

- Windows 95
- Windows NT Workstation

■ **Manage disk resources. Tasks include:**

- Creating and sharing resources
- Implementing permissions and security
- Establishing file auditing

Exam objectives are subject to change at any time without prior notice and at Microsoft's sole discretion. Please visit Microsoft's Training & Certification website (www.microsoft.com/Train_Cert) for the most current exam objectives listing.

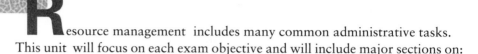

Resource management includes many common administrative tasks. This unit will focus on each exam objective and will include major sections on:

- User and Group Management
- Profiles and Policies
- Remote Administration
- Disk Resource Management

After reviewing each objective, you can focus on how to put everything together in the last section:

- Managing Resources in an Enterprise Environment

User and Group Management

User and group management are common administrative tasks. This section will focus on how to manage NT users, user rights, groups, account policies, and how you can audit account management. All of these tasks will be accomplished through the User Manager for Domains utility.

Managing NT Users

To create and manage users, use the User Manager for Domains utility. NT Server has only two default user accounts, Administrator and Guest (the Guest account is disabled by default). This means you will probably have to create users.

In order to create and manage users, you must be logged on as a member of the Administrators or Account Operators group. The following subsections will cover the creation and management of NT user accounts.

Creating User Accounts

Once you are in User Manager for Domains, you can create a user by selecting User ➤ New User. Figure 3.1 illustrates the New User dialog box.

FIGURE 3.1

The New User
Dialog Box

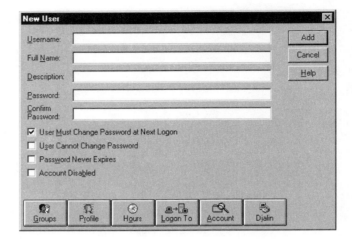

The options for creating a new user are shown in Table 3.1.

TABLE 3.1

The New User Dialog
Box Configuration
Options

Option	Description
Username	A unique ID used to identify the user. The username can be up to 20 characters and is typically a combination of alphanumeric characters. The following characters are NOT allowed: " / \ [ ] ; :	= , + * ? < >. Username is the only required field for creating a new user. It is actually a property of the User's Security ID (SID) and can be changed.
Full Name	Designed to provide the user's first and last name, for informational purposes.
Description	Can be used to provide further information for the user, such as title, department, or location.
Password and Confirm Password	Specifies the user's initial password.

	Option	Description
T A B L E 3.1 *(cont.)* The New User Dialog Box Configuration Options	User Must Change Password at Next Logon	Checked by default. This option forces the user to change his or her password the first time he or she logs on.
	User Cannot Change Password	Not specified by default. This option prevents a user from changing his or her password. This option is typically used for guest, service, and shared accounts.
	Password Never Expires	This option allows you to override the password expiration in the Account Policy. This is typically used for guest and service accounts.
	Account Disabled	Keeps an account from being accessed. This option is used for accounts that are not currently being used, but might be used again in the future, and it is used for template accounts. Improves overall account security posture.

You can also specify user properties, which will be covered in the next subsection during user creation.

Managing User Accounts

Each user account has associated properties. These properties specify:

- To which groups the user belongs
- Profile information
- The hours during the week when the user can log on
- From which computers the user account can log on
- Account expiration and type

Groups

Groups are used to assign and specify collections of local and global users to simplify assignment of permissions and properties. Groups will be covered in more detail in the Managing NT Groups section.

If users are logged on before they are added to a group, they must log off and log on again so that their access tokens will be updated.

Profile

By clicking the Profile button in the User Properties dialog box, you open the User Environment Profile dialog box (see Figure 3.2). This dialog box is used to configure roaming profile paths, logon scripts, and the user's home directories.

FIGURE 3.2

The User Environment Profile Dialog Box

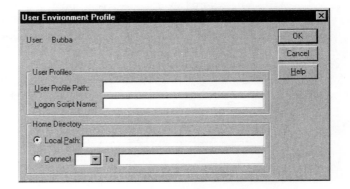

The options you can specify are listed in Table 3.2.

TABLE 3.2

The User Environment Profile Dialog Box Defined

Option	Description
User Profile Path	This option is normally left blank, indicating that the user will use a local profile. If the user will use a roaming profile, this box is filled with a UNC path pointing to the location of the User Profile, usually on PDC or BDC.
Logon Script Name	Specifies a logon script that will run every time the user logs on. This is normally a .BAT or .EXE file. By default, NT will look for logon scripts in the NETLOGON share of the authenticating domain controller.

T A B L E 3.2 *(cont.)*	Option	Description
The User Environment Profile Dialog Box Defined	Home Directory	Allows you to specify a home directory for the user. Home directories normally are used as a place for users to store their personal data files. You can specify that the home directory be on a local or network drive. The *%USERNAME%* variable can be used to substitute the user's logon name. It is one of several variables that can be used to modify the path based on user information.

When a user logon script is defined, you can specify a file name, but not a UNC path. The authenticating server will look for the logon script in its NETLOGON share which is the \winnt\system32\repl\import\scripts folder. If users could potentially be authenticated by multiple servers, you should use directory replication to manage your logon scripts. Directory replication is covered in Unit 2.

Hours

Logon hours are used to specify when a user is permitted to log on and access the network. By default, a user can log on 24 hours a day, seven days a week. You could limit this for:

- Security reasons
- Backup purposes

Hours can only be set on a per-user basis. There is no option for defining hours as a system policy, or even a group policy. The quickest way to manage this for existing users is to highlight all users who should have the time restrictions applied through the User Manager for Domains main dialog box, then select Properties so that you can manage the properties of all highlighted users at the same time.

Logon To

The Logon Workstations dialog box specifies from which computers the user can log on to the domain. By default, a user can log on from any client. Logon To can limit this ability to eight or fewer clients, specified by Computer (NetBIOS) Name. For example, you might limit (for security) the Administrator account to being able to log on only from certain workstations within the domain.

Account

The Account user property specifies two items:

- If the account has an expiration date, for example, for temporary employees
- Whether the account is a global account or a local account

The next section defines the NT user rights.

Managing NT User Rights

User rights are used to specify the system tasks to which users and groups have access. User rights come in two types, regular user rights and advanced user rights. To specify user rights, use User Manager for Domains, Policies ≻ User Rights. The regular user rights are defined in Table 3.3.

T A B L E 3.3: NT User Rights

User Right	Description	Default Membership
Access this computer from the network	Allows a user to connect to this computer from another network location.	Administrators, Everyone
Add workstations to the domain	Allows a user to add NT computers to the domain.	Account Operators, Administrators
Backup files and directories	Overrides any permissions to allow a user to back up the file system.	Administrators, Server Operators, Backup Operators
Change the system time	Used to change the computer's internal system time.	Administrators, Server Operators

T A B L E 3.3: NT User Rights *(continued)*

User Right	Description	Default Membership
Force shutdown from a remote system	Not currently implemented.	Administrators, Server Operators
Load and unload device drivers	Used to load and unload device drivers dynamically.	Administrators
Log on locally	Allows the user to log on at the local computer. Normally users do not log on at NT servers; they log on to the domain through network clients.	Account Operators, Administrators, Backup Operators, Print Operators, Server Operators
Manage auditing and security log	Used to view audit log files if auditing has been enabled. Also allows you to define NTFS and printer auditing, but does not allow you to configure auditing through User Manager for Domains.	Administrators
Restore files and directories	Overrides any permissions to allow a user to restore the file system.	Administrators, Server Operators, Backup Operators
Shut down the system	Allows users to shut down the computer.	Account Operators, Administrators, Backup Operators, Print Operators, Server Operators
Take ownership of files or other objects	Allows a user to take ownership of an NTFS file or folder or other object, such as a printer.	Administrators

Managing NT Groups

Normally you assign user rights and permissions to a group as opposed to an individual user. It is much easier for an administrator to manage and troubleshoot group permissions as opposed to individual users.

NT supports two types of groups; local groups and global groups. In this section, you will review:

- Local groups
- Global groups

- Local and global group interaction
- Default NT groups

Local Groups

Local groups have the following characteristics:

- The purpose of a local group is to assign resource permissions to a single entity of users and global groups.
- Local groups can be created on any computer running the NT operating system.
- When you create a local group, it resides in the NT computer's local SAM database.
- Local groups can contain:
  - Users from the local SAM database
  - Users from within the domain
  - Users from trusted domains
  - Global groups from within the domain
  - Global groups from trusted domains

Global Groups

Global groups have the following characteristics:

- A global group logically groups users who have similar network requirements.
- Global groups can reside only on NT domain controllers.
- Global groups can contain only users from within the local domain.

Local Group and Global Group Interaction

Local groups and global groups are designed to work as follows:

1. At the NT computer that contains a shared network resource, create a local group and assign the access permissions the local group will require.

2. From a domain controller (or computer with server administrative tools), create a global group that contains the users who need to access the resource.

3. At the NT computer that contains the shared network resource, add the global group from Step 2 as a member of the local group created in Step 1.

For example, Rick, Kevin, and Katie are users within your domain who need to access the EMAIL share on the member server APPS. You should manage the groups as shown in Figure 3.3.

FIGURE 3.3

Group Interaction

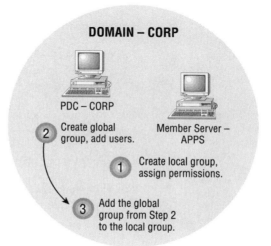

Default NT Groups

By default, NT servers (domain controllers) include several built-in groups. The idea is that every network will have some common requirements. The default groups already have been assigned the permissions and user rights they require to manage a specific task. Administration is easier because you only need to add your users to the predefined groups.The default NT groups are defined in Table 3.4.

T A B L E 3.4: Default NT Groups

Group	Global or Local	Description	Default Members
Domain Administrators	Global	Used to logically group all users who will administer the domain.	Administrator
Domain Users	Global	Used to logically group all users within a domain.	Any user, including the default Administrator account, created in the domain with the exception of the Guest account
Domain Guests	Global	Used to logically group all of the domain guest accounts.	Guest
Administrators	Local	This group has the rights to manage accounts, resources, and the NT operating system.	Administrator and the Domain Admins global group
Account Operators	Local	This group can only manage NT accounts. For example, you can create, modify, and delete users, local groups, and global groups.	None assigned
Backup Operators	Local	Backup operators can back up and restore the NT domain servers.	None assigned
Print Operators	Local	This group can share and stop sharing printers and manage existing printers.	None assigned
Replicator	Local	This is a special group which is used if you use directory replication.	None assigned
Server Operators	Local	Members of this group can manage NT server resources such as: sharing and stop sharing resources, lock or override a lock on a server, manage (even format) the servers hard disks, and back up and restore the server.	None assigned
Guests	Local	Guests don't have default rights. You must assign them rights to the resources to which they require access.	Guest and the Domain Guests global group

In addition there are special groups which do not appear in the User Manager for Domains, but which are used in the NT security model. They appear in other parts of the NT operating system (such as when NTFS permissions are set). These include:

- Everyone

- Network

- Interactive

Everyone includes all users who can access a computer. This includes guests, network users, and interactive users.

Network users are users who connect and use the resources of a computer over the network.

An interactive user is a user who is logged on locally at the computer which contains the resources he or she is accessing.

Difference between Domain Users and Everyone

The use of Domain Users versus Everyone becomes very significant in a multi-domain environment. Take the following example:

Assume that you have two domains, EAST and WEST. Between EAST and WEST, there is a two-way trust relationship defined (see Figure 3.4).

FIGURE 3.4

Difference between Groups Everyone and Domain Users

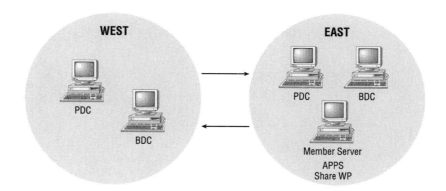

The EAST domain contains a member server called APPS, which has a share called WP. When defining permissions for this share, the following options can be applied:

- You could assign permissions to group Everyone. This would allow users from domain EAST and WEST to access the resource because all users are part of Everyone.

- You could assign permissions to group Domain Users. This includes only users from the EAST domain, so users from the WEST domain could not access the resource.

> Use group Everyone to assign permissions when you want to include users from trusted domains. Use group Domain Users when you want only users from within your domain to be able to access resources.

Difference between Domain Admins and Administrators Group

The distinction between Domain Admins and Administrators Group is important. The PDC in the following example is configured so Kim and Elaine are members of Administrators and Brett and Matt are members of Domain Admins.

Assume that you have the setup shown in Figure 3.5.

FIGURE 3.5

Differences between Group Administrators and Domain Admins

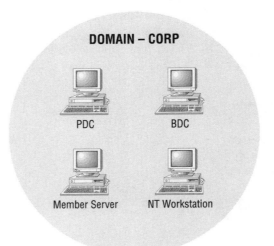

- Because Kim and Elaine are members of the Administrators group, they can manage the PDC and the BDC. This is because the PDC and the BDC share the same SAM database. They can't manage the member server or the NT workstation.

- Brett and Matt have much more power. The Domain Admins group is automatically added to the Administrators group on the PDC, as well as any computers that are added to the domain. This means that they have administrative rights over the PDC, BDC, member server, and the NT workstation.

When you add computers to the domain (NT member servers or NT workstations) the Domain Admins group is automatically added to the local Administrators group. The Domain Users group is automatically added to the local Users group and the Domain Guests group is automatically added to the local Guests group. If you have a member server or an NT workstation that Domain Admins should not have access to, you can remove the Domain Admins global group for the member server or workstations local group Administrators.

In the next section, you'll learn how to manage account policies.

Administering Account Policies

Account policies are used to specify password and account restrictions. To access the Account Policy dialog box (see Figure 3.6), select Policies ➤ Account in the main window of User Manager for Domains. These options are defined in Table 3.5 and Table 3.6.

FIGURE 3.6

The Account Policy Dialog Box

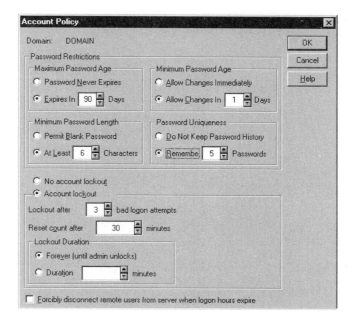

T A B L E 3.5 Password Restrictions	**Password Restriction**	**Description**	**Values**
	Maximum Password Age	Maximum number of days a password can be valid. (Default: 42 days)	1–999
	Minimum Password Age	Minimum number of days a password can be valid. (Default: Allow changes immediately)	1–999
	Minimum Password Length	Specifies whether or not a password is required and how many characters it must be. (Default: Permit Blank Password)	1–14
	Password Uniqueness	Specifies how many unique passwords must be used before a user can reuse a password. (Default: Do not keep password history)	1–24

T A B L E 3.6 Account Restrictions	**Account Restrictions**	**Description**	**Values**
	No account lock-out or Account lockout	Specifies whether or not account lockout should be enabled. (Default: No account lockout)	This is set or not set, the following options within the table assume account lockout is enabled.
	Lockout after	Specifies how many attempts a user can make when trying to log on. (Default if lockout turned on: 5)	1–999
	Reset count after	Specifies how many minutes between failed logon attempts before account is reset. (Default if lockout turned on: 30)	1–99,999 minutes

TABLE 3.6 *(cont.)* Account Restrictions	Account Restrictions	Description	Values
	Lockout duration	Specifies how long an account should be locked if the account lockout restrictions are exceeded. You can specify forever (administrator must unlock in User Manager for Domains) or a set duration in minutes. (Default if lockout turned on: 30)	1–99,999 minutes

If you are using the master domain model defined in Unit 1, you only need to define the account policies in the master domain, because all of the accounts are centralized in the master domain, and the resource domains should not contain users.

The next section will review how you can audit accounts management.

Auditing Accounts Management

You can audit changes made to the accounts database by using User Manager for Domains, then accessing Policies ➤ Audit. To enable auditing, click on Audit These Events in the Audit Policy dialog box (see Figure 3.7).

FIGURE 3.7

The Audit Policy Dialog Box

Audit Policy

Domain: DOMAIN

○ Do Not Audit

● Audit These Events:

	Success	Failure
Logon and Logoff	☐	☐
File and Object Access	☐	☐
Use of User Rights	☐	☐
User and Group Management	☐	☐
Security Policy Changes	☐	☐
Restart, Shutdown, and System	☐	☐
Process Tracking	☐	☐

OK   Cancel   Help

Once auditing is enabled, you can choose what success events, failure events, or both you want to manage. Audit options are defined in Table 3.7.

Audit Option	Description
Logon and Logoff	This option tracks an event in the audit log anytime a user logs on, logs off, or makes a network connection.
File and Object Access	This option must be enabled prior to auditing NTFS or printer events. If you enable this option, and you enable NTFS and/or printer auditing, the specified events will be written to the audit log.
User of User Rights	This option records any user rights that are used with the exception of events that relate to logon and logoff. User rights were covered in the "Managing NT User Rights" subsection in this unit.
User and Group Management	This audit option allows you to track changes to users and groups. Examples would include creating, modifying, and deleting users or groups. It also tracks events to user accounts (such as renaming a user account, disabling or enabling a user account, or resetting a password).
Security Policy Changes	Allows you to track any changes in the Policies option of User Manager for Domains. Security policies include Account Policies, Users Rights Policies, Audit Policies, and the management of trust relationships.
Restart, Shutdown, and System	Tracks any system shutdowns or restarts in the audit log. System refers to any events that relate to system security of the security log, such as clearing the security log through Event Viewer.
Process Tracking	Tracks process-related events such as program activation, indirect object accesses, some forms of handle duplication, and process exit.

To view the results of your audit, use Event Viewer and select the Security log. In the next section, you will learn how to manage NT profiles and system policies.

Profiles and System Policies

Profiles and system policies are used to manage NT user and workstation configurations.

User profiles are used used to configure user settings such as desktop appearance, program groups, shortcuts, and network connections. Profiles come in different types, local or roaming, and you can make them read-only by imposing mandatory profiles.

System policies configure the user environment and what actions the user can perform. System policies can be applied to users, groups, and specific computers. System policies are implemented by making changes to the registry with the System Policy Editor.

Local User Profiles

By default, NT uses a local profile. When a user logs on for the first time, a profile is created on the local NT computer in a directory called \WINNT\PROFILES in a subdirectory that matches the users logon name. For example, Katie's profile would be stored in \WINNT\PROFILES\KATIE. This works well if you only log on in one location. To use or access a user's profile from any network client, you must use a roaming profile.

Roaming User Profiles

Roaming profiles make a profile accessible over the network. This is especially useful for users who may have more than one workstation or who move around. This subsection defines how to create a roaming profile, and how to copy a profile from one user to another.

Creating Roaming Profiles

To create a roaming profile, complete the following steps:

1. Create a network share in a folder on a domain controller that contains the user profile.

2. In the User Environment Profile dialog box (see Figure 3.2), specify the UNC path to the directory that contains the roaming profile.

3. To invoke the roaming profile, open the System Control Panel, select the User Profiles Tab, and change the selected profile by using the Change Type button and setting the Roaming Profile option.

Copying Profiles from One User to Another

Commonly used profiles are stored in each user's home directory. This means that they will need to be copied from the default \WINNT\PROFILES folder. This cannot be accomplished through a simple copy. To copy User Profiles, you must use Control Panel ➤ System ➤ User Profiles tab shown in Figure 3.8.

FIGURE 3.8

User Profiles Tab
Dialog Box

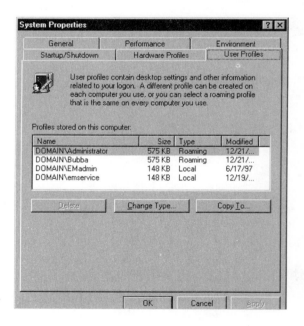

To copy a profile, simply click on the profile you want to copy, then click the Copy button. Then supply the destination path and your profile will be copied.

User profiles should never be copied through utilities like NT Explorer because they will not copy the entire profile properly.

Mandatory User Profiles

By default, profiles are read-write. The actual profile file is called NTUSER.DAT. You may not want users to change their profiles, possibly for control purposes or because the profile is shared by a group of users. You can specify that the profile is mandatory by renaming NTUSER.DAT to NTUSER.MAN.

Remember, if a mandatory profile is unavailable (for example, if the server that stores the profile goes down), the user will not be able to log on successfully.

System Policies

System policies are used to configure the user's environment. They are configured through the System Policy Editor. System policies work by editing the registry to reflect whatever settings you have imposed. System policies can be applied to:

- Users
- Groups
- Computers

System policies should reside in the \WINNT\SYSTEM32\REPL\IMPORT directory, which is the NETLOGON share. NT system policies are named NTCONFIG.POL.

System policies can be created for multiple groups. If a user belongs to multiple groups that have system policies defined, you can specify which group has the highest priority through System Policy Editor ➢ Options ➢ Group Priority.

Remote Administration

Remote administration makes it possible to administer an NT domain from a Windows 95 client or a Windows NT Workstation client. These administration tools can be installed from the NT Server distribution CD.

Windows 95

A Windows 95 computer that installs the NT administrative tools can access the following utilities:

- User Manager for Domains
- Server Manager
- Event Viewer

NT Workstation

An NT Workstation that installs the NT administrative tools gets a much wider selection of administrative tools. They include:

- User Manager for Domains
- Server Manager
- DHCP Manager
- WINS Manager
- System Policy Editor
- Services for Macintosh (adds extensions to File Manager and Server Manager)
- Remote Access Administrator
- Remoteboot Manager

Main Remote Administration Utilities

The main administrative utilities that are used are:

- User Manager for Domains
- Server Manager

The User Manager for Domains utility was discussed earlier in the "User and Group Management" section. The Server Manager utility can also be used for remote management. This is a very powerful tool that allows you to:

- Manage NT computer, Domain, or Workgroup properties remotely
- Manage users, shares, and services on remote NT servers and workstation computers
- Manage computers and other properties of a domain or workgroup

In addition, when you install the remote administration tools on Windows 95 or Windows NT Workstations, the schema of Explorer and My Computer are extended to allow you to support and manage remote NTFS security and network printers.

 When managing domains across a slow link, you can reduce the amount of network traffic generated by selecting the Low Speed Connection option in User Manager for Domains or Server Manager. You won't see listing information, but you can still manage many domain functions. The benefit of this option is that it allows you to complete management tasks more quickly.

The next section will cover the management of disk resources.

Disk Resource Management

In this section, you will learn about disk resource management through creating and sharing resources, permissions, security, and file auditing.

Creating and Sharing Resources

It is possible to create and share resources on FAT and NTFS partitions. In order to create a network share, you must be logged on as a member of the Administrators or Server Operators groups.

You can create shares through the NT Explorer, My Computer, WinFile (File Manager), and Server Manager.

Assume that you're using NT Explorer. To create a share, click on the folder you want to share, then go to File ➤ Sharing. You'll see the Sharing tab page (see Figure 3.9).

FIGURE 3.9

The Sharing Tab Page

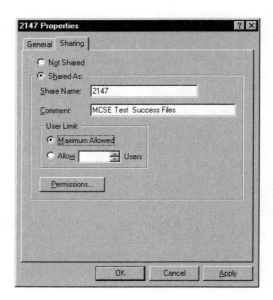

From the main dialog box, you can configure the options shown in Table 3.8.

TABLE 3.8

Sharing Dialog Box Options

Option	Description
Not Shared or Shared As	Specifies whether or not the folder can be shared. If the folder is shared, the following configuration options can be applied.
Share Name	Name users will see when browsing through utilities like Network Neighborhood.
Comment	Allows an optional informational comment.
User Limit	Allows you to specify whether or not the share should be connection limited, and if so, how many users can access the share concurrently.
Permissions	These are covered in Table 3.9.

In addition, you can specify which permissions will apply for users and groups to the share. By default, the share permissions allow Full Control to the Everyone group, but you can limit this by manipulating permissions in the Access Through Share Permissions dialog box (see Figure 3.10).

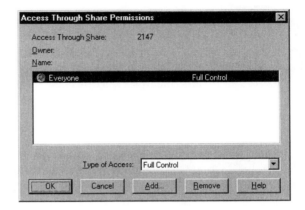

The permissions are defined in Table 3.9.

Share Permission	Description
No Access	No Access means that you do not have access to the shared folder. Even if you have other permissions through your user or group memberships, you will not be able to access the share, because No Access overrides all other permissions.
Read	Read can be used to view files and folders, view data, and run programs.
Change	With Change, you incorporate Read with the ability to add files and folders, edit data, and delete files and folders.
Full Control	This is the whole enchilada, with Full Control you get everything that Read and Change offer with the ability to change share permissions and take ownership.

With the exception of No Access, your access permissions will be cumulative, meaning you will receive the highest level of access that has been granted through your user account or group memberships.

Permissions and Security

In this section, permissions refer to directory and file level (also called local) security that can only be applied to NTFS formatted files and folders. NTFS security is more detailed than share permissions and it allows very specific control over directory and file resources.

NTFS (local) security applies to users who are logged in locally to a computer and users who access the same resource over the network. When share security has been applied, the more restrictive permissions of NTFS and sharing will be enforced.

To apply local security, you can use NT Explorer, My Computer, and Win-File (File Manager). In this case, assume that you are using NT Explorer. To assign local security, you would take the following steps:

1. Within NT Explorer, click the NTFS file or folder to which you want to apply permissions.

2. Go to File ➤ Properties.

3. Click on the Security tab

4. Click the Permissions option to see the Directory Permissions dialog box (see Figure 3.11). Note: Individual file permissions are rarely used.

FIGURE 3.11

The Directory Permissions Dialog Box

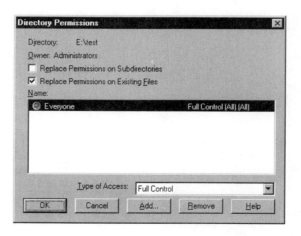

The default permissions are that group Everyone has Full Control. You can modify this for whatever is appropriate for your environment. The default permissions assignments are:

- Permissions are not replaced on subdirectories.

- Permissions are replaced on files within the parent directory.

The NTFS (local) permissions are defined in Table 3.10.

	Permission	Description	Applies to Folder	Applies to File
T A B L E 3.10 Local NTFS Permissions Defined	No Access	User has no rights to the specified resource. This right overrides any other rights the user may have through the user account or through group memberships.	✓	✓
	List	Displays a list of files and folders within the current directory, also allows you to change to subdirectories.	✓	
	Read	Allows you to read files and execute programs. Read also inherently includes the list permission.	✓	✓
	Add	Only used to add files and directories to the specified directory.	✓	
	Add and Read	Just like it sounds, combines the permissions of Add and Read.	✓	
	Change	Gives you the combined permissions of List, Add, and Read. In addition, you can edit files and delete data within a folder or file.	✓	✓
	Full Control	Gives you the combined permissions of all other rights. In addition, you can take ownership of files and directories.	✓	✓

	Permission	Description	Applies to Folder	Applies to File
T A B L E 3.10 *(cont.)* Local NTFS Permissions Defined	Special Directory Access	Used to customize access permissions for folders. You can choose from Read, Write, Execute, Delete, Change Permissions, and Take Ownership.	✓	
	Special File Access	Used to customize access permissions for files. You can choose from Read, Write, Execute, Delete, Change Permissions, and Take Ownership.		✓

File Auditing

You can audit file events on NTFS partitions. To enable file auditing, you must first enable auditing of File and Object Access through User Manager for Domains ➤ Policies ➤ Audit. Once this is completed, you can configure file auditing through NT Explorer, My Computer, or WinFile (File Manager).

To enable and configure auditing, complete the following steps:

1. Use NT Explorer and select the file or folder you want to audit.

2. Select File ➤ Properties ➤ Security tab.

3. You will see the Directory Auditing dialog box (see Figure 3.12). From this box, specify which users or groups you want to audit and which events you want to track.

The options you can audit are:

- Read
- Write
- Execute
- Delete
- Change Permissions
- Take Ownership

FIGURE 3.12

The Directory Auditing
Dialog Box

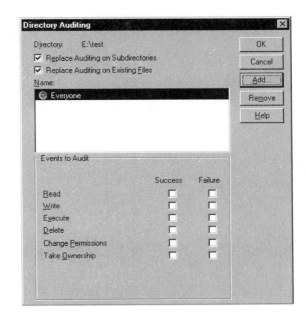

Once you have enabled auditing, you can view the results through the Security log within Event Viewer.

In the next section, you'll learn how everything fits together when you manage resources in an enterprise environment.

Managing Resources in an Enterprise Environment

In Unit 1, you learned about trust relationships. In this unit, you learned about NT users, groups (local and global groups), and resource management. In this section, you'll learn how these pieces all fit in an enterprise environment. The following checklist states what you'll need to do:

1. Make sure you establish the correct trust relationship.

2. In the domain where the user exists, create a global group on the PDC and add the users.

3. In the domain where the resources exist, create a local group on the computer that contains the resource. Assign the access permissions that are required.

4. Add the global group to the local group.

This is a very important topic on this exam. You should be very familiar with this concept!

Study the following examples.

Enterprise Management Example #1

Assume that you have the following scenario:

You have two domains, NORTH and SOUTH. Michelle is a user in the NORTH domain and she requires access to the \\SALES\DATA share that is located in the SOUTH domain.

When answering this type of question, take a moment to sketch the scenario, it should look like Figure 3.13.

FIGURE 3.13

Enterprise Management Example #1

The first step is to determine the proper trust relationship. In this case, the SOUTH domain must trust the NORTH domain (see Unit 1 for more information on trust relationships).

The second step is to create a global group in the NORTH domain. Add Michelle to this group.

The third step will be to create a local group on the SALES member server. The access permissions required should be assigned to the local group.

The fourth and final step is to add the global group to the local group.

Enterprise Management Example #2

This example will be more complex. Assume that you have three users: Brad, Rhoda, and Lars. They are required to back up the domain controllers, member servers, and NT workstations in the EAST and WEST domains. The three users are part of the WEST domain. This example is illustrated in Figure 3.14.

F I G U R E   3.14

Enterprise Management Example #2

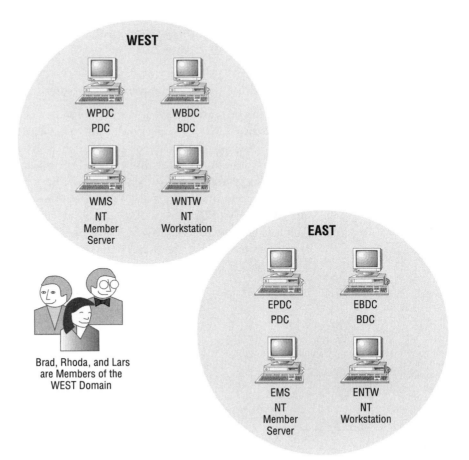

Going back to our checklist of what needs to be done:

1. Define the trust relationship.

In this case, users in the WEST domain need to access resources in the EAST domain. You will need to set up a one-way trust where the EAST domain trusts the WEST domain.

2. In the domain where the users exist, create a global group and add the users.

On the WEST domain, create a group called Global Backup. Add Brad, Rhoda, and Lars to this group.

3. At each resource, create a local group and assign the necessary permissions.

In this case, each NT computer already has a local group, Backup Operators, who already have been assigned permissions to back up and restore the computer.

4. Add the global group to the local group.

This will be more involved. For the domain controllers (PDC and BDCs) you only add the Global Backup global group to the Backup Operators local group on the PDC because the PDC sends a copy of its SAM to the BDCs. This should be done for both domains. Because each NT member server and NT workstation contains its own local SAM database, you'll have to add the Global Backup global group to the local group, Backup Operators, on each NT member server and each NT workstation in both domains.

If this unit seems long, there's a reason. The majority of the exam questions are drawn from this objective. To make sure that you understand everything, review the following study questions and practice exam.

User and Group Management

1. The _____ built variable can be used to substitute a user's name for things like logon scripts and user profile paths.

2. What is the best way to prevent an NT account that is not currently being used (but will be used in the future) from posing a security risk?

_____

3. The authenticating server will look for logon scripts in this folder during the logon process.

_____

4. By default, these two groups can change the system time on a domain controller.

_____

_____

5. In addition to managing the Administrators local group, the _____ built-in local group can manage NT user and group accounts.

6. In addition to managing the Administrators local group, the _____ built-in local group can manage NT server resources.

7. True or False. Logon hours can be defined as a system policy.

8. True or False. You can specify how many concurrent logons each user can have through User Manager for Domains system policy.

9.   What would you do if you wanted a user to back up the NT domain PDC and BDCs, but you did not want him or her to perform restore operations?

_____

10.   What is the minimum assignment you can make so that a user can view and manage the logs generated through auditing?

_____

11.   When assigning permissions, when would you use the Domain Users group and when would you use the Everyone group?

_____

12.   When assigning administrative permissions, when would you assign a user to the Administrators group and when would you assign a user to the Domain Admins group?

_____

13.   When managing NT groups, you should create a _____ group on the PDC and add your users. At the resource the users need to access, you create a _____ group and assign access permissions to this group. Finally, you add the _____ group to the _____ group.

14.   True or False. Local groups can reside on NT domain controllers, NT member servers, and NT Workstations.

15. True or False. Global groups can reside on NT domain controllers, NT member servers, and NT Workstations.

16. True or False. A global group can contain users from within its domain or users from trusted domains.

17. When you add a computer to a domain, the _____ account is automatically added to the NT computers local Administrators group.

18. What service would you use to maintain a copy of all of the logon scripts on each PDC and BDC within a domain?

_____

19. What audit option would you select to determine which administrator was doing the most administrative work?

_____

20. What password restriction defines how many unique passwords a user must have before he or she can recycle and use previous passwords?

_____

21. What account policy allows you to protect your server if someone tries to break in by using a valid user name and guessing user passwords?

_____

22. If a user activates account lockout and the duration has been set to forever, how is the account unlocked?

_____

23. In order to enable NTFS and printer auditing, you must choose to audit the
_____ option in User Manager for Domains auditing.

24. In order to audit system events such as management of trust relationships, you must enable this audit option.

_____

25. To view the audit logs generated from NT account auditing, you would use the
_____ utility.

Profiles and Policies

26. By default, user profiles are created in the _____
folder.

27. The file that stores the user profile is called _____ by
default.

28. How are mandatory profiles created?

_____

29. By default, the authenticating domain controller will look for a file called
_____ to determine if a system policy file has been
defined.

30. What utility is used to define a roaming profile?

_____

31. What utility is used to copy a user profile?

_____

32. What happens if a user has been assigned a mandatory profile, and the mandatory profile is
unavailable?

_____

33. How does the system policy know which group policy to implement if a user is a member of
multiple groups that have had system policies defined?

_____

34. The _____ utility is used to create and manage NT
system policies.

35. True or False. You can use the NT Explorer to copy a user profile from one user to another.

36. System policies can be applied to:

_____

_____

_____

37. System policies work by editing the _____ and applying the system policy that has been defined.

Remote Administration

38. What two platforms can the NT remote administration tools be installed on using the NT
Server 4.0 CD?

_____

_____

39. What remote administration utility would you use from your Windows NT Workstation to create a share on a remote NT Workstation?

_____

40. When working from home, you want to speed up administration when using User Manager for
Domains or Server Manager, what option should you use?

_____

41. True or False. You could use the DHCP Manager utility from a Windows 95 computer that had the remote administration tools installed.

42. The schema of the _____ and _____ utilities are expanded on NT workstations and Windows 95 computers that have the NT remote administration utilities installed.

43. The _____ utility is used to manage NTFS permissions on NT workstations and Windows 95 computers that have the NT remote administration utilities installed.

Disk Resource Management

44. In order to create a network share, you must be a member of one of these groups:

_____

_____

45. True or False. You can audit file events on FAT or NTFS partitions.

46. Terry is a user who is accessing a share called DATA. Through the DATA share, she has combined access rights of Read. The share resides on an NTFS folder also called DATA. Through NTFS permissions, Terry has Full Control permissions. What are Terry's rights when she accesses the share?

_____

47. True or False. You can apply NTFS permissions to files and folders, but share permissions can be applied only to folders.

48. True or False. The default permissions on a share are that group Everyone has Full Control.

49. Jill is a member of SALES, SALES MANAGERS, and SALES TEMPS. Jill requires access to the \\SALES\DATABASE share. The following permissions have been assigned:

SALES   Change

SALES MANAGERS   Full Control

SALES TEMPS   Read

What are Jill's effective rights to this share?

_____

50. Jack is a member of SALES, SALES MANAGERS, and SALES TEMPS. Jack requires access to the \\SALES\DATABASE share. The following permissions have been assigned:

SALES   Change

SALES MANAGERS   Full Control

SALES TEMPS   No Access

What are Jack's effective rights to this share?

_____

51. Your Sales users use a program called SALESDB.EXE. You are concerned that you may not have enough licenses to support the number of users who run this application. What file audit option would you use to track usage of this file?

_____

52. Because of the sensitive nature of the payroll files located on the D:\PAYROLL folder (which is NTFS), you want to track any time data is read or written in this directory, whether the attempt is successful or unsuccessful. What audit options should you track?

_____

53. What NTFS access permission allows you to see the contents of a folder, but does not allow you to read the data within the files?

_____

Managing Resources in an Enterprise Environment

SCENARIO A

Kevin and Katie are Sales Managers in the SALES domain. The accounting database is located in the ACCT domain. Kevin and Katie require access to a share located on a member server called \\ACCTSERVER\ACCTDB.

The following series of questions will be based on Scenario A.

54. In this example, domain _____ is trusted and domain _____ is trusting.

55. In the SALES domain, you will create a _____ group called Sales Managers.

56. In the ACCT domain, you will create a _____ group called Account DB Users.

57.   The _____ group will have the database access permissions assigned to it.

58.   The _____ (local or global) group will have the users added to it.

59.   The Sales Managers group will reside on the _____ computer.

60.   The Account DB Users group will reside on the _____ computer.

61.   You will add the _____ group to the _____ group to complete the scenario.

SCENARIO B

You have a group of users (Cindy, Todd, and Otto) who need to be able to manage the backups for the SALES, ACCT, and CORP domains. Each domain consists of a PDC, two BDCs, NT member servers, and NT Workstations. Cindy, Todd, and Otto are all users in the CORP domain.

The following series of questions will be based on the Scenario B.

62.   What trust relationships need to be defined so that Cindy, Todd, and Otto will have access to the SALES and ACCT domains?

_____

63. Is there a default global group already created that will allow these users to be logically grouped together? If so, what is it called?

_____

64. Once Cindy, Todd, and Otto have been associated with a global group, what needs to be done so that they can back up the domain controllers in the SALES, ACCT, and CORP domains?

_____

65. How do you give Cindy, Todd, and Otto additional permissions to include backing up all of the NT member servers?

_____

66. How do you give Cindy, Todd, and Otto further permissions to include backing up all of the NT Workstations?

_____

SCENARIO C

You have two domains, US and ASIA. A two-way trust relationship is defined between the two domains. Dustin is a member of US\Domain Admins and Ryan is a member of ASIA\Domain Admins.

The following series of questions will be based on Scenario C.

67. True or False. By default, Dustin has administrative rights in the ASIA domain.

68. What needs to be done to allow all Domain Admins from the US domain to have administrative rights in the ASIA domain, without allowing Domain Admins from the ASIA domain to have administrative rights in the US domain.

69. You have a member server in the US domain called APPS. The APPS server has a share called \\APPS\COMMON. The following access rights have been assigned:

Everyone   Read

Domain Admins   Full Control

What access will the Domain Users group from ASIA have to this share?

70. You have a member server in the US domain called APPS. The APPS server has a share called \\APPS\COMMON. The following access rights have been assigned:

Domain Users   Read

Domain Admins   Full Control

What access will the Domain Users group from ASIA have to this share?

71. You have a member server in the US domain called APPS. The APPS server has a share called \\APPS\COMMON. The following access rights have been assigned:

Domain Users   Read

Domain Admins   Full Control

What access will Ryan have to this share?

72. You have a member server in the US domain called APPS. The APPS server has a share called \\APPS\COMMON. The following access rights have been assigned:

Everyone   Read

Domain Admins   Full Control

What access will Ryan have to this share?

SAMPLE TEST

3-1   You are the network administrator for a large NT network. Part of your job description allows you to work from home every other Friday. At home you use an NT Workstation with an ISDN connection to work. Your ISDN connection is having problems and you have had to fall back to your old 9600 analog modem.

The administration tools are installed on your computer, and most of your work is through User Manager for Domains and Server Manager. You are going crazy because the connection is so slow. What option can you select through User Manager for Domains and Server Manager that will reduce the amount of traffic sent through the connection so that you can complete your management tasks more quickly?

   A. From Options, select the Minimize Network Traffic option.

   B. From Options, select the Low Speed Connection option.

   C. From Connection, select the Minimize Network Traffic option.

   D. From Connection, select the Low Speed Connection Option.

3-2   You are the network administrator for a large NT network. Because you are very concerned with network security, you defined the System Policies as shown here:

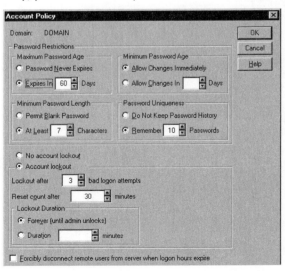

SAMPLE TEST

One of your users, Adam, changes his password on Friday before he goes home. On Monday, when he tries to log on he can't remember his password. After three tries he receives an error message stating that his account has been locked out. What needs to be done so that Adam can log on again?

  A. You must assign Adam a new password When 30 minutes have elapsed since Adam locked his account, he should be able to log on again.

  B. You must assign Adam a new password and then clear the Account Disabled box in the User Properties dialog box for the account Adam.

  C. You must assign Adam a new password, then in the User Properties box for the user account Adam, check the Override Account Lockout box.

  D. You must assign Adam a new password, then in the User Properties dialog box for the user account Adam, clear the Account Locked Out box.

3-3   Your company has recently decided to install Windows NT as its network operating system. You have been hired to design the network architecture. You have decided to use the master domain model with CORP as the master domain, and to use EAST and WEST as resource domains. Users in the CORP domain will require access to resources in EAST and WEST.

A specific requirement you have is that the sales department must be able to access a share on the member server SALES called DATA. This server is a part of the EAST domain. These users should be able to view any data, but not change it.

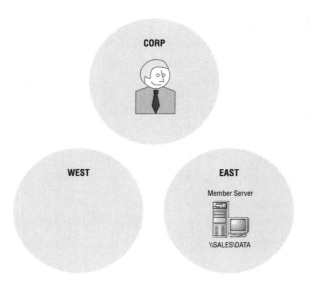

What do you do? Choose all that apply.

    A. Create one-way trusts so that CORP trusts EAST and WEST.

    B. Create one-way trusts so that EAST and WEST trust CORP.

    C. Create a two-way trust between CORP and EAST and CORP and WEST.

    D. Create a global group in CORP called Global Sales. Add the members of the Sales department to this group. Create a local group on the SALES server called Sales Data. Assign the Sales Data group Read permission to the DATA share. Add the global group Global Sales to the local group Sales Data.

    E. Create a local group in CORP called Local Sales. Add the members of the Sales department to this group. Create a global group on the SALES server called Sales Data. Assign the Sales Data group Read permission to the DATA share. Add the local group Local Sales to the global group Sales Data.

    F. Create a global group in EAST called Global Sales. Add the members of the Sales department to this group. Create a local group on the SALES server called Sales Data. Assign the Sales Data group Read permission to the DATA share. Add the global group Global Sales to the local group Sales Data.

S A M P L E   T E S T

3-4   Your network uses the master domain model. You support about 15,000 users and have designated 5 users as members of the Domain Admins global group and about 50 users as members of the Account Operators local group. The primary task of these users is to offload administrative tasks related to user and group management. You want each of these users to be accountable for any changes he or she makes. You decide to implement auditing. What event should you choose to audit?

    A. Enable success and failure in auditing for User and Group Management.

    B. Enable success and failure in auditing for Use of User Rights.

    C. Enable success and failure in auditing for Changes to SAM database.

    D. Enable success and failure in auditing for Use of User Manager for Domains.

3-5   Your network uses the master domain model. CORP is the master domain and EAST and WEST are the resource domains.

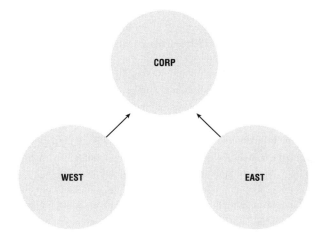

You have been having a problem because some users are not logging off when they leave for the day, and your backup program does not allow you to back up open files. This means that critical files are not backed up on a daily basis. You define a policy so that users cannot be logged on from 1:00 A.M. to 4:00 A.M. when the backups are in progress. How do you implement this policy?

A. Configure the logon hours through the CORP system policy.

B. Configure the logon hours through the CORP, EAST, and WEST system policies.

C. Configure the logon hours for group EVERYONE.

D. Configure the logon hours for each individual user in the CORP domain.

3-6 You have been assigned the task of evaluating your domains system policies. You notice that the Maximum Password Age has been set to 30. This option forces the users to change their passwords, but you notice that if you rotate between two passwords, it allows you to use the same passwords over and over again. Which policy should you define to enforce the spirit of the restriction and require users to use unique passwords every 30 days?

A. Click the Require Unique Passwords radio button in User Manager for Domain ➤ Policies ➤ Account Policy dialog box.

B. Specify that the Minimum Password Age is 30 in User Manager for Domain ➤ Policies ➤ Account Policy dialog box.

C. In the Password Uniqueness box, click the Remember _____ Passwords radio button and specify how many passwords will be remembered in User Manager for Domain ➤ Policies ➤ Account Policy dialog box.

D. Click the Require Unique Passwords radio button and specify the number of passwords that will be remembered in User Manager for Domain ➤ Policies ➤ Account Policy dialog box.

3-7   Your network consists of a single domain with a PDC, two BDCs, and 500 NT workstations. Your users are allowed to create and manage whatever user profiles they desire. The only specification is that each user's profile should be stored in his or her home directory and each user should be able to access his or her profile from any workstation from which he or she logs on. What do you do? Choose two answers.

    A. Specify that the profiles are to be roaming through Control Panel ➤ System ➤ User Profiles tab.

    B. Specify that the profiles are to be roaming, by specifying a UNC path to the profile through User Manager for Domains on each user's Profile property.

    C. Specify that the profiles are to be copied through Control Panel ➤ System ➤ User Profiles tab.

    D. Specify that the profiles are to be copied through NT Explorer.

3-8   Your network consists of two domains, EAST and WEST. There is a two-way trust relationship defined between the two domains. Corporate policy dictates that the administrators in the EAST domain should have administrative rights in the WEST domain, but administrators in the WEST domain should not be able to administer the EAST domain. How do you configure this?

    A. Add the EAST Domain Admins group to the WEST Domain Admins group.

    B. Add the EAST Domain Admins group to the WEST Administrators group.

    C. Add the EAST Administrators group to the WEST Domain Admins group.

    D. Add the EAST Administrators group to the WEST Administrators group.

SAMPLE TEST

3-9 Your network consists of two domains, EAST and WEST. There is no trust relationship defined. The EAST domain contains a member server called SALES that has a share called DATA. The EAST\Data Users local group has the Read permission assigned to this share. Other than the DATA share, most of the files on the server are actually required by users in the WEST domain, so you decide to move the SALES member server to the WEST domain. Once moved, you create a local group called WEST\Data Users and assign this group Read to the DATA share. How do you provide access to the EAST\Data Users? Choose two answers.

    A. Define a one-way trust so that EAST trusts WEST.

    B. Define a one-way trust so that WEST trusts EAST.

    C. Add the EAST\Data Users local group to the WEST\Data Users local group.

    D. Create a global group on the EAST domain called Domain Data Users, and add the users from the EAST domain who need to access the \\SALES\DATA share. Add this global group to the WEST\Data Users local group.

    E. Create a global group on the WEST domain called East Data Users, and add the users from the EAST domain who need to access the \\SALES\DATA share. Add this global group to the WEST\Data Users local group.

3-10 Rhonda began working for the company as a contract worker. She has recently decided to join the company and should now be allowed to access the D:\DATA folder on her computer. This partition is NTFS and has the following permissions assigned. Rhonda is a member of the Data Entry, Sales Managers, and Sales Temps groups. What are Rhonda's effective permissions for D:\DATA?

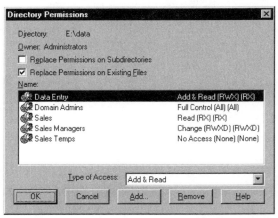

A. Read

B. Add and Read

C. Change

D. No Access

3-11   Your superiors at corporate headquarters think there are some anomalies in your NT security. They suspect that a member of the Domain Admins group has been accessing areas of the network that they are on their honor not to access. Corporate headquarters sends an auditor, Kade, to watch your network in more detail. Kade should be able to define auditing on any NTFS partition on any domain controller. He also needs to be able to view the audit logs that are generated. What is the minimum assignment so that Kade can perform his task?

    A. Make Kade a member of the Administrators local group.

    B. Make Kade a member of the Account Operators local group.

    C. Make Kade a member of the Server Operators local group.

    D. Assign Kade the Manage Auditing and Security Log user right.

    E. Assign Kade the Manage NTFS and Auditing user right.

3-12   Your Sales department consists of 20 users. You create a template to create a user profile that will define a custom desktop to be shared by all of the Sales users. After you create the custom profile, what should you do to make the profile mandatory so that no Sales user can modify the desktop?

    A. Specify that the profile be mandatory through Control Panel ➤ System ➤ User Profiles tab.

    B. Specify that the profile be mandatory through the System Profile Editor.

    C. Rename the `NTUSER.DAT` file to `NTUSER.MAN`.

    D. Place the shared user profile on an NTFS partition and apply NTFS permissions to the `NTUSER.DAT` file.

```
┌──────────────────── S A M P L E   T E S T ────────────────────┐
```

3-13 You are the network administrator. Your domain consists of a PDC, two BDCs, 50 NT Work-stations, and 50 Windows 95 computers. You have an NT workstation on your desk that has the NT administrative tools installed. You need to create a share on the SALES member server. What utility do you use?

    A. User Manager for Domains

    B. Server Manager

    C. NT Explorer

    D. File Manager

3-14 You have decided to create a system policy file that will specify the policies for the NT users and groups in your domain. You use the System Policy Editor utility to define the policies. Where should the file be saved?

    A. \winnt\system32\repl\import\policy.dat

    B. \winnt\system32\policies\ntconfig.dat

    C. \winnt\system32\repl\import\scripts\ntconfig.pol

    D. \winnt\system32\policies\ntconfig.pol

3-15 You have hired three users (Larry, Curly, and Moe) who will operate and manage backup oper-ations for your domain. Your domain consists of a PDC, three BDCs, 10 member servers, and 150 NT Workstations.

    Required Element: Larry, Curly, and Moe should be able to back up the PDC and the BDCs.

    Optional Elements: Larry, Curly, and Moe should be able to back up the member servers.

    Larry, Curly, and Moe should be able to back up the NT workstations.

    Proposed Solution: Create a global group on the PDC called Domain Backups. Add Larry, Curly, and Moe to the global group. Add the Domain Backups global group to the Backup Operators local group on the PDC.

What does the proposed solution offer?

    A. It meets the required element and both optional elements.

    B. It meets the required element and one optional element.

    C. It meets the required element, but not the optional elements.

    D. It does not meet the required or the optional elements.

3-16   You have hired three users (Larry, Curly, and Moe) who will operate and manage backup operations for your domain. Your domain consists of a PDC, three BDCs, 10 member servers, and 150 NT Workstations.

    Required Element: Larry, Curly, and Moe should be able to back up the PDC and the BDCs.

    Optional Elements: Larry, Curly, and Moe should be able to back up the member servers.

    Larry, Curly, and Moe should be able to back up the NT workstations.

    Proposed Solution: Create a local group on the PDC called Domain Backups. Add Larry, Curly, and Moe to the local group. Add the Domain Backups local group to the Backup Operators local group on the PDC.

What does the proposed solution offer?

    A. It meets the required element and both optional elements.

    B. It meets the required element and one optional element.

    C. It meets the required element, but not the optional elements.

    D. It does not meet the required or the optional elements.

3-17   You have hired three users (Larry, Curly, and Moe) who will operate and manage backup operations for your domain. Your domain consists of a PDC, three BDCs, 10 member servers, and 150 NT Workstations.

    Required Element: Larry, Curly, and Moe should be able to back up the PDC and the BDCs.

    Optional Elements: Larry, Curly, and Moe should be able to back up the member servers.

    Larry, Curly, and Moe should be able to back up the NT workstations.

Proposed Solution: Create a global group on the PDC called Domain Backups. Add Larry, Curly, and Moe to the global group. Add the Domain Backups global group to the Backup Operators local group on the PDC. Add the Domain Backups global group to the local group Backup Operators on each member server.

What does the proposed solution offer?

A. It meets the required element and both optional elements.

B. It meets the required element and one optional element.

C. It meets the required element, but not the optional elements.

D. It does not meet the required or the optional elements.

3-18   Kim has been hired to help offload some of the NT administrative work. One of her main responsibilities is to create and manage network shares on the NT domain controllers and member servers. What is the minimum rights assignment that Kim will require?

A. Give Kim the Create Network Shares user right.

B. Give Kim the Manage Network Shares user right.

C. Make Kim a member of Server Operators.

D. Make Kim a member of the Administrators group.

3-19   Your NT network consists of two domains, NORTH and SOUTH. The domains are configured with a two-way trust. Users in the NORTH domain require access to the \\APPS\EMAIL share that is located in the SOUTH domain. What do you need to configure for this access?

A. Create a global group in the NORTH domain called App Users. Add the users from the NORTH domain. Create a local group on the APPS server called Email Users. Assign access permissions to Email Users. Add the App Users global group to the Email Users local group.

B. Create a global group in the SOUTH domain called App Users. Add the users from the NORTH domain. Create a local group on the APPS server called Email Users. Assign access permissions to Email Users. Add the App Users global group to the Email Users local group.

C. Create a global group in the NORTH domain called App Users. Add the users from the NORTH domain. Create a global group on the APPS server called Email Users. Assign access permissions to Email Users. Add the App Users global group to the Email Users global group.

D. Create a local group in the NORTH domain called App Users. Add the users from the NORTH domain. Create a global group on the APPS server called Email Users. Assign access permissions to Email Users. Add the App Users local group to the Email Users global group.

3-20   Your network consists of two domains, NORTH and SOUTH. There is a one-way trust relationship defined so that the NORTH domain trusts the SOUTH domain. Brad is a user in the SOUTH domain. Brad will be responsible for managing all server operations for domain controllers in the NORTH and SOUTH domains. What do you need to do to allow Brad to do his job?

A. In the NORTH domain, create a global group called Domain Server Managers, and add Brad to this group. Add this global group to the Server Operators local groups on the PDC in the NORTH and SOUTH domains.

B. In the SOUTH domain, create a global group called Domain Server Managers, and add Brad to this group. Add this global group to the Server Operators local groups on the PDC in the NORTH and SOUTH domains.

C. In the NORTH domain, create a local group called Server Managers, and add Brad to this group. Add this local group to the Server Operators local groups on the PDC in the NORTH and SOUTH domains.

D. In the SOUTH domain, create a local group called Server Managers, and add Brad to this group. Add this local group to the Server Operators local groups on the PDC in the NORTH and SOUTH domains.

S A M P L E   T E S T

3-21   Your network consists of two domains US and EUROPE. The US domain contains a global group called Domain Sales Managers. This group needs to access a share within the EUROPE domain, \\france\data. What do you need to do?

    A. Configure a one-way trust so that US trusts EUROPE. Create a global group on the FRANCE server called Data Users. Grant access permissions to the Data Users group. Add the US\Domain Sales Managers group to the Data Users group.

    B. Configure a one-way trust so that EUROPE trusts US. Create a local group on the FRANCE server called Data Users. Grant access permissions to the Data Users group. Add the US\Domain Sales Managers group to the Data Users group.

    C. Configure a one-way trust so that US trusts EUROPE. Create a local group on the FRANCE server called Data Users. Grant access permissions to the Data Users group. Add the US\Domain Sales Managers group to the Data Users group.

    D. Configure a one-way trust so that EUROPE trusts US. Create a local group on the FRANCE server called Data Users. Grant access permissions to the Data Users group. Add the US\Domain Sales Managers group to the Data Users group.

3-22   Your company uses the single-domain model. You have a PDC and two BDCs. You are in the process of installing a server that will be used by your legal department. Several lawyers have stressed that extremely sensitive data will be stored on the server; therefore, only two senior lawyers should have complete access to the data. How do you configure the server?

    A. Install the server as a member server, remove the Administrators group from the Domain Admins group on the server, and add the two senior lawyers.

    B. Install the server as a member server, remove the Domain Admins group from the Administrators group on the server, and add the two senior lawyers.

    C. Install the server as a BDC, remove the Administrators group from the Domain Admins group on the server, and add the two senior lawyers.

    D. Install the server as a BDC, remove the Domain Admins group from the Administrators group on the server, and add the two senior lawyers.

3-23 You are using User Manager for Domains to create a template account that will define users who are associated with the MIS group. When defining the user's home directory, what variable would you use to substitute the user's name for the variable?

    A. %LogonName%

    B. %Username%

    C. %LogonName

    D. %UserName

3-24 You have two domains, NORTH and SOUTH. Susan is a user in the NORTH domain. You want Susan to be able to manage all user management for the NORTH and SOUTH domains. Which of the two following tasks must be complete?

    A. Configure a one-way trust where the NORTH domain trusts the SOUTH domain.

    B. Configure a one-way trust where the SOUTH domain trusts the NORTH domain.

    C. Create global group in the NORTH domain that contains Susan's account. Add this group the Account Operators local group on the PDC in both domains.

    D. Create a global group in the NORTH domain that contains Susan's account. Add this group to the Server Operators local group on the PDC in both domains.

    E. Create a global group in the NORTH domain that contains Susan's account. Create a global group in the SOUTH domain that contains Susan's account. Add the global group from each domain to the Server Operators local group on the PDC in both domains.

3-25   You have created a system policy file for SALES, MANAGERS, and EXECUTIVES. Todd is a member of all of these groups. How do you determine which system policy Todd will use?

    A. In User Manager for Domains, specify which group is Todd's primary group.

    B. In the System Policy Editor, specify the priority level of each group.

    C. Create multiple policy files, one for each group. In User Manager for Domains, in the Profiles box, specify which policy file the user account Todd will use.

    D. In User Manager for Domains, specify the priority level of each group.

UNIT

4

Connectivity

Test Objectives: Connectivity

■ Configure Windows NT Server for interoperability with NetWare servers by using various tools. Tools include:

- Gateway Services for NetWare
- Migration Tool for NetWare

■ Install and configure multiprotocol routing to serve various functions. Functions include:

- Internet router
- BOOTP/DHCP Relay Agent
- IPX router

■ Install and configure Internet Information Server.

■ Install and configure Internet services. Services include:

- World Wide Web
- DNS
- Intranet

■ Install and configure Remote Access Server (RAS). Configuration options include:

- Configuring RAS communications
- Configuring RAS protocols
- Configuring RAS security

Exam objectives are subject to change at any time without prior notice and at Microsoft's sole discretion. Please visit Microsoft's Training & Certification website (www.microsoft.com/Train_Cert) for the most current exam objectives listing.

NT Sever ships with a variety of connectivity services, and this unit will cover many of the connectivity options. The first section will cover NetWare connectivity. This includes Gateway Services for NetWare and Migration Tool for NetWare. You will also learn about MultiProtocol routing through the RIP for Internet Protocol, DHCP Relay Agent, and the RIP for NWLink IPX/SPX Compatible Transport protocol services. The Internet Information Server (IIS) will be discussed along with other Internet services including DNS. The final section will review Remote Access Server (RAS) connectivity including RAS communications, RAS protocols, and RAS security.

NetWare Connectivity

One of NT's greatest strengths is its ability to exist in a heterogeneous network environment. To support mixed networks of NT and NetWare, NT ships with Gateway Services for NetWare (GSNW). In order to ease shifts from existing NetWare servers to NT Servers, Microsoft includes the Migration Tool for NetWare utility.

To help alleviate confusion, Table 4.1 provides an overview of the protocol and services that are related to NetWare connectivity.

T A B L E 4.1: Overview of NetWare Connectivity Protocols and Services

Protocol or Service	Platform Installed On	Main Features	Benefits	Drawbacks
NWLink IPX/SPX Compatible Transport	Any NT platform	This is an easily configured, routable protocol. Used by itself, it provides access to other servers running NetBIOS applications.	Used to support CSNW, GSNW, and Migration Tool for NetWare.	By itself, it provides no access for NT users trying to access NetWare resources or NetWare users trying to access NT resources.

T A B L E 4.1: Overview of NetWare Connectivity Protocols and Services *(continued)*

Protocol or Service	Platform Installed On	Main Features	Benefits	Drawbacks
Client Services for NetWare (CSNW)	Only installed in NT Workstations	Allows an NT user to access NetWare file and print resources.	Provides better performance than GSNW.	Requires a user account and license on the NetWare server and takes up resources on the NT Workstation.
Gateway Services for NetWare (GSNW)	Only installed on NT Servers	Allows clients attached to the NT Server to access NetWare file and print resources.	Only one user connection is used on the NetWare server and no additional software is required on client computers.	GSNW provides slower access to clients who are going through the gateway as opposed to using a NetWare redirector on their client computers.
File and Print Services for NetWare	NT Servers	Allows the NT server to emulate a NetWare server so that NetWare users can access NT file and print resources.	NetWare users can access NT file and print resources.	Does not ship with NT and you have to purchase it separately.

Gateway Services for NetWare

Gateway Service for NetWare (GSNW) provides access to NetWare file and print resources for users who are logged in locally at the NT server or clients that are attached and have access to the NT server (see Figure 4.1).

Benefits of GSNW

- Any clients attached to the NT Server through a network connection (where the server is running GSNW) can access NetWare file and print resources.

- Users logged in locally at the NT Server can access NetWare file and print resources.

- The GSNW connection requires only one NetWare license, regardless of the number of users accessing the gateway.

FIGURE 4.1

GSNW Access

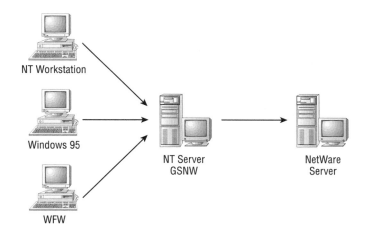

Drawbacks of GSNW

- GSNW typically provides a slower connection than CSNW. Performance will depend on the number of users connected to the NetWare server.

- All users who access the Gateway will have the same permissions on the NetWare server.

Prerequisites for Installing GSNW

GSNW can be installed only on NT servers. Before GSNW can be installed, the following prerequisites should be met.

Prerequisites for the NT Server

The NT server must be running the NWLink IPX/SPX Compatible Transport protocol.

Prerequisites for the NetWare Server

The NetWare server requires the following setup:

- A user account must be created on the NetWare server that will act as the gateway account.

- A NetWare group named NTGATEWAY must be created on the server to which you will connect.

- The user you created for the gateway users must be added to the NTGATEWAY group.

You can assign the permissions to resources that gateway users need to access through the NetWare user or the NTGATEWAY group.

Installing and Configuring GSNW

To install GSNW, access Control Panel ➤ Network ➤ Services tab. Once you are in the Services dialog screen, click the Add button and select Gateway (and Client) Services for NetWare. After you specify the location of the distribution files and install the required files, you must restart your computer. If not installed previously, the NWLink IPX/SPX network protocol will also be installed.

Once GSNW has been installed, you will see a new icon in Control Panel for GSNW. This icon is used to configure GSNW. GSNW is configured two ways: basic configuration and the gateway configuration.

GSNW Basic Configuration

When you double-click the GSNW Control Panel icon, you will see the Gateway Service for NetWare dialog box (see Figure 4.2).

FIGURE 4.2

The Gateway Service for NetWare Dialog Box

Gateway Service for NetWare
Username: Administrator
● Preferred Server
Current Preferred Server: <None>
Select Preferred Server: <None>
○ Default Tree and Context
Tree:
Context:
Print Options
☐ Add Form Feed
☑ Notify When Printed
☑ Print Banner
Login Script Options
☐ Run Login Script
OK
Gateway...
Cancel
Help
Overview

The options that can be configured in the main dialog screen are defined in Table 4.2.

	GSNW Option	Description
TABLE 4.2 Gateway Service for NetWare Configuration Options	Preferred Server	Used to specify the default NetWare server to which you will connect. This is used to specify a NetWare 2.*x* or 3.*x* server.
	Default Tree and Context	Used to specify a default tree and context. Tree and context are associated with the Novell Directory Services (NDS) used by NetWare 4.*x* servers.
	Print Options	Defines the print options that will be used when NT gateway users send print jobs to NetWare print queues. You can specify whether Add Form Feed, Notify When Done, and Print Banner functions are enabled and/or disabled. By default, the Notify and Banner functions are enabled.
	Login Script Options	Specifies whether or not NetWare login scripts will be used by the gateway users when accessing the NetWare resources.

GSNW Gateway Configuration

To configure the GSNW gateway account, click the Gateway button illustrated in Figure 4.2. The GSNW Configure Gateway dialog box (see Figure 4.3) will appear.

FIGURE 4.3

The GSNW Configure Gateway Dialog Box

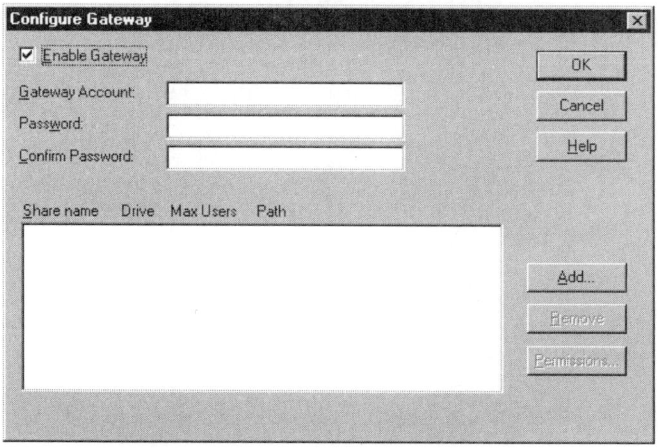

In the Configure Gateway dialog box, you can configure the options shown in Table 4.3.

	Configure Gateway Option	Explanation
T A B L E 4.3 GSNW Configure Gateway Configuration Options	Enable Gateway	Checked, this box enables the gateway. Unchecked, the gateway is disabled.
	Gateway Account	Used to specify the NetWare user account that has been configured as the gateway account and is a member of the NetWare group NTGATEWAY.
	Password and Confirm Password	Used to specify the NetWare Gateway account user password.
	Share box	Allows you to configure or modify shares of NetWare file resources for the gateway users.

In this section, you learned how to provide connectivity to NetWare file and print resources. In the next section, you will learn how to migrate information from a NetWare server to an NT server.

Migration Tool for NetWare

The Migration Tool for NetWare is used to migrate specific objects from a NetWare server to an NT server. This is typically used when a NetWare server is being replaced by an NT server. The following sections will cover:

- Items that can and can't be migrated
- The prerequisites to using the Migration Tool for NetWare
- Running and configuring the Migration Tool for NetWare

Objects That Can Be Migrated

The Migration Tool for NetWare can be configured to migrate specific NetWare objects from NetWare to NT. You can migrate NetWare 2.*x*, 3.*x*, or 4.*x* servers.

It is important to note that the Migration Tool for NetWare does not support NetWare 4 NDS or Novell Directory Services. This means you must be running in bindery emulation mode to migrate from a NetWare 4.*x* NDS server.

NetWare Items That Can Be Migrated

- User accounts
- Group accounts
- Directories and files that you specify
- NetWare permissions on the directories and files that are migrated

In order for file and directory permissions to be migrated, the destination NT directory must be NTFS.

NetWare Items That Cannot Be Migrated

- User passwords
- Login scripts
- Print queues and print servers
- User Account Manager and Workgroup Manager specifications

Prerequisites to Using the Migration Tool for NetWare

In order to use the Migration Tool for NetWare, the following requirements must first be met:

- You must be logged in with administrative rights on the NetWare side and on the NT side.
- You must be migrating to an NT domain controller if you are migrating user and group information.
- The NWLink IPX/SPX Compatible transport protocol must be installed on the NT server.
- The NT server must have GSNW installed.

Running and Configuring the Migration Tool for NetWare

Once you have met the prerequisites for running the Migration Tool for Net-Ware, you can run this utility from Start ➤ Programs ➤ Administrative Tools (Common) ➤ Migration Tool for NetWare.

The utility can also be run from the command line as boot drive from `\WINNT\SYSTEM32\NWCONV.EXE`.

The Migration Tool for NetWare dialog box (see Figure 4.4) will appear.

FIGURE 4.4

The Migration Tool for NetWare Dialog Box

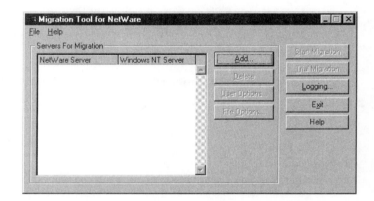

The first option you will configure is the source NetWare server and the destination NT server using the Add... button and then selecting the servers in the Select Servers For Migration dialog box. You can select any number of Net-Ware to NT server mappings. Once you have selected the servers that will be used in the Migration, you can then configure the User and Group options, the File Options, Trial or Actual migration, and the Logging options that will be used for the migration.

User and Group Migration Options

Once you have selected the servers that will participate in the migration, the User Options button that was shown in Figure 4.4 will become active. If you click this button, you will see the dialog box shown in Figure 4.5.

FIGURE 4.5

The User and Groups
Dialog Box from
Migration Tool
for NetWare

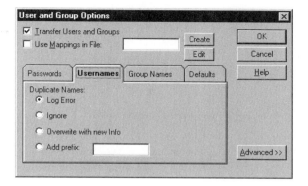

From this screen, you can select to configure:

- That users and groups will or will not be transferred

- Whether or not a mapping file will be used

- How passwords should be specified for transferred users

- How usernames will be specified if duplication exists

- How group names will be specified if duplication exists

Transfer Users and Groups

In Figure 4.5, the first check box, Transfer Users and Groups, which is selected by default, is used to specify if NetWare users and groups will be transferred. If this box remains selected, then you can configure: Mapping File, Password Specification, Duplicate Usernames, DuplicateGroup Names, Account Policy Defaults, File Options for Migration, Trial or Actual Migration, and Logging Options for Migration.

Mapping File

The Use Mappings in File check box specifies whether or not a mapping file should be used. The mapping file is used to specify how users, groups, and passwords will be used on the NT server. If a mapping file has not been previously created, the Create button will cause a new one to be opened and it can be edited at this point.

For example, let's assume that you have a user, Kevin Smith, who has a user account named Kevin on the NetWare server. You can specify that Kevin will be transferred to the NT server as SmithK. Additionally, you can specify that his password will be "buzz" through the use of a mapping file. This is the most user-intensive method, but it provides the best continuity of password security during the migration process.

Password Specification

As noted earlier, passwords can't be transferred from the NetWare side to the NT side. So, unless you specify the use of a mapping file that has password data, you must specify what will happen to the every migrated user's password. The choices are defined in Table 4.4.

TABLE 4.4 Password Options for the NetWare Migration	Password Option	Description
	No Password	Users will have no initial password on the NT server. This is the default selection.
	Password is Username	All users will have their migrated usernames as their initial passwords.
	Password is:	Specifies a generic password that will be used initially by all of the users that were migrated from the NetWare server.
	User Must Change Password	The default check box will set the User Must Change Password check box in the NT User Account that is created in the SAM.

None of these options are secure, so it's a good idea to use the mapping file.

Duplicate Usernames

It's possible to have an existing name on the NT domain that matches a name that exists on the NetWare server that is being migrated. Because NT does not allow duplicate usernames, you can specify what will happen in this event through the Usernames tab in the Users and Groups dialog box. Table 4.5 lists your options.

TABLE 4.5	Username Option	Description
Duplicate Username Resolution in a NetWare Migration	Log Error	Specifies that an error should be reported in the ERROR.LOG file. This is the default selection.
	Ignore	Causes no action to be taken, so if you are migrating a user that already exists, the migration will ignore the new user in favor of the existing NT user.
	Overwrite with new Info	Specifies that if a user already exists on the NT side, and a conflict exists, the NT user should be overwritten with the NetWare user.
	Add Prefix	Specifies that the prefix you select should be added to the NetWare user account if a conflict exists. For example, Kevin might have the prefix NW added and become NWKevin. Because NT usernames can be changed, this is the preferred method of transfer.

Duplicate Group Names

You specify how duplicate group names should be handled through the Group Names tab of the User and Group Options dialog box. The options that you can configure are:

- Log error
- Ignore
- Add prefix

These options are similar to the username options that were defined in Table 4.5.

Account Policy Defaults

The Defaults tab of the User and Group Options dialog box is used to specify how account management should be handled during the migration. The options you can choose from are shown in Table 4.6.

TABLE 4.6 Account Defaults During NetWare Migration	Account Policy	Description
	Use Supervisor Defaults	Specifies that default NetWare account restrictions will be applied as opposed to the default NT account restrictions. This includes things like NT account policy criteria like minimum password and password expiration date. This is the default selection.
	Add Supervisors to the Administrators Group	This option is used to add NetWare Supervisor equivalents to the NT Administrators local group on the domain controller. This option is not selected by default.

File Options for Migration

Once you have selected the servers that will participate in the migration, the File Options button, as shown in Figure 4.4, becomes active. By clicking this button, you will see the screen shown in Figure 4.6.

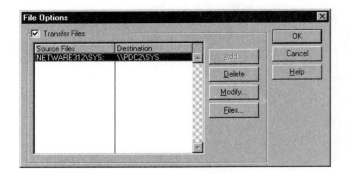

FIGURE 4.6

The File Options Dialog Box for NetWare Migration

Within the File Options dialog box, the Transfer Files box is selected by default to specify that you want to transfer directories and files. With this box checked, you can specify the directories and files you want to migrate as well as the destination directory.

When choosing the destination directory, you can specify that a new share be created and the properties of the destination directory. As noted earlier, if you want NetWare permissions to be migrated, you must select an NTFS partition as your destination directory.

Trial or Actual Migration

Before you perform the actual NetWare migration, you should perform a trial migration. A trial migration goes through all of the steps of a real migration, but it does not actually transfer any data. This allows you to see if any errors will occur, and it gives you a chance to correct those errors before an actual migration is performed. Conduct as many trial migrations as required, until the trial runs error free or produces errors that can't be resolved.

Logging Options for Migration

During the NetWare migration, you can choose what logging information will be recorded. You can choose from:

- Pop-up Errors which will produce a pop-up box every time an error is encountered

- Verbose User/Group Logging which provides verbose information on users and groups transferred

- Verbose File Logging which provides verbose information on file and directory migrations

Now that you have learned about NetWare connectivity, we'll move on to MultiProtocol routing.

MultiProtocol Routing

One common assumption that can be made about an enterprise environment is that somewhere within the network routing is involved. In order to support routing, NT Server uses a service called the MultiProtocol Router or MPR. You might think this is a single service you install, but it's actually a set of three different network services that you can install. The network services are:

- Routing Information Protocol (RIP) for Internet Protocol (IP) (Referred to as Internet Router in the objectives)

- DHCP Relay Agent (Referred to as BOOTP/DHCP Relay Agent in the objectives)

- RIP for NWLink IPX/SPX Compatible Transport (Referred to as IPX Router in the objectives)

This section will provide a routing overview, then will examine RIP for IP, the DHCP Relay Agent, and RIP for NWLink IPX Compatible Transport protocol.

Routing Overview

Routing is used to connect two or more network segments together. Commonly routers are used to:

- Connect dissimilar topologies (for example, Ethernet and Token Ring)
- Segment a high-traffic network into two or more subnets to reduce local network traffic
- Connect a local area network (LAN) to a wide area network (WAN)

As noted in Unit 1, the TCP/IP and the NWLink IPX/SPX protocols have routing capabilities.

RIP for Internet Protocol

TCP/IP is the most commonly used protocol with NT. To route between IP subnets, you can use static route tables or you can install RIP for IP, which uses dynamic route tables. This section will describe both options.

Static IP Route Tables

Static route tables must be manually configured in order to support routing. One reason you would use static route tables is because they do not generate network traffic like dynamic routing does.

In order to set up a router that will use static route tables, you must first have an NT Server with at least two network cards. In this case, we'll assume that they are connecting two IP subnets, subnet 131.103.1.0 and subnet 131.103.2.0 as shown in Figure 4.7.

Notice that each card in Figure 4.7 must be configured with an IP address from the subnet to which it will connect. In this case, Network Card 1 uses the IP address 131.103.1.20 and Network Card 2 uses the IP address 131.103.2.20.

The term multihomed is used to refer to an NT server that has two or more network cards installed and configured.

F I G U R E   4.7

IP Router Example

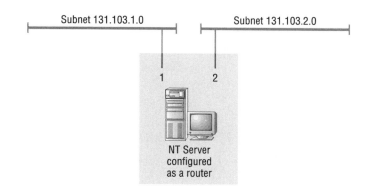

Subnet 131.103.1.0   Subnet 131.103.2.0

1   2

NT Server
configured
as a router

Network Card 1 – 131.103.1.20
Network Card 1 – 131.103.2.20

Once the network cards have been installed and configured, you need to make sure that IP Forwarding is enabled as shown in Figure 4.8. You can verify that this is configured by selecting Start ➤ Settings ➤ Control Panel ➤ Network ➤ Protocols ➤ TCP/IP Protocol ➤ Properties button ➤ Routing tab.

F I G U R E   4.8

Microsoft TCP/IP Routing Tab Dialog Box

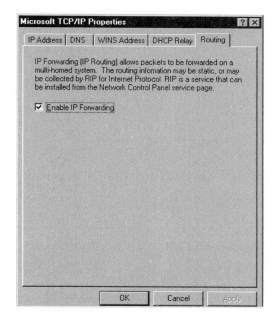

Microsoft TCP/IP Properties

| IP Address | DNS | WINS Address | DHCP Relay | Routing |

IP Forwarding (IP Routing) allows packets to be forwarded on a multi-homed system. The routing information may be static, or may be collected by RIP for Internet Protocol. RIP is a service that can be installed from the Network Control Panel service page.

☑ Enable IP Forwarding

OK   Cancel   Apply

The ROUTE command can then be used to manually configure your router tables.

> For more information on the ROUTE command, access NT Help through Start (Help (Windows NT Commands ➤ Windows NT Commands ➤ R ➤ route.

Dynamic Routing with RIP for IP

Assuming you don't want the headaches involved with manually managing your router tables, you can choose to install RIP for IP. Once this service is installed, the RIP router will exchange routing information with other routers on the network. Anytime routing information changes, the router will note the change and propagate the changes to other routers on the network.

RIP for IP is the easy way of managing routing, but it comes with the price of increasing network traffic. RIP routers broadcast their RIP tables periodically so that all routers on the network can remain synchronized.

DHCP Relay Agent

DHCP is a TCP/IP service based on an earlier protocol called Bootstrap Protocol or BOOTP. BOOTP was originally designed for diskless workstations that had no way to store an IP configuration. The administrator would configure a BOOTP server and the clients could then get IP information from the BOOTP server.

The next evolution was DHCP. DHCP is also designed to provide clients with IP configuration information. As seen in Unit 2, a DHCP server can be defined with a range or with IP addresses (called *scope*), which can be leased to DHCP clients.

By default, a DHCP server will serve only DHCP clients on its own subnet. Assume that you are configured as shown in Figure 4.9.

FIGURE 4.9
DHCP Configuration Example

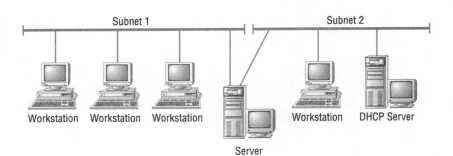

The clients on Subnet 2 will be able to obtain IP configuration information because the DHCP server is on their subnet, but the clients on Subnet 1 will need to rely on manual configuration because no DHCP server exists on their segment.

To overcome this problem, you could use one of two solutions:

- Install a DHCP server on each subnet.

- Install the DHCP relay agent on the router.

The DHCP Relay Agent is used to broadcast DHCP messages between a DHCP server and a router.

Because you may not have the resources to install a DHCP server on each subnet, you may choose to install the DHCP Relay Agent.

To install the DHCP Relay Agent, use Control Panel ≻ Services ≻ Add ≻ DHCP Relay Agent. After the support files are copied over, you will need to restart your computer.

To activate the DHCP Relay Agent, you must specify the DHCP Servers IP address in the Control Panel ≻ Network ≻ Protocols tab ≻ TCP/IP Protocol DHCP Relay tab as shown in Figure 4.10.

FIGURE 4.10

DHCP Relay Configuration Tab Dialog Screen

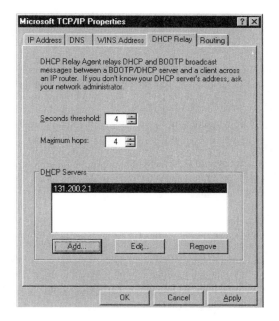

RIP for NWLink IPX/SPX Compatible Transport

The IP and IPX protocols are similar in many ways, including the way they are routed.

However, one major difference between IP and IPX is their usage. While IP is a de facto industry standard, IPX is more of a proprietary protocol that was developed by Novell. So while IP is pretty much used by all network operating systems, IPX is mainly used in environments that support Novell NetWare. This point is made so you can note that NT IPX routing is compatible with the Novell IPX router specification.

Like IP, IPX routing can be configured manually through static route tables or dynamically through RIP for IPX. In this section, you will learn about both options.

Static IPX Routing

In order to go from one subnet to another, you must know what path or direction to take. You can accomplish this by enabling RIP routing and then manually configuring the IPX route tables. As noted in the IP section, you must have at least two network cards in your NT Server that are configured with the correct network address for the subnet to which they will attach.

To confirm that RIP Routing for IPX is enabled, access the dialog box shown in Figure 4.11. To access this box, select Start ➢ Settings ➢ Control Panel ➢ Network ➢ Protocols ➢ NWLink IPX/SPX Compatible Transport ➢ Properties button ➢ Routing tab.

The IPXROUTE command can then be used to manually configure your router tables.

For more information on the IPXROUTE command, access NT Help through Start (Help (Windows NT Commands ➢ Windows NT Commands ➢ I ➢ ipxroute.

Dynamic Routing with RIP for IPX

If you don't want the administrative overhead associated with manually adding IPX routes, you can install RIP for NWLink IPX, which will configure and manage IPX route tables for you dynamically.

When you install RIP for NWLink IPX, you will actually use the services of RIP and SAP (Service Advertising Protocol). SAP is used by NetWare to broadcast services. This is somewhat similar to the way NT uses NetBIOS with the browser service to advertise resources.

FIGURE 4.11

NWLink IPX/SPX Routing Tab Dialog Box

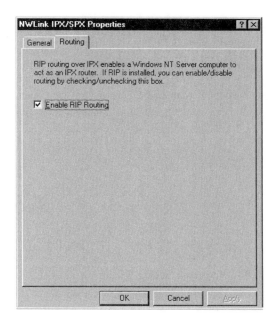

You also have the option of enabling NetBIOS Broadcast Propagation (broadcast of type 20 packets). This must be enabled if you have Microsoft clients using NWLink to connect to the NT server. Failure to enable this option will mean that NetBIOS functions (such as browsing) running on the NWLink IPX protocol will not function properly.

In the next section, you will learn how the Internet Information Server (IIS) can be used to provide NT connectivity.

Internet Information Server and Internet Services

NT Server 4.0 originally shipped with Internet Information Server 2.0 and has been updated to 3.0 with the release of Service Pack 2. Currently IIS 4.0 is available from Microsoft's Web site. IIS is used to publish and host Internet services for internal networks (intranets) and the worldwide Internet.

The main service protocols that comprise IIS are:

- Hypertext Transfer Protocol (HTTP)
- File Transfer Protocol (FTP)

Although the Gopher service is also included in IIS, it is almost never used either on the Internet or in corporate intranets. Therefore, it is not covered in this testing guide. This section will focus on Internet connectivity through the IIS services and the DNS service.

IIS

Install IIS as a service through Control Panel ➤ Network ➤ Services. Then specify that you want to install Internet Information Server by using the Add... button. You will want to install the most current version. Check the Microsoft website for current version information.

Once you install IIS, you will have a new program group called Microsoft Internet Server (Common) on the computer on which IIS was installed. A utility called Internet Service Manager lives in this program group. You can configure WWW and FTP through this utility. The main screen is shown in Figure 4.12.

FIGURE 4.12

Internet Service Manager Main Dialog Box

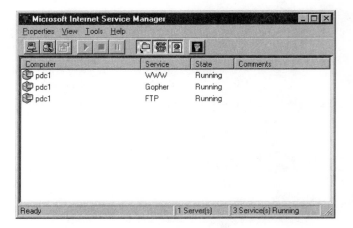

The following subsections overview the purpose and configuration of the IIS WWW and FTP services. You will also learn about virtual directories and virtual servers.

World Wide Web (WWW) Service

WWW or the Web is used to provide a graphical interface for viewing documents on the Internet. WWW uses the HTTP protocol as a client-server process. The client uses WWW to navigate the Web and request HTML files. HTML files can contain text, graphics, audio, and video data. The WWW server in turn stores the HTML data.

When you install IIS, the WWW service is automatically installed. To configure WWW, double-click on the WWW service depicted in Figure 4.12. You will see a dialog screen similar to Figure 4.13.

F I G U R E 4.13

WWW Service Properties Dialog Screen

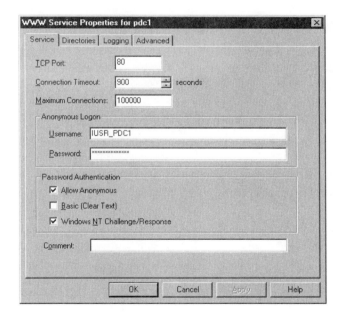

Through the WWW service properties, you can configure:

- Service

- Directories

- Logging

- Advanced

These options are defined in the following subsections.

Service

The WWW Service Property tab is shown in Figure 4.13 and the service properties are defined in Table 4.7.

T A B L E 4.7:   WWW Service Properties

Service Property	Description
TCP Port	Allows you to specify the TCP port on which you want the WWW service to run. By default, the WWW service uses port 80.
Connection Timeout	Specifies how long a connection should be held open if no user activity is detected. By default a connection will be held open for 900 seconds without activity.
Maximum Connections	This number specifies the maximum number of concurrent connections the WWW service will support. This is set to 100,000 by default.
Anonymous Logon	Species whether or not anonymous logons are allowed. By default, the WWW service will use an account called IUSR_*computername*. This account name is created when IIS is installed and can be managed through User Manager for Domains. If a password is specified in this dialog box, it must match the password that is specified through User Manager for Domains.
Password Authentication	Specifies which password authentication method will be required for WWW clients. You can select more that one uthentication method. The authentication methods include: Allow Anonymous which uses no authentication; Basic (Clear Text) which is encoded and is supported by most Web browsers; and Windows NT Challenge/Response which offers the highest level of encryption and will encrypt the username and password. Default settings are Allow Anonymous and Windows NT Challenge/Response selected.
Comment	Used for informational purposes.

Directories

The WWW Directories Property tab is shown in Figure 4.14 and the properties are defined in Table 4.8.

FIGURE 4.14

WWW Directories
Property Dialog Box

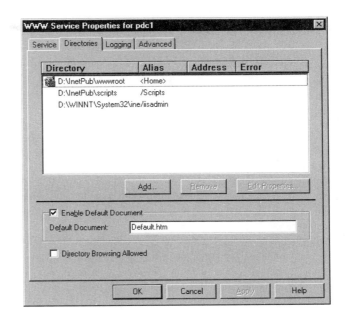

FIGURE 4.14

WWW Directories
Property Dialog Box

TABLE 4.8: WWW Directories Properties

Directory Property	Description
Directories	This property specifies the directories that will be used by the WWW service. You can specify Directories (the path of the directories to be used by WWW), Alias (the path for virtual directories, covered in more detail later in this section), Address (the IP address for virtual servers), and Error (which will list any system errors reported).
Enable Default Document	Specifies that a default document be displayed if the remote client does not request a specific document in the directory.
Directory Browsing Allowed	This option will allow the remote client to obtain a listing of directories and files that are hosted by the WWW service.

Logging

You can configure the WWW service to support logging features. Logging is used to determine how much use you have through the WWW service (i.e., how long each client is attached to the WWW service), to determine what files users are accessing, and to help identify any security violations. You can configure Logging through the dialog screen shown in Figure 4.15.

FIGURE 4.15

WWW Logging Property Dialog Box

You can configure the logging options shown in Table 4.9.

T A B L E 4.9: WWW Logging Properties

Logging Property	Description
Enable Logging	Enables the logging feature. Selected by default.
Log Format	When you choose to enable logging, you can log to a Standard format (default) or the NCSA format. NCSA logs follow the format defined by the National Center for Supercomputing Applications.

T A B L E 4.9:   WWW Logging Properties *(continued)*

Logging Property	Description
Automatically open new log	Specifies how often a new log should be generated. You can choose from daily (default), weekly, monthly, or when the file reaches a certain size (whatever size you specify).
Log file directory	Allows you to specify the location of your log files. By default, log files are stored in the NT boot drive in \WINNT\System32\LogFiles.
Log to SQL/ODBC Database	Specifies that the log file should be saved in an SQL or ODBC (Open Database Connectivity) database as opposed to the file logging. If you use this option, you must specify the location of the database and a username and password that is valid for the database application.

Once you enable logging, you can view the log file which contains information about: Client's IP address, Client's username, Date, Time, Service, Computer name, IP address of server, Elapsed time, Bytes received, Bytes sent, Service status code, Windows NT status code, Name of the operation, and Target of the operation.

Advanced

You can configure the WWW service to support advanced features. The advanced features mainly relate to security for the WWW service. The Advanced tab of the WWW service is shown in Figure 4.16.

Through the advanced tab of the WWW service property, you can define which computers are granted or denied access to the WWW service. This is based on the computers' IP addresses and subnet masks.

You can also specify the amount of bandwidth allowed by Internet services by configuring the Limit Network Use by all Internet Services on this computer and specifying the maximum number of kilobits per second that will be allowed.

Next, you will learn how to configure the FTP service.

FIGURE 4.16

WWW Advanced
Property Dialog Box

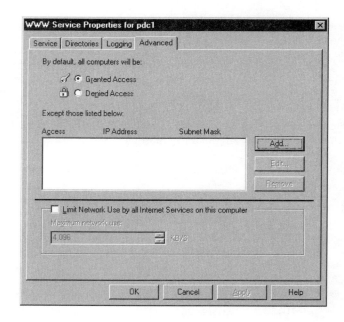

File Transfer Protocol (FTP) Service

The FTP service is a TCP/IP protocol service used to transfer files between a local and a remote host. The IIS Server contains the FTP service as a default component. You can configure the following properties for FTP as shown in Figure 4.17.

Through the FTP service properties, you can configure:

- Service

- Messages

- Directories

- Logging

- Advanced

These options are defined in the following subsections.

Service

The Service property as shown in Figure 4.17 is very similar to the WWW Service property previously defined. The differences are that the TCP port number for FTP is 21, the maximum number of connections is 1,000 (due to the continuous nature of FTP connections), and there is no option to support encrypted passwords (meaning no MS-CHAP encryption option).

F I G U R E   4.17

FTP Service Properties
Dialog Screen

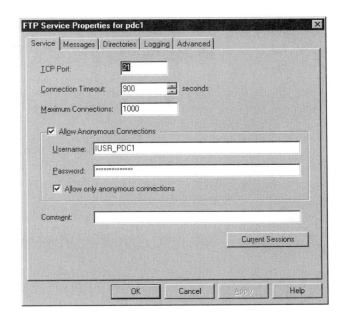

F I G U R E   4.17

FTP Service Properties
Dialog Screen

Messages

The Message property is unique to FTP and is shown in Figure 4.18.

F I G U R E   4.18

FTP Messages Service
Property Dialog Box

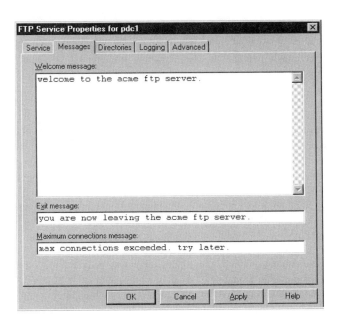

This dialog box allows you to specify the message users see when:

- They access the FTP server
- They exit the FTP server
- They access the FTP server, but the maximum concurrent connections have already been exceeded

Directories

The Directories property of the FTP service is shown in Figure 4.19. This is similar to the WWW Directories property, but it allows you to specify whether the Directory Listing Style will be UNIX or MS-DOS based. FTP does not support virtual servers.

FIGURE 4.19

FTP Directories Service
Property Dialog Box

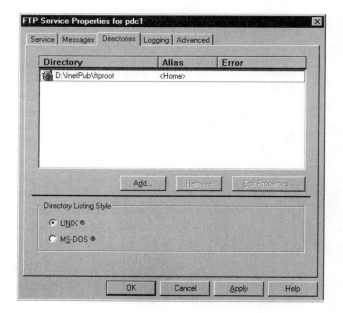

Logging

The Logging property is similar to the WWW Logging property that was previously covered.

Advanced

The Advanced property is similar to the WWW Logging property that was previously covered.

Virtual Directories and Virtual Servers

A virtual directory is a directory that exists on a remote computer, but appears as if it physically exists on the computer that hosts the IIS server. A virtual server is a single computer that has IIS installed, but appears to remote users as multiple Internet servers.

Creating Virtual Directories

To create a virtual directory, point to a UNC name through the WWW or FTP Directories service property tab.

Creating Virtual Servers

Creating a virtual server is more complex. To create a virtual server:

- You must have an IP address for the primary server and an IP address that will be used for each virtual server.

- You must use Control Panel ➤ Network to assign the multiple IP addresses to your LAN adapter.

- Through the Internet Service Manager, assign each virtual server its own IP address through the Directories tab of the WWW service. FTP does not support this.

The next section will review the DNS service.

DNS

The Domain Name System (DNS) Service is used to map TCP/IP Fully Qualified Domain Names (FQDNs) to IP addresses. DNS is based on a hierarchical name service structure. Domain names (also called host names) are used to identify resources on intranets or on the Internet.

An example of DNS usage is the IP address 209.1.78.150, which is used by sybex.com. It's much easier for humans to remember sybex.com, rather than the IP address. DNS servers are manually configured and maintained by system administrators.

Remote Access Server

Remote access allows you to access remote network resources or access the main network from a remote location. NT does this through remote access server service and remote access client service. The remote access server software ships with NT Server and is called Remote Access Server or RAS. The remote access client software ships with NT Workstation, Windows 95, and Windows for Workgroups and installs as a service that is accessed through Dial-Up Networking on NT/95 operating systems. The NT Server CD also provides remote client software for other clients.

Installing RAS is fairly easy. It consists of two main steps:

1. Install the RAS service from Control Panel ➤ Network ➤ Services.

2. Install and configure the communication devices (Modem, ISDN, X.25 PAD) that RAS will use.

In this section, you will learn about RAS communications, RAS protocols, RAS security, and RAS dial-up clients.

RAS Communications

RAS servers support a variety of communication options. You can communicate through:

- PSTN
- ISDN
- X.25
- RS-232 null modem cables
- PPTP

Each of these communication options is defined in Table 4.10.

T A B L E   4.10:   RAS Communication Options

RAS Communication Type	Description
PSTN	PSTN is the Public Switched Telephone Network and using PSTN is associated with good-old analog modems.

T A B L E   4.10:   RAS Communication Options *(continued)*

RAS Communication Type	Description
ISDN	Integrated Services Digital Network (ISDN) is associated with digital communications. Instead of using modems with ISDN, you use ISDN adapters.
X.25	X.25 refers to a packet-switching network that uses the X.25 protocol. X.25 networks have been declining in popularity as the Internet has taken over in popularity.
RS-232 null modem cables	Serial cable used to connect two computers together. The cable is specially configured so that the transmit and receive wires are crossed on one side. This method could be used to test and troubleshoot RAS by removing the communication hardware from the connection path.
PPTP	Point-to-Point Tunneling Protocol (PPTP) is used to support RAS via Internet connections. PPTP can be a cost-effective way to support long distance connections, since you are able to take advantage of the Internet's infrastructure.

RAS Protocols

RAS supports WAN protocols and LAN protocols.

The WAN protocols supported through RAS are:

- SLIP (Serial Line Internet Protocol)

- PPP (Point to Point protocol)

The LAN protocols supported through RAS are:

- NetBEUI

- IPX (NWLink in NT)

- TCP/IP

These protocols are described in the following subsections.

WAN Protocols

The WAN protocols associated with RAS are SLIP and PPP.

SLIP

SLIP is an older protocol that was originally developed for UNIX computers. It is not commonly used in Microsoft networks. RAS can use SLIP as a dial-out protocol, but it does not support SLIP for dial-in connections. The disadvantages of SLIP are:

- No error checking

- No security

- No flow control or data compression

PPP

PPP is the default WAN protocol used when you install RAS. It offers the following benefits:

- Supports encrypted logons

- Supports NetBEUI, IPX, and TCP/IP

- Optimized for low-bandwidth connections

LAN Protocols

The LAN protocols supported through the RAS server are NetBEUI, IPX, and TCP/IP.

This section will cover the configuration option that is used by all three protocols, then it will look at specific configurations for each protocol.

To configure the LAN protocols, select Control Panel ➤ Network ➤ Services, then check the protocol you want to configure and click the Configure button.

Common Configuration for All Protocols

Each network protocol can be configured to allow access to the Entire Network or This Computer Only.

The Entire Network option allows RAS clients to act as clients to the network. The client can access any network resources to which the user account has permissions.

The This Computer Only option allows users to access resources only on the RAS server. This provides better security for the rest of the network.

NetBEUI

As noted in Unit 1, NetBEUI is the simplest network protocol, and it requires the least amount of overhead. If your clients don't require the services of IPX or TCP/IP, NetBEUI will provide the best performance.

Other than the Entire Network or This Computer Only option, NetBEUI requires no configuration.

IPX

As shown in Figure 4.20, the IPX protocol requires more configuration. The configuration options for IPX are defined in Table 4.11.

FIGURE 4.20

The RAS Server IPX Configuration Dialog Box

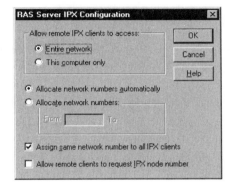

TABLE 4.11

RAS Server IPX Configuration Options

RAS IPX Configuration Option	Description
Allocate network numbers automatically	Default option used to assign any IPX network number that is not in use by the RAS server.
Allocate network numbers	Allows you to specify the range of network numbers. You provide the start range, and the end range will be filled in automatically based on the number of ports you have defined.
Assign same network numbers to all IPX clients	Specifies that only one network address be used by all RAS clients. This option helps reduce RIP traffic and is activated by default.
Allow remote clients to request IPX node number	Allows remote clients to pick their own network addresses. You run a security risk with this option because a client can impersonate another node with the same address.

TCP/IP

TCP/IP is the most commonly used protocol. The TCP/IP configuration box is shown in Figure 4.21 and the configuration options are defined in Table 4.12.

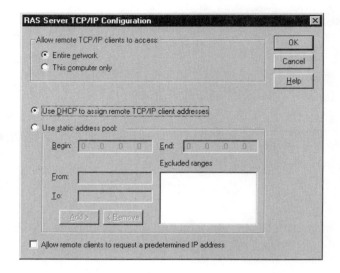

RAS TCP/IP Configuration Option	Description
Use DHCP to assign remote TCP/IP client addresses	Allows a RAS client to get an IP address from a DHCP server. If a DHCP server is not available, you must use the next option. This is the default option.
Use static address pool	Allows the assignment of IP addresses from a scope that you define. The scope requires an address for the network adapter in the RAS server and an IP address for each RAS client. The range must be valid for the subnet where the RAS server is located. Multiple exclusions can be created in the single defined scope.
Allow remote clients to request a predetermined IP address	Allows the RAS clients to select their own IP address. This address must be valid for the subnet where the RAS server is located.

TCP/IP is the only protocol that supports the Windows Sockets API. If your users require access to applications that use the Windows Sockets API, you must configure TCP/IP for your RAS server. If you are using multiple protocols, TCP/IP should be listed first in the bindings order.

RAS Security

You can make your RAS server more secure by applying security and dictating who can use RAS, dial-back requirements, and encryption methods.

Specifying Authorized RAS Users and RAS Call Back

One of the first steps in setting up RAS security is to determine who should be able to use RAS and if any call-back options should be applied.

You can specify whether or not a user is authorized for RAS through:

- Remote Access Admin (shown in Figure 4.22)
- User Manager for Domains (through the Dialin property box of each user)

You can assign RAS access to users from within your domain or trusted domains. To assign users permissions from trusted domains, select the Server option in the Remote Access Admin utility and then specify which users should have RAS access.

The Remote Access Admin utility can be used to manage the RAS communication ports; start, stop, and pause the RAS service; or assign RAS permissions. To assign RAS permissions, select Users ➢ Permissions.

The same dialog box that is used to specify dial-in permissions is used to specify call-back security. Call-back security is defined in Table 4.13.

FIGURE 4.22

The Remote Access Permissions Dialog Box

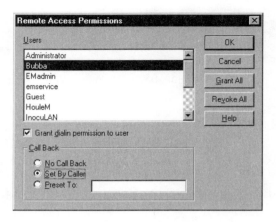

TABLE 4.13

RAS Call-Back Security

Call-Back Option	Description
No Call Back	Call back is not used
Set By Caller	The caller specifies the number that will be called back. This option is often used so the caller does not bear the costs of long distance calls and so remote access locations can be tracked.
Preset To	This option specifies the number that will be called back. This option is used for accounts that are sensitive, such as administrative accounts, that will always RAS in from a fixed location.

RAS Encryption

As noted earlier, RAS encryption is supported for PPP clients. You can configure RAS encryption through Control Panel ≻ Network ≻ Services ≻ Remote Access Service ≻ Properties. Once you access the dialog box shown in Figure 4.23, you can choose from:

- Allow any authentication including clear text
- Require encrypted authentication
- Require Microsoft encrypted authentication

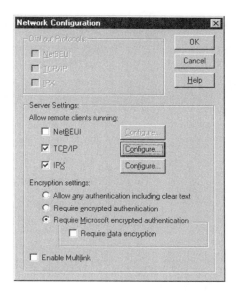

FIGURE 4.23

The Remote Access
Service Network Con-
figuration Dialog Box

These options are described in Table 4.14.

TABLE 4.14	**RAS Encryption**	**Description**
RAS Encryption Options	Allow any authentication including clear text	The least secure method, but it supports many levels of encryption including MS-CHAP, SPAP, and PAP. This option is useful if you have a variety of clients dialing in and you want to support whatever encryption they are using.
	Require encrypted authentication	Supports the MS-CHAP and SPAP encryption methods, but not PAP. This method requires that clients use encrypted passwords.
	Require Microsoft encrypted authentication	The most secure encryption method. This option uses MS-CHAP encryption and is the only encryption option that also allows you to specify that both data and the user's password should be encrypted. This is the default.

RAS Dial-Up Clients

Once the RAS server has been installed, you must install the RAS client software. Depending on the client platform you are using, setup will differ. This section will focus on how to install and configure an NT RAS client.

Installing RAS Client Software

To install the RAS client software on an NT client, follow the same procedure as RAS for NT Server. Once that is completed, choose the My Computer icon from the desktop, then click the Dial-Up Networking icon. You will specify:

- A phone book entry (where you'll call your RAS server)
- The communication device you'll use
- The telephony dialing properties (where you are calling from)

During the installation of the RAS client software (also called dial-up networking or DUN), you can also configure your RAS connection, which is covered in the next section.

Configuring RAS Client Software

Once the dial-up networking software has been installed, you will see the screen shown in Figure 4.24. To configure the RAS connection on the client software, click the More button shown in Figure 4.24, and choose the Edit Entries and modem properties selection. You will see the figure shown in Figure 4.25.

FIGURE 4.24

The Dial-Up Networking
Dialog Box

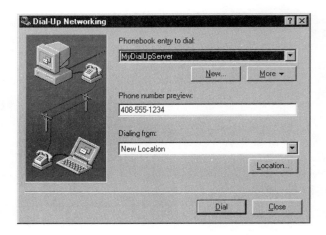

FIGURE 4.25

The Edit Phonebook
Entry Dialog Box

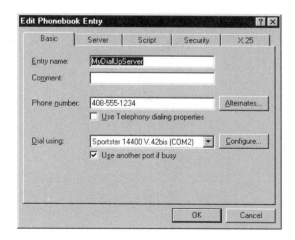

From the dialog box shown in Figure 4.25, you can configure the client DUN properties. Two of the most important configuration tabs are:

- Server
- Security

These tabs are covered in the following subsections.

Server Tab

As shown in Figure 4.26, the Server tab allows you to configure the connection for the server to which you will connect. These options are defined in Table 4.15.

FIGURE 4.26

Dial-Up Networking
Server Property Tab

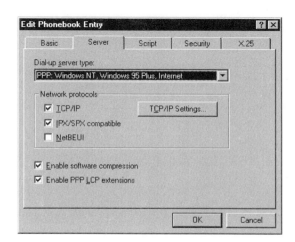

TABLE 4.15	Server Option	Description
Dial-Up Networking Server Property Tab Options	Dial-up server type	Allows you to specify the type of connection you are using: • A PPP connection to attach to Windows NT, Windows 95 Plus, or the Internet • A SLIP connection to the Internet • A connection to a Windows NT 3.1 or Windows for Workgroups computer
	Network Protocols	Allows you to specify the dialin protocol(s) you will use. You can choose from TCP/IP, IPX/SPX compatible, or NetBEUI. You must have a protocol in common with the RAS server you are calling. TCP/IP and IPX/SPX are selected by default.
	Enable software compression	Offers software compression that is used in addition to modem hardware compression. Selected by default.
	Enable PPP LCP extensions	Specifies that you want to enable enhancement features for PPP. This can cause problems if you connect to a server running outdated PPP software. Selected by default.

Security Tab

The security tab specifies the authentication and encryption method you want to use. The options are shown in Figure 4.27 and defined in Table 4.16.

FIGURE 4.27

Dial-Up Networking Security Property Tab

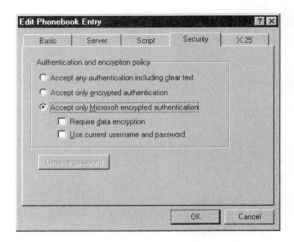

TABLE 4.16 Dial-Up Networking Security Property Tab Options	Authentication Option	Description
	Accept any authentication including clear text	Specifies that the client can specify any authentication that is requested by the server, including no authentication (which could happen if you were connecting to a non-Microsoft server).
	Accept only encrypted authentication	Specifies that you can authenticate with any encryption method except PAP. This is more secure than the previous option.
	Accept only Microsoft encrypted authentication	Specifies that you want to use the MS-CHAP encryption method to authenticate. This assumes that you will connect to a Microsoft server. This is the most secure authentication method and allows you the option of also encrypting any data that is sent. This also allows use of data encryption and current usernames and passwords. Selected by default.

Now that you've reviewed NT connectivity, it's time to put your knowledge to the test.

NetWare Connectivity

1. You must install _____ on an NT Server that will be used to connect to NetWare servers running client/server applications, such as an SQL server.

2. The _____ service is used on NT Servers to provide NT users with connectivity to NetWare file and print resources.

3. The _____ utility is used to migrate NetWare users, groups, and data to NT servers.

4. The _____ protocol is required if you install GSNW on an NT server.

5. When installing GSNW, you must create a group called _____ on the _____ (NT or NetWare) server.

6. When using the Migration Tool for NetWare the _____ option gives you the greatest control over how users, groups, and passwords are migrated from NetWare to NT.

7. Before you can use the Migration Tool for NetWare, the _____ protocol and the _____ service must be installed on the NT Server.

8. What needs to be configured so NT users do not have banner pages printed when printing to NetWare queues through GSNW?

_____

9. True or False. You can configure whether or not NetWare login scripts will be used by users who attach to NetWare servers through GSNW.

10. True or False. You must create a user on the NT server that has GSNW installed that will act as a GSNW service account.

11. What username option would you choose in Migration Tool for NetWare if you wanted the NetWare account to overwrite the NT account if duplicate account names existed?

---

12. What username option would you choose in Migration Tool for NetWare if you wanted the NT account to be used and the NetWare account ignored in the event that duplicate account names exist?

---

13. What Migration Tool for NetWare option provides the most security for user passwords during migration?

---

14. What Migration Tool for NetWare option will automatically add Supervisor equivalents from the NetWare environment to the NT Administrators group?

---

15.   What software is required on an NT Server to allow NetWare users to access NT file and print resources?

_____

16.   What software can be installed on NT Workstations to allow access to NetWare file and print resources?

_____

17.   True or False. You must create a user account for each NT user who will access the NetWare server though GSNW.

18.   True or False. GSNW can be installed on NT Workstations or NT Servers.

19.   True or False. When configuring the GSNW gateway, you must provide a Gateway account and password. This gateway account is a NetWare user . The specified password is for the NetWare user account.

20.   True or False. Any client who can attach to the NT Server running GSNW can access the resources to which the gateway user (through user or group membership) has rights.

21.   What requirement must be met on the NT Server in order to transfer NetWare file and directory permissions when transferring files and directories through Migration Tool for NetWare?

_____

22.   True or False. NetWare print queues and printers can be migrated with Migration Tool for NetWare.

23.   True or False. NetWare user passwords can be migrated with Migration Tool for NetWare.

24.   True or False. NetWare group accounts can be migrated with Migration Tool for NetWare.

25.   True or False. NetWare login scripts can be migrated with Migration Tool for NetWare.

26.   True or False. NetWare permissions for migrated directories and files can be migrated with Migration Tool for NetWare.

27.   How do you specify that NetWare account restrictions should be enforced rather than NT account policies when configuring Migration Tool for NetWare?

_____

28.   Which logging option will cause a pop-up message to appear during a NetWare migration if any errors occur?

_____

29.   Which logging option will provide detailed information about user and group transfers during a NetWare migration?

_____

30.   What option should you configure in Migration Tool for NetWare if you want to identify possible migration errors before they are actually committed?

_____

MultiProtocol Routing

31. List the three services that comprise the MultiProtocol Router.

_____

_____

_____

32. The _____ service is used to provide DHCP support for network segments that do not have a DHCP server installed.

33. The _____ service is used to support dynamic routing in a network using the TCP/IP transport protocol.

34. The _____ service is used to support dynamic routing in a network using the NWLink IPX/SPX Compatible Transport protocol.

35. An NT Server configured as a router using the TCP/IP protocol must have the network cards configured with IP addresses from _____ (same or different) network addresses.

36. The _____ command is used to configure static routing tables in networks using TCP/IP.

37. The_____ command is used to configure static routing tables in networks using NWLink IPX/SPX Compatible Transport protocol.

38. When you install RIP for IPX, you also install the _____
protocol, which is used to broadcast NetWare resources.

39. You have an NT Server using NWLink IPX/SPX as its primary transport protocol. The server
acts as a router and has RIP for NWLink IPX installed. What must be enabled to allow
Microsoft Windows clients using NWLink as their primary transport protocol to access the
NT Server correctly?

_____

40. You are using TCP/IP with two network segments. Segment A has a DHCP server. Segment B
has no DHCP server, but it has an NT server on the segment. The two segments are connected
through a router. On what computer should the DHCP Relay Agent be installed so that clients
located on Segment B can use DHCP services?

_____

Internet Information Server and Internet Services

41. The _____ service is used to map IP addresses to
domain names.

42. The _____ IIS service is used to transfer files between
local and remote hosts.

43. The _____ IIS service is used to provide a graphical
interface used to view documents on the Internet.

STUDY QUESTIONS

44.   What is the difference between an intranet and the Internet?

_____

45.   How do you create a virtual server in IIS?

_____

46.   When using IIS, what is the definition of a virtual directory?

_____

47.   How do you specify whether or not anonymous connections can be used for the WWW service in IIS?

_____

48.   What account is used for anonymous connections for the IIS WWW and FTP services?

_____

49.   What utility is used to configure IIS WWW and FTP service properties?

_____

50.   What password authentication method would you configure for the IIS WWW service if you wanted the highest level of security?

_____

51.   How do you limit access to the IIS FTP service?

_____

52.   True or False. You can configure auditing for IIS through the Internet Service Manager.

53.   How do you specify that users see a document called `welcome.htm` if no file is specified when connecting to your IIS server?

_____

54.   You have installed IIS and are using the WWW service. Only 10 people should have access to the WWW server. How do you configure the WWW service to allow only these specific users access?

_____

55.   You have enabled logging for the FTP service. Where will the log file be created by default?

_____

56.   You are allowing anonymous connections to the WWW service through IIS. What password authentication method should be used to support the anonymous connections?

_____

57.   True or False. The DNS server will automatically create mappings of IP addresses to domain names.

Remote Access Server

58. What RAS encryption setting should you use if you require data encryption in addition to password encryption?

_____

59. What utilities can be used to specify which NT users can dial in to a RAS server?

_____

_____

60. What dial-back options of RAS allow users to dial in from any location?

_____

_____

61. What RAS TCP/IP configuration option allows you to specify a range of IP addresses that can be assigned to RAS clients?

_____

62. What RAS TCP/IP configuration option allows you to allow RAS clients to get their IP configuration information from a DHCP server?

_____

63. What configuration is required on the RAS server and on RAS clients so that RAS clients can specify the IP address they will use?

_____

64. What three transport protocols are supported for dial-in RAS clients on a RAS server?

_____

_____

_____

65. What encryption setting would you use on the RAS server if you support a variety of RAS clients, some using Microsoft client software, some using non-Microsoft client software?

_____

66. As a RAS client, you dial in to a UNIX server using the SLIP protocol. How should password encryption be configured?

_____

67. The _____WAN protocol is used for clients who dial in to an NT RAS server.

68. You would use the _____RAS communication option if you wanted to support your RAS environment over Internet connections.

69. Which RAS call-back option specifies the highest level of security?

_____

70. You have installed RAS on your NT server. You require that all passwords be encrypted through RAS. You support Microsoft and non-Microsoft clients. What encryption option should you choose?

_____

71. Which RAS communication option uses analog phone lines with modems?

_____

72. True or False. NT RAS supports SLIP for dial-in connections, but does not support SLIP for dial-out connections.

73. True or False. NT RAS supports PPP for dial-in and dial-out connections.

74. What RAS protocol would be installed if your RAS clients were connecting to NetWare servers?

_____

SAMPLE TEST

4-1 Your network uses the TCP/IP protocol. You have two subnets connected through a router as shown:

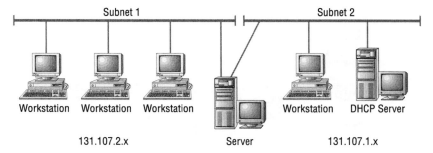

Clients on the 131.107.2.x subnet should be able to get their IP configurations from the DHCP server located on subnet 131.107.1.x. What needs to be done to make this possible?

A. You should install RIP for IP on the NT server that acts as the router.

B. You should install the DHCP Router Service on the NT server that acts as the router.

C. You should install the DHCP Relay Agent service on the NT server that acts as the router.

D. You should configure the TCP/IP properties on each client on subnet 131.107.2.x to specify the IP address of the DHCP server on subnet 131.107.1.x.

SAMPLE TEST

4-2   Your network supports a variety of NetWare and NT resources as shown in the following graphic:

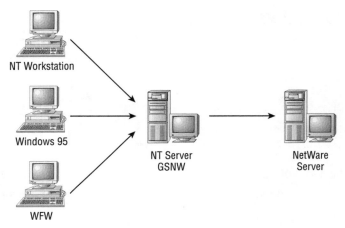

All of your Windows 95 and NT workstation clients use only the Microsoft redirector software. To access the NetWare file and print resources, they must go through the NT server that has GSNW installed. Whenever the gateway users send print jobs to the NetWare printers, the job is always appended with a blank page of paper. What do you do to prevent the blank page from printing?

A. On the NetWare server, specify that the form feed should be disabled on the print queue.

B. On the NetWare server, specify that form feed should be disabled for the print server.

C. On the NT server, create a printer that points to the NetWare print device. Specify that the printer has form feed disabled.

D. On the NT server, configure the Gateway for NetWare service property so that the Add Form Feed option is not checked.

SAMPLE TEST

4-3 Previously your network used NetWare servers exclusively. You have now decided to use NT Servers as your network servers. You use the Migration Tool for NetWare to transfer all users, groups, and data to a PDC called NTS1. What needs to be done so that all of the NetWare clients will now be able to access the NT Server?

    A. Install CSNW on each computer.

    B. Install GSNW on the NT server.

    C. Install the Microsoft File & Print Service on the NetWare server.

    D. Install CSNW on the NT server.

4-4 Your company is an ISP and provides Internet services to many companies. Several of the companies have registered domain names and have contracted you to design, develop, and maintain their Web sites. You will use IIS to host each Web site. Three of the companies belong to the same parent corporation. They have provided you with a server that should host each of the three individual company's Web sites. How do you create the three virtual servers? (Choose two answers.)

    A. You will need a unique IP address for the primary server and each virtual server. Then you must assign all of the IP addresses to the network adapter in the server hosting IIS.

    B. You will need a unique IP address for the primary server and each virtual server. You will need a network adapter for each virtual server. Assign one IP address to each network adapter installed in the server hosting IIS.

    C. You need to have only one IP address. Assign the IP address to the network adapter hosting IIS.

    D. Create a home page for each virtual server and link it to the virtual server through Internet Service Manager.

    E. Use Internet Service Manager and assign a unique IP address to each virtual server's WWW folder.

4-5 You have configured your RAS server to support dial-in and dial-out capability. When using the RAS server to dial out, clients connect to an ISP. The ISP uses a UNIX server that only supports SLIP connections. How should you configure the authentication and encryption policy?

   A. Allow any authentication including clear text.

   B. Accept any encrypted authentication.

   C. Allow SLIP authentication.

   D. Accept only Microsoft encrypted authentication.

4-6 Your network consists of NetWare and NT resources. Several of the NT users require access to NetWare resources. You decide to install GSNW on an NT server to which the NT users connect. What must be done on the NetWare server to allow access? Choose all that apply.

   A. Create a group called NTGATEWAY.

   B. Create a group called NWGATEWAY.

   C. Create a user account that is a Supervisor equivalent and is part of the NTGATEWAY group.

   D. Create a user account that has permissions to the NetWare resources to which the NT users require access. Add this user to the NTGATEWAY group.

   E. Create a user account that is a Supervisor equivalent and is part of the NWGATEWAY group.

   F. Create a user account that has permissions to the NetWare resources to which the NT users require access. Add this user to the NWGATEWAY group.

4-7 Your network consists of an NT domain called CORP that contains a PDC, a BDC, and three member servers. You also have two NetWare 3.*x* servers that will be migrated to the NT servers. Some users have accounts on the NT domain and on the NetWare servers. Other users only have accounts on the NetWare servers. You want to migrate the NetWare users to NT, but you do not want any of the NT accounts to be overwritten. What do you do?

A. Migrate all of the users. After the migration is complete, delete any duplicate accounts.

B. In the Migration Tool for NetWare User and Group options box, select the Overwrite with New Info option.

C. In the Migration Tool for NetWare User and Group options box, select the Combine Duplicate Names option.

D. Use a mapping file to specify how NetWare users will be migrated to the NT environment.

4-8 Your company is a Microsoft Solution Provider and hosts a Web site to provide technical support for its clients. Specifically, the IIS server uses FTP to provide support software to your clients. For security purposes, how do you limit access to the FTP service to specific users?

A. In the Internet Service Manager, specify which users are granted access to the FTP service through the Security tab of the FTP service property.

B. In the Internet Service Manager, specify which computers have been granted access to the FTP service by specifying the computers NetBIOS name in the Security tab of the FTP service property.

C. In the Internet Service Manager, specify which computers have been granted access to the FTP service by specifying Granted Access To and providing the IP address in the Advanced tab of the FTP service property.

D. In the Internet Service Manager, specify which users have been granted access to the FTP service by specifying Granted Access To and specifying the NT logon name in the Advanced tab of the FTP service property.

4-9 You company uses TCP/IP as its transport protocol. You have installed RAS on an NT server that provides network access for your roaming network users. In addition to having RAS installed, your server also has IIS installed. You have configured IIS security so that user access is determined by IP address. How do you configure RAS so that each client uses a preassigned IP address?

    A. Use the Remote Access Admin utility to configure each RAS client to use a predetermined IP address based on the logon name.

    B. Configure the RAS server TCP/IP properties to allow each client to request a predetermined IP address, then configure each RAS client with the preassigned IP address.

    C. Create a `lmhosts` file on the RAS server that defines the IP address for each RAS client. Configure the RAS TCP/IP properties to use the `lmhosts` file. Through the NetBIOS computer name, clients will get their preassigned IP address from the mapping in the `lmhosts` file.

    D. Create a `hosts` file on the RAS server that defines the IP address for each RAS client. Configure the RAS TCP/IP properties to use the `hosts` file. Through the NetBIOS computer name, clients will get their preassigned IP address from the mapping in the `hosts` file.

4-10 Your network consists of an NT domain and two NetWare servers. One of the NT Servers has RAS installed. The RAS clients will dial in to the RAS server to access a BTRIEVE database located on one of the NetWare servers. How should the RAS server be configured?

    A. Make sure the RAS server has the IPX protocol installed.

    B. Make sure the RAS server is using the NetBEUI protocol and the NetWare server also has NetBEUI installed.

    C. Through Remote Access Admin, configure the RAS server to support SAP broadcasting.

    D. Through the RAS network configuration in the IPX protocol properties box, check the support NetWare NetBIOS application box.

SAMPLE TEST

4-11   Your NT server is configured as a RAS server. You use TCP/IP as your primary transport protocol. You have a DHCP server on the same segment as the RAS server. How do you configure the RAS server so that the RAS clients can have their IP addresses assigned through the DHCP server?

   A. In the TCP/IP properties of RAS configuration, specify the Use DHCP to assign remote TCP/IP client addresses option.

   B. In the TCP/IP properties of RAS configuration, specify that remote clients be allowed to request IP configuration from a DHCP server, then configure each RAS client as a DHCP client.

   C. Select the Use Static IP address pool option when configuring the TCP/IP RAS property. This allows the RAS server to act as a DHCP server.

   D. RAS clients are not able to get their IP addresses from a DHCP server unless the DHCP server is on the same computer that hosts the RAS server.

4-12   Your company is a legal firm that supports lawyers who access the company network locally and remotely. When the network is accessed remotely, it is accessed from Windows 95 clients calling in to a RAS server. You have been asked to develop a security policy with the following conditions:

   Required elements: Passwords should be encrypted during transmission.

   Optional elements: Data should be encrypted during transmission.

   Only specified users should be able to access the network via the RAS server, but they should be able to access the network from any location.

   Proposed solution: Specify that only specified lawyers can use RAS through the Remote Access Admin utility. Specify that each lawyer use the Preset to: callback option. Configure the RAS server to Require encrypted authentication.

What does the stated solution provide?

   A. It meets the required element and both optional elements.

   B. It meets the required element and one optional element.

   C. It meets the required element, but not the optional elements.

   D. It does not meet the required or the optional elements.

4-13   Your company is a legal firm that supports lawyers who access the company network locally and remotely. When the network is accessed remotely, it is accessed from Windows 95 clients calling in to a RAS server. You have been asked to develop a security policy with the following conditions:

Required elements: Passwords should be encrypted during transmission.

Optional elements: Data should be encrypted during transmission.

Only specified users should be able to access the network via the RAS server, but they should be able to access the network from any location.

Proposed solution: Specify that only specified lawyers can use RAS through the Remote Access Admin utility. Specify that each lawyer use the Preset to: callback option. Configure the RAS server to Require Microsoft encrypted authentication. In addition, specify that data should be encrypted.

What does the stated solution provide?

   A. It meets the required element and both optional elements.

   B. It meets the required element and one optional element.

   C. It meets the required element, but not the optional elements.

   D. It does not meet the required or the optional elements.

$$\boxed{\textbf{S A M P L E \quad T E S T}}$$

4-14   Your company is a legal firm that supports lawyers who access the company network locally and remotely. When the network is accessed remotely, it is accessed from Windows 95 clients calling in to a RAS server. You have been asked to develop a security policy with the following conditions:

Required elements: Passwords should be encrypted during transmission.

Optional elements: Data should be encrypted during transmission.

Only specified users should be able to access the network via the RAS server, but they should be able to access the network from any location.

Proposed solution: Through Remote Access Admin, grant each lawyer dial-in permission and specify that each lawyer use the Set By Caller call-back option. Configure the RAS server to Require Microsoft encrypted authentication. In addition, specify that data should be encrypted.

What does the stated solution provide?

A. It meets the required element and both optional elements.

B. It meets the required element and one optional element.

C. It meets the required element, but not the optional elements.

D. It does not meet the required or the optional elements.

4-15   Your company is a legal firm that supports lawyers who access the company network locally and remotely. When the network is accessed remotely, it is accessed from Windows 95 clients calling in to a RAS server. The lawyers need access to the law firm's IIS server. You want the IIS server to be as secure as possible. What security options should be implemented? Choose all that apply.

A. Configure the IIS server to only allow access to specific users.

B. Configure the IIS server to only allow access to specific computers NetBIOS names.

C. Configure the IIS server for logging.

D. Configure the IIS server for auditing.

E. Configure the IIS server to allow only specified IP addresses.

F. Configure the IIS server so that it requires the NT Challenge/Response authentication method.

4-16   You are installing an NT server that will function as a router in a TCP/IP network. What needs to be configured on the NT Server so that packets will route correctly between the two subnets? Choose all that apply.

    A. Install the SAP agent.

    B. Install the NetBIOS agent.

    C. Install RIP for Internet Protocol.

    D. Install RIP for NWLink IPX/SPX.

    E. Enable IP forwarding in the TCP/IP protocol properties.

    F. Enable IPX forwarding in the NWLink IPX/SPX Compatible Transport protocol properties.

    G. Enable NetBIOS broadcast propagation (broadcast of type 20 packets).

4-17   You are installing an NT server that will function as a router in a network using NWLink IPX/SPX Compatible Transport protocol. What needs to be configured on the NT Server so that packets will route correctly between the two subnets? Choose all that apply.

    A. Install the SAP agent.

    B. Install the NetBIOS agent.

    C. Install RIP for Internet Protocol.

    D. Install RIP for NWLink IPX/SPX.

    E. Enable IP forwarding in the TCP/IP protocol properties.

    F. Enable IPX forwarding in the NWLink IPX/SPX Compatible Transport protocol properties.

    G. Enable NetBIOS broadcast propagation (broadcast of type 20 packets).

4-18 Your company has a network that consists of NT servers, NetWare servers, NT Workstations, and Windows 95 clients. The NT Workstations and the Windows 95 clients only have Microsoft redirector software installed. How can you provide access to the NetWare servers for these clients?

    A. Install CSNW and NWLink IPX/SPX Compatible Transport protocol on each Windows NT Workstation and Windows 95 computer.

    B. Install GSNW and NWLink IPX/SPX Compatible Transport protocol on an NT Server to which all of the client computers can attach.

    C. Install File and Print Services for NetWare on an NT Server to which all of the client computers can attach.

    D. Install only the NWLink IPX/SPX Compatible Transport protocol on each computer that requires access to the NetWare servers.

4-19 What prerequisite should be met before GSNW can be installed on NT Server?

    A. You should be running NWLink IPX/SPX Compatible Transport protocol.

    B. You should be running CSNW on the computer on which GSNW will be installed.

    C. You should have created a GSNW service account through the User Manager for Domains that has the "logon as a service" user right.

    D. You should have installed RIP for NWLink IPX/SPX Compatible Transport protocol.

4-20 Which of the following items can be migrated from a NetWare server to an NT server using Migration Tool for NetWare? Choose all that apply.

    A. User accounts

    B. User passwords

    C. Login scripts

    D. Directories and files

    E. Permissions on directories and files

4-21 You are migrating NetWare users and groups to your NT domain through Migration Tool for NetWare. If duplicate names exist between the NetWare and NT servers, you want the NetWare user account to overwrite the NT user account. How should you configure the Migration Tool for NetWare?

A. Specify Ignore in the Usersnames tab.

B. Specify Overwrite with new Info in the Usersnames tab.

C. Specify Add Prefix in the Usersnames tab.

D. Specify Merge Users in the Usersnames tab.

4-22 Which of the following services are considered part of the MultiProtocol Router? Choose all that apply.

A. RIP for IP

B. RIP for NWLink IPX/SPX Compatible Transport

C. DHCP Relay Agent

D. RIP for NetBEUI

E. DNS Relay Agent

4-23 Which command is used to configure static IP route tables?

A. IPCONFIG

B. IPROUTE

C. TRACERT

D. ROUTE

4-24 Which of the following authentication methods can be used with the IIS WWW service to encrypt user passwords as they are transmitted over the network?

    A. Allow anonymous

    B. Basic (Clear Text)

    C. Windows NT Challenge/Response

    D. Microsoft encrypted authentication

4-25 You are using IIS to publish documents to the public. You want to create a virtual directory. What do you do?

    A. You will need to have a unique IP address for the primary server and each virtual directory. Then you must assign all of the IP addresses to the network adapter in the server hosting IIS.

    B. You will need to have a unique IP address for the primary server and each virtual directory. You will need to have a network adapter for each virtual server. Assign one IP address to each network adapter installed in the server hosting IIS.

    C. Point to the virtual directory by using a UNC name through the WWW or FTP Directories service tab.

    D. Point to the virtual directory by specifying the IP address of the computer that the virtual folder exists on through the WWW or FTP Directories service tab.

UNIT

5

Monitoring and Optimization

Test Objectives: Monitoring and Optimization

■ Establish a baseline for measuring system performance. Tasks include creating a database of measurement data.

■ Monitor performance of various functions by using Performance Monitor. Functions include:

- Processor
- Memory
- Disk
- Network

■ Monitor network traffic by using Network Monitor. Tasks include:

- Collecting data
- Presenting data
- Filtering data

■ Identify performance bottlenecks.

■ Optimize performance for various results. Results include:

- Controlling network traffic
- Controlling server load

Exam objectives are subject to change at any time without prior notice and at Microsoft's sole discretion. Please visit Microsoft's Training & Certification website (www.microsoft.com/Train_Cert) for the most current exam objectives listing.

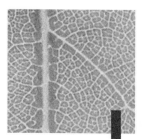

In order to monitor and optimize your NT Server, NT ships with the Performance Monitor and Network Monitor utilities. This unit will overview how to use these utilities, and how to create baselines to manage performance. In addition, you'll see key values that should be monitored for the four main server components through Performance Monitor.

Baseline Measurement of System Performance

One goal of network management is to maximize computer and network performance. Most administrators use a *baseline* to accomplish this goal. A baseline is a snapshot record of your computer's or network's current performance statistics that can be used for analysis and planning purposes.

Before creating a system baseline, you should consider the following items:

- What are you trying to measure through your baseline?

- What tools should you use to measure system performance?

- How do you analyze the data you collect?

- How can you optimize system performance based on the data you collect?

- How has optimization affected system performance?

- How can your baselines help you predict future needs?

Baseline Standard Determination

Before you create your first baseline, you should determine what areas you want to baseline. For example, do you want to measure system performance or do you want to measure network capacity? If you are new to performance monitoring, it is probably a good idea to monitor the key areas of system performance: processor, memory, disk access, and network access. Each of these areas are covered in greater detail throughout this unit.

Tools for Measuring System Performance

To help you monitor your system performance, NT Server 4.0 ships with two utilities, Performance Monitor and Network Monitor.

Performance Monitor is used to measure specific resources on your NT computer. You can view the data in a variety of formats, and you can even export the data to a spreadsheet or database application.

Network Monitor is used to capture and display network traffic between an NT Server and other computers on the network. This data can then be used to determine network optimization, and it can also be used to identify possible network problems.

Both of these utilities are covered in greater detail in this unit.

Analyzing Collected Data

When collecting data, you should first try to create a measurement for an environment with no load (or as little load as possible). This will provide your baseline data point from which you can later compare. Remember that new baselines must be reestablished after major hardware and software configuration changes.

Later, when you are operating within a representative production environment, collect another set of data for your established baseline metrics. This will give you an idea of the load your operating environment puts on your system resources.

Based on the data you collect, you can then determine if a particular component is causing a bottleneck. A *bottleneck* is a system resource that is inefficient compared to the rest of the system as a whole.

The Performance Monitor section of this unit will give some basic tips for identifying common system bottlenecks.

System Optimization

If you determine through your analysis of collected data that you have a bottle-neck, the next logical step is to try to eliminate the bottleneck. Do this through *system optimization,* which might include reconfiguring the network hardware and computer locations, or adding new resources (for example, adding memory or off-loading tasks to another computer).

Analyzing Optimization Effects

When optimizing your system, you should always baseline your environment before and after you make any changes. This helps ensure that the bottleneck is eliminated and that any changes have been beneficial to system performance.

Planning System Growth through Baselines

You can also use your baselines to perform trend analysis. If you create base-lines on a regular basis, you can use the data to spot trends in system usage. For example, if your Processor Utilization increases by 5% a month, you can pro-actively manage system resources before a bottleneck occurs.

In the following sections, you will learn how to monitor and optimize NT computers and the network.

Using Performance Monitor

The Performance Monitor utility is used to measure performance and aid in the optimization of NT workstations and servers either locally or remotely.

This unit will overview how Performance Monitor is organized, key components to track, and the views that can be selected through Performance Monitor.

Organization of Performance Monitor

Performance Monitor is organized in a hierarchical structure. You track per-formance by selecting items you want to monitor. The top level of the structure is computer (see Figure 5.1), which is broken down into objects, which are fur-ther broken down into counters. These terms are defined in Table 5.1.

F I G U R E 5.1

Organization of Performance Monitor

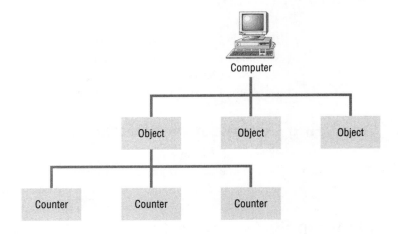

T A B L E 5.1: Organization of Performance Monitor

Organization Option	Description	Example
Computer	Specifies which computer you will monitor. You can monitor the local computer through Performance Monitor, or you can monitor remote computers (assuming that you have administrative rights to do so).	Any computer's NetBIOS name.
Object	Each computer contains objects, the computer's resources and processes, the sum of which is the computer. There are default objects which exist in all NT computers, and there are objects that are present or not present depending on the computer's configuration.	Cache, Logical Disk, Memory, Processor.
Counter	Counters further isolate specific areas within each object. For example, Memory is a fairly broad option. By further subdividing memory into discrete counters, you can track specific counters that relate to the area of memory you want to monitor.	The object Memory contains counters for Available bytes, Pages per second, and the number of committed bytes.

In addition, each object can also have multiple instances. For example, if you have two physical hard drives, you would have two instances of the object PhysicalDisk (which would allow you to track each disk as a separate entity).

Key Server Components to Monitor

The key objects you track through Performance Monitor are processor, memory, disk, and network.

Processor

The processor object is used to track how hard your CPUs are working. The key counters you should watch are defined in Table 5.2.

T A B L E 5.2: Processor Counters to Watch

Counter	Description	Desirable Values	Likely Cause of Problem
Processor/ %Processor Time	The percentage of the time the processor is busy performing useful tasks.	Below 80%	Not enough horsepower for the applications you are running. Either add another processor, upgrade the processor you have, or move applications to another server.
Processor Interrupts per second	This is the number of device interrupts the processor is handling each second.	Below 3,500 on a Pentium or RISC computer	Poorly written program or device driver, or a failing piece of hardware.
System Processor Queue Length	The number of outstanding requests the processor has in the queue.	Under 4	Not enough horsepower for the applications you are running. Either add another processor, upgrade the processor you have, or move applications to another server.

If you have multiple processors in your computer, the %Total Processor Time counter will show you how your processors are performing collectively.

Memory

Memory (or lack thereof) is one of the most likely bottlenecks you can encounter. Memory is broken up into two areas: your physical RAM and your page file.

The three counters you should monitor to view your memory statistics are:

- The Cache object, Data Map Hits% counter
- The Memory object, Pages/Sec
- The Memory object, Available Bytes

The Data Map Hits% counter specifies the percentage of requests that can be processed through physical RAM as opposed to needing to access the data from disk.

The Pages/Sec counter specifies the number of pages that were written or read from disk because the pages were not available through physical RAM, or cache memory. The acceptable range for this counter is considered to be 0–20.

The Available Bytes counter shows how much RAM is available for caching. This should be at least 4MB or greater than 20% of physical memory, whichever is greater.

If you suspect that lack of memory is the problem, add more physical RAM.

Disk

The first thing you should do to monitor disk performance is to enable disk counters by executing the DISKPERF -y command. Once this command has been issued, you must then restart the computer for the disk counters to collect information.

Disk counters are tracked through the Physical Disk and Logical Disk objects. Physical Disk relates to the physical hard drive. For example, you might have two physical hard drives, drive 0 and drive 1. Logical Disk refers to the disk partition. For example, Disk 0 might be broken down into Logical Drive C: and Logical Drive D:. Logical disks are also referred to as disk partitions.

Table 5.3 defines the counters you should add to monitor your disk's performance.

T A B L E 5.3: Performance Monitor Disk Counters

Object	Counter	Description	Desired Value
LogicalDisk or Physical Disk	Average Disk Queue Length	This is the average number of outstanding requests that the disk is waiting to process. This number should not exceed two.	0–2
LogicalDisk or Physical Disk	% Disk Time	This is the percentage of time that the disk is busy processing read or write requests.	Under 50%

If you suspect that the disk channel is the bottleneck, you can take the following actions:

- Use RAID 0 or RAID 5 to take advantage of disk striping.

- Use faster disks and disk controllers.

- Put all disks on individual controllers.

- Balance heavily used files by moving them to a less frequently used disk channel.

Network

You can monitor your network statistics through the NetBEUI, TCP/IP, and NWLink objects. The objects you track will depend on the protocols you are using.

It is important to note that in order to track the TCP/IP or Network Interface-related counters, you must first install the SNMP (Simple Network Management Protocol) service on the computer on which you want to track TCP/IP statistics. To install SNMP, add the service from Control Panel ➤ Network ➤ Services tab.

If you only want to track Network Interface counters, you can install the Network Monitoring Agent instead of SNMP. To install NMA, add the service from Control Panel ➤ Network ➤ Services tab.

If you suspect that your network channel is the bottleneck, you should take the following action:

- Buy network adapter cards that take advantage of the full bus width on your computer.

- Segment busy networks into two or more subnets.

Performance Monitor Views

Performance Monitor offers four views that are used to track and analyze the data you collect. The views are chart, alert, log, and report. These views are described in Table 5.4.

T A B L E 5.4:   Performance Monitor Views

View	Description
Chart	Chart is the default view. It displays what is being tracked in real-time. You can view the chart through a graph or a histogram.

T A B L E 5.4: Performance Monitor Views *(continued)*

View	Description
Alert	Alert is used to specify threshold conditions that will trigger an alert. You specify an alert by choosing a counter, then specifying that an alert be generated because a threshold is over or under a value you define. In addition, you can specify a filename to be run if an alert is generated.
Log	Log is used to save data to a log file. This is normally the view that would be used if you were creating a baseline for analysis or historical record.
Report	Report view textually reports the objects and counters you have defined in real-time. This view is useful when you are tracking a large number or counters that are difficult to read through the chart view.

In the next section, you will learn to monitor network capacity through the Network Monitor utility.

Network Monitor

The Network Monitor that ships with NT Server 4.0 is a limited version of the Network Monitor utility that ships with Microsoft's Systems Management Server (SMS) Back Office product. It is limited so that you can only collect data that is sent or received by the NT server on which the Network Monitor agent has been installed. It will also capture frames from network broadcasts.

By default, Network Monitor is not installed. To install the Network Monitor, use Control Panel ➢ Network ➢ Services, then add the Network Monitor Tools and Agent. Once the Network Monitor is installed, you can then:

- Collect data

- Present data

- Filter data

Each of these tasks are covered in the following subsections.

Data Collection

To collect data, access the Network Monitor utility through Start ➤ Programs ➤ Administrative Tools (Common) ➤ Network Monitor. You will see the screen shown in Figure 5.2.

FIGURE 5.2

Network Monitor Main
Dialog Screen

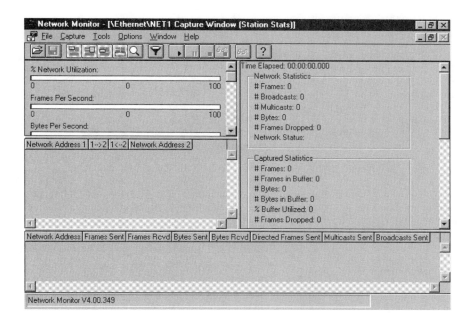

To initiate a data capture, select Capture ➤ Start from the screen shown in Figure 5.2.

Once the data has been collected, choose Capture ➤ Stop from the Network Monitor utility. The next subsection will review how data is presented once it is collected.

Data Presentation

Once you have captured data, the Network Monitor main screen will provide you with general information through the main screen. You can also display captured data by listing all frames captured and then viewing specific frames.

Data Presentation Main Screen

During and after a data collection, you will see a dialog box as shown in Figure 5.3.

FIGURE 5.3

Network Monitor Main
Screen after Data
Collection

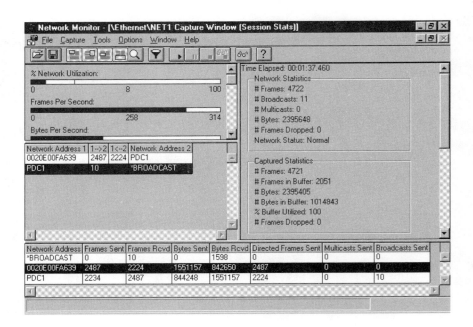

The main screen presents data through four summary panes. They are:

- Bar graphs
- Session statistics
- Station statistics
- Summary statistics

These panes are defined in the following subsections.

Bar Graphs

Bar graphs provide real-time information on network activity. The bar graphs provide information on:

- % Network Utilization
- Frames per Second

- Bytes per Second

- Broadcasts per Second

- Multicasts per Second

If you look at % Network Utilization in Figure 5.3, you can get an idea of the information available for the bar graphs. The blue bar represents the % Network Utilization that was occurring when the data capture was stopped. The vertical black line in the Utilization bar graph marks the highest utilization that occurred during the capture and the value 8 that is listed under % Network Utilization shows that the network utilization averaged 8% during this sample capture.

Session Statistics

Session statistics are displayed below the bar graphs. Session statistics show all data communication between the host computer and any computers that communicate with the host.

In Figure 5.3, you can see that PDC1, the host, is communicating with network card 0020E00FA639. During this session 2,487 frames were sent from 0020E00FA639 to PDC1, and 2,224 frames were sent from PDC1 to 0020E00FA639. You can also see any broadcast frames or multicast frames that were generated during the capture.

Station Statistics

Station statistics are shown at the bottom of the Network Monitor main screen. They show cumulative statistics for frames transmitted between the host computer and any computers that communicated with the host during the capture period. Station statistics include information about:

- Network Address

- Frames Sent

- Frames Received

- Bytes Sent

- Bytes Received

- Directed Frames Sent

- Multicasts Sent

- Broadcasts Sent

Total Statistics

The total statistics are shown on the right side of Figure 5.3. The total statistics are cumulative, per the session. Total statistics include:

- Network Statistics
- Captured Statistics
- Per Second Statistics
- Network Card Media Access Control (MAC) Statistics
- Network Card Media Access Control (MAC) Error Statistics

Once you have reviewed the main screen, you can view the frames generated through the capture by selecting Capture ➤ Display Captured Data from the main screen of Network Monitor.

Displaying Captured Data

Once you display captured data, you will see a screen similar to Figure 5.4.

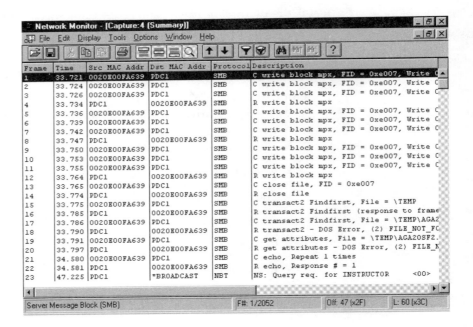

FIGURE 5.4

Captured Data from Network Monitor

The display shows all data that was captured, from the first frame descending to the last frame.

To see a specific frame, double-click the frame from the screen depicted in Figure 5.4. You will see a screen similar to Figure 5.5.

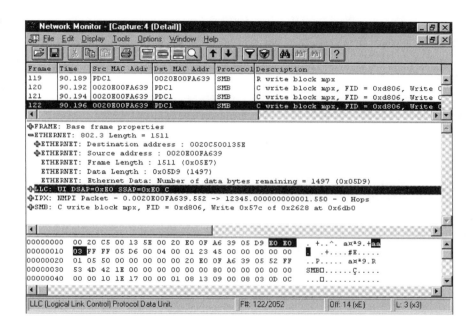

Each frame will have three parts:

- Summary Pane
- Detail Pane
- Hexadecimal Pane

Summary Pane

The summary pane shows all of the frames from the capture period. In Figure 5.5, the summary pane is at the top of the screen. This screen shows the frame you are currently viewing. In the summary screen, you can see columns for:

- Frame number (relative to all frames in capture)
- Time (time relative to capture process)

- Source MAC address (hardware address of computer that sent the frame)

- Destination MAC address (hardware address of computer that received the frame)

- Protocol (network protocol used to transport the frame)

- Description (summary of the frame)

- Source other address (network address of computer that sent the frame)

- Destination other address (network address of computer that received the frame)

- Type other address (specifies network protocol used)

Detail Pane

Displays the protocol information for the frame that is highlighted in the summary pane. The protocol information is displayed from the lowest protocol to the highest protocol (protocols from the lowest OSI layers to the highest OSI layers). The + sign indicates that more information is available if you double-click the protocol.

Hexadecimal Pane

By selecting protocol information in the detail pane, you will display the hexadecimal format in the bottom of the screen. The hexadecimal information can be used for advanced troubleshooting.

The next section will overview how to filter data.

Data Filtering

Even during a short capture, you can collect an overwhelming amount of frames. To help you identify relevant frames, Network Monitor comes with a filtering feature. Filters can be configured based on:

- Specific protocol

- Specific (MAC) media access control address

- Protocol property

To create a data filter, choose Display ➤ Filter within the dialog box shown in Figure 5.5. You will see a dialog box, as shown in Figure 5.6.

FIGURE 5.6

Default Display Filter
Dialog Box

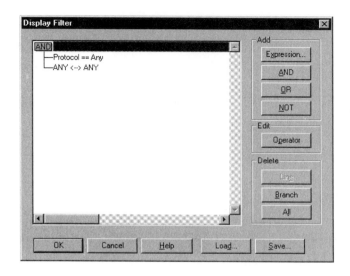

FIGURE 5.6

Default Display Filter
Dialog Box

To create a filter, specify the characteristics of the frames you want to display. For example, assume that you want to display only frames that use the DHCP protocol. By double-clicking the Protocol==Any line shown in Figure 5.6, you bring up the dialog box shown in Figure 5.7.

F I G U R E 5.7

Network Monitor
Expression Filter
Dialog Box

Using the dialog box shown in Figure 5.7, you can disable all protocols except DHCP. Your filter can then be defined as shown in Figure 5.8.

FIGURE 5.8
Network Monitor Display Filter Defined for DHCP Frames Only

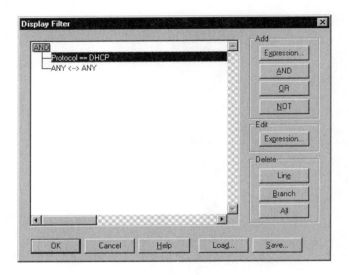

The display filters would be set in the same manner for station address and protocol property.

The next section will address performance optimization.

Performance Optimization

Performance optimization can apply to network traffic and server load.

Network Traffic

Network traffic can be optimized in the following ways:

- Use network cards that use the full width of your system bus.

- Only use necessary network protocols.

- Disable the server service on workstations that do not share their local resources.

- Subnet network segments with excessive traffic.

- Use faster network cards.

Server Load

NT Server can be optimized for system performance based on how the server is being used. To optimize server performance, choose Control Panel ➤ Network ➤ Services ➤ Server ➤ Properties. You will see the screen shown in Figure 5.9.

FIGURE 5.9

Server Service Optimization Dialog Screen

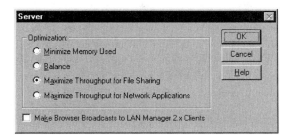

Table 5.5 defines the server optimization options.

TABLE 5.5

Server Service Optimization Options

Server Optimization Option	Description
Minimize Memory Used	This option is used if the server supports fewer than 10 connections or is being used as a desktop computer.
Balance	Used to support up to 64 client connections.
Maximize Throughput for File Sharing	Used to support servers that mainly act as file and print servers. Domain controllers would use this option. This is the default setting.
Maximize Throughput for Network Applications	Supports servers configured as application servers, for example, an NT Server running SQL.

This concludes the optimization unit. Answer the following questions to test your knowledge.

Baseline Measurement of System Performance

1.   What two main utilities are used to create baselines of system performance?

_____

_____

2.   True or False. Baselines collected at regular intervals can help you plan for system growth.

3.   True or False. If possible, you should take your first baseline during a period of no activity so you have a reference to compare to a baseline taken when you are operating within production hours.

4.   True or False. Baselines should be taken during nonproduction hours so you don't place an additional load on the server during work hours.

Using Performance Monitor

5.   How do you enable the disk counters for Performance Monitor?

_____

6.   List the four Performance Monitor views.

_____

_____

_____

7. List the four areas most likely to cause bottlenecks in an NT computer.

_____

_____

_____

_____

8. The most likely bottleneck is _____.

9. If the %Disk Time counter of the LogicalDisk object is above _____%, a disk bottleneck is indicated.

10. If the Processor Queue Length counter of the System object is above _____, it may indicate the _____ is the bottleneck.

11. True or False. You are using Performance Monitor on your NT Server. You notice that %Processor Time is at 10%. Based on this statistic, a processor bottleneck is likely.

12. If the Average Disk Queue Length counter of the LogicalDisk object is above _____, it may indicate that there is a disk bottleneck.

13. The_____ view is used in Performance Monitor to view data in a graphical real-time chart.

14. You would use the _____ view in Performance Monitor if you wanted to save data so it could be used to track system baselines over time.

15. If the Pages/Sec counter of Memory were over _____, a memory bottleneck might be indicated.

16. True or False. When viewing the Available Bytes of the Memory object, you should have at least 2MB of available RAM.

17. The _____ view in Performance Monitor is used to generate messages or run a specific program if the threshold you define is over or under the specified value.

18. True or False. It is possible to monitor a remote computer with Performance Monitor.

Network Monitor

19. True or False. You can monitor all stations' network activity on the network segment that has the version of Network Monitor installed that ships with NT Server 4.

20. How would you determine how the network bandwidth was being utilized during a capture with Network Monitor?

_____

21. True or False. Through Station statistics in Network Monitor, you can identify all stations that communicated with the server during the capture period.

22.   List the three properties that can be filtered through Network Monitor.

_____

_____

_____

23.   How do you determine which node generated the most traffic during a capture through Network Monitor?

_____

24.   How do you install Network Monitor for an NT Server that will collect and manage the data collected through Network Monitor?

_____

25.   How would you define a filter for Network Monitor that displayed only frames that used the DHCP protocol?

_____

26.   True or False. You can design a filter through Network Monitor that will display only frames generated by a client with a specific MAC address.

27.   True or False. The summary pane of frames captured through Network Monitor will list the source and destination MAC addresses, as well as the username of the logged-on user.

Performance Optimization

28.   How do you access the optimization settings for the server service?

_____

29.   Which server optimization method is used for servers supporting application servers?

_____

30.   What server optimization method would you use if you used NT Server as your desktop computer?

_____

31.   What server optimization method would you use for an NT Server that mainly supports file and print applications or would be used as a Domain Controller?

_____

32.   List the four NT Server optimization options.

_____

_____

_____

_____

33.   What is the maximum recommended number of connected users for the Balance server optimization setting?

_____

SAMPLE TEST

5-1 You are using Network Monitor on your NT Server to analyze your network traffic. You install the Network Monitor on your PDC. After initiating a data capture, you find that thousands of frames have been captured. You only want to examine traffic that is related to the Browser service. How do you configure the filter?

  A. Protocol==Browser

  B. Filter==Browser

  C. Service==Browser

  D. Search==Browser

5-2 You are using Network Monitor on your NT Server to analyze the network traffic being generated by the server. The server is using the TCP/IP protocol and acts as a DHCP server, a WINS server, and a DNS server. After initiating a data capture, you find that thousands of frames have been captured and you are only interested in looking at traffic relating to IP address assignment. What protocol filter do you use?

  A. Protocol==DHCP

  B. Protocol==WINS

  C. Protocol==DNS

  D. Protocol==NetBIOS

5-3 You are experiencing slow network performance during the early morning and late afternoon. You notice that the slowdown is occurring during peak logon hours. You suspect that the problem is caused by a lack of network bandwidth or because the PDC does not have enough horsepower. While trying to isolate the problem, you install the Network Monitor on the PDC. How do you determine how much network bandwidth is being used for network traffic to or from the PDC?

  A. Start a capture during a peak period, and view the % Network Utilization bar graph.

  B. Start a capture during a peak period, and view the Frames per Second bar graph.

C. Start a capture during a peak period, and view the % Bandwidth Utilization bar graph.

D. Start a capture during a peak period, and view the # Frames Sent bar graph.

5-4 Your PDC has been experiencing slowdowns and you have decided to use Performance Monitor to try to isolate the bottleneck. You specify counters for Memory, Processor, PhysicalDisk, LogicalDisk, and NWLink IPX. After you collect data for several hours, you import the data to a spreadsheet. You notice that the PhysicalDisk and LogicalDisk counters are all flat. What caused this result?

A. You did not have any disk activity during the capture period.

B. You need to install and start the Diskperf service.

C. You need to run DISKPERF -y at the command line, and restart the computer.

D. You need to run PERFDISK -y at the command line, and restart the computer.

5-5 You have decided to establish a baseline for your NT Server that will be used for analysis purposes over time. How do you establish a baseline?

A. Create a baseline during random periods of the day.

B. Create a baseline during a period of no activity, then create another baseline during a period of typical usage. This can be used for comparative purposes over time.

C. Create a baseline during periods of no activity by generating activity through simulations. This way you will not affect performance during working hours by running Performance Monitor.

D. Create a baseline that runs for 24 hours. This will give you good, average statistics so that you are not just looking at periodic spikes in activity.

5-6   You have an NT Server that acts as an applications server. One of your Windows 95 clients (called CLIENT1) has had problems connecting the server. Your network uses the TCP/IP protocol and the NWLink protocol. You install Network Monitor on the NT Server and initiate a capture. During the capture period, thousands of frames are collected. How do you filter the data so that only frames from CLIENT1 are displayed?

   A. Configure the filter to display only frames from the user who is logged on at CLIENT1.

   B. Configure the filter display to display only frames based on the NetBIOS name CLIENT1.

   C. Configure the filter display to display only frames from CLIENT1's MAC address.

   D. Configure the filter display to display only frames based on the NWLink address of CLIENT1.

5-7   You have an NT Server that acts as a PDC, a DHCP server, a DNS server, and a WINS server. You want to make sure the system has no bottlenecks, so you use Performance Monitor and record the following statistics:

Object	Counter Value	Value
Processor	%Processor Time	68
Processor	Interrupts Per Second	2,990
System	Processor Queue Length	5
Memory	Pages Per Second	16
Logical Disk	Average Disk Queue Length	1
Logical Disk	%Disk Time	35

Based on these values, what component is the most likely bottleneck?

A. Memory

B. Processor

C. Disk subsystem

D. No bottleneck is indicated

5-8   You have an NT Server that acts as a PDC, a DHCP server, a DNS server, and a WINS server. You want to make sure the system has no bottlenecks, so you use Performance Monitor and record the following statistics:

Object	Counter Value	Value
Processor	%Processor Time	87
Processor	Interrupts Per Second	3,000
System	Processor Queue Length	1
Memory	Pages Per Second	10
Logical Disk	Average Disk Queue Length	1
Logical Disk	%Disk Time	35

Based on these values, what component is the most likely bottleneck?

A. Memory

B. Processor

C. Disk subsystem

D. No bottleneck is indicated

5-9   You have an NT Server that acts as a PDC, a DHCP server, a DNS server, and a WINS server. You want to make sure the system has no bottlenecks, so you use Performance Monitor and record the following statistics:

Object	Counter Value	Value
Processor	%Processor Time	50
Processor	Interrupts Per Second	1,500
System	Processor Queue Length	1
Memory	Pages Per Second	5
Logical Disk	Average Disk Queue Length	1
Logical Disk	%Disk Time	15

Based on these values, what component is the most likely bottleneck?

A. Memory

B. Processor

C. Disk subsystem

D. No bottleneck is indicated

5-10 You have an NT Server that acts as a PDC, a DHCP server, a DNS server, and a WINS server. You want to make sure that the system has no bottlenecks, so you use Performance Monitor and record the following statistics:

Object	Counter Value	Value
Processor	%Processor Time	68
Processor	Interrupts Per Second	2,990
System	Processor Queue Length	1
Memory	Pages Per Second	16
Logical Disk	Average Disk Queue Length	3
Logical Disk	%Disk Time	70

Based on these values, what component is the most likely bottleneck?

A. Memory

B. Processor

C. Disk subsystem

D. No bottleneck is indicated

5-11   You have an NT Server that acts as a PDC, a DHCP server, a DNS server, and a WINS server. You want to make sure the system has no bottlenecks, so you use Performance Monitor and record the following statistics:

Object	Counter Value	Value
Processor	%Processor Time	68
Processor	Interrupts Per Second	2,990
System	Processor Queue Length	3
Memory	Pages Per Second	32
Logical Disk	Average Disk Queue Length	1
Logical Disk	%Disk Time	35

Based on these values, what component is the most likely bottleneck?

A. Memory

B. Processor

C. Disk subsystem

D. No bottleneck is indicated

5-12   You have an NT Server that has IIS installed. The IIS server contains all of your company's corporate information, and it is accessed by thousands of employees. What server optimization option should you use?

A. Minimize Memory Used

B. Balance

C. Maximize Throughput for File Sharing

D. Maximize Throughput for Network Applications

5-13   Your domain consists of a PDC, a BDC, and 30,000 clients. The domain controller's primary function is to authenticate logon requests. How should the server service optimization be configured for maximum server optimization?

   A. Minimize Memory Used

   B. Balance

   C. Maximize Throughput for File Sharing

   D. Maximize Throughput for Network Applications

5-14   You have an NT Server that has SQL installed. The main purpose of the server is to support the SQL application. How should the server service optimization be configured for maximum server optimization?

   A. Minimize Memory Used

   B. Balance

   C. Maximize Throughput for File Sharing

   D. Maximize Throughput for Network Applications

UNIT

6

Troubleshooting

Test Objectives: Troubleshooting

- Choose the appropriate action to take to resolve installation failures.

- Choose the appropriate course of action to take to resolve boot failures.

- Choose the appropriate action to take to resolve configuration errors. Tasks include:
  - Backing up and restoring the registry
  - Editing the registry

- Choose the appropriate course of action to take to resolve printer problems.

- Choose the appropriate course of action to take to resolve RAS problems.

- Choose the appropriate course of action to take to resolve connectivity problems.

- Choose the appropriate course of action to take to resolve resource access problems and permissions problems.

- **Choose the appropriate course of action to take to resolve fault-tolerance failures. Fault-tolerance methods include:**
  - Tape backup
  - Mirroring
  - Stripe set with parity

- **Perform advanced problem resolution. Tasks include:**
  - Diagnosing and interpreting a blue screen
  - Configuring a memory dump
  - Using the Event Log service

Exam objectives are subject to change at any time without prior notice and at Microsoft's sole discretion. Please visit Microsoft's Training & Certification website (www.microsoft.com/Train_Cert) for the most current exam objectives listing.

One skill all MCSEs must have is the ability to troubleshoot common problems. This unit will cover common troubleshooting topics. This includes installation errors, boot failures, configuration errors, printer problems, RAS problems, connectivity problems, resource access problems, and fault-tolerance failure. In addition, you'll learn about advanced problem resolution through blue-screen or stop-screen interpretation, memory-dump configuration, and the Event Viewer utility.

Troubleshooting Installation Errors

Installation errors can have many causes. Some of the common causes are:

- Media errors
- Hardware that is not on the HCL (hardware compatibility list)
- Incorrect hardware configuration
- Problems connecting to the domain controller
- Blue screen or stop messages

Table 6.1 contains tips for troubleshooting common installation errors.

TABLE 6.1: Common Installation Errors

Errors	Possible Solutions
Media errors	You could have a bad floppy or the NT Server CD may be corrupt. If you suspect that you have media errors, try a different set of setup disks (possibly even creating a fresh set) or another NT Server CD.
Hardware not on the HCL	NT is picky about the hardware it uses. You should verify that all of the hardware you are using is on the HCL.

T A B L E 6.1:   Common Installation Errors *(continued)*

Errors	Possible Solutions
Incorrect hardware configuration	Check hardware components such as network card, video adapter, sound card, modems, etc. for configuration settings. There must be no overlap in IRQ, base memory, base I/O addresses, or DMA. In addition, the software configurations must match the hardware configurations. In some cases, configuration settings (such as those made by Windows 95 Plug-n-Play routines) must be manually configured or disabled through utilities.
Problems connecting to the domain controller	If you are installing a BDC or are joining a domain during installation, your computer will contact the PDC. Common errors that would prevent you from contacting the PDC are incorrect spelling of the PDC's name, incorrect network settings, or the PDC not being currently on-line.
Blue-screen or stop messages	Blue-screen or stop messages during installation can be caused by incorrect or outdated drivers being initialized. If this is a problem, don't let NT auto-detect your mass storage device. Instead, manually identify the mass storage you are using, and provide the correct driver. You should be able to get the correct driver from the manufacturer's web site.

In the next section, you'll learn how to identify and correct boot failures.

Troubleshooting Boot Failures

When troubleshooting boot failures, you must first identify which file is causing the boot error, then correct the problem.

NT Boot Files

The primary files used to boot NT on an Intel platform are:

- NTLDR
- BOOT.INI
- BOOTSECT.DOS
- NTDETECT.COM
- NTOSKRNL.EXE

These files are described in Table 6.2. Table 6.3. includes the error that will occur if there is a problem with the boot file.

T A B L E 6.2 NT Boot Files	**Boot File**	**Description**
	NTLDR	This file is used to control the NT boot process.
	BOOT.INI	This configuration file is responsible for building the menu choices that are displayed during boot up. If you select an NT option, it also provides the ARC pathname location of the boot partition on which NT is installed.
	BOOTSECT.DOS	This file is used to load any operating system that was installed prior to NT. This file is loaded if you choose an alternate operating system during the boot process.
	NTDETECT.COM	This file is used to detect installed hardware and add the hardware it detects to the registry.
	NTOSKRNL.EXE	The is the NT OS kernel.

If you are using an SCSI controller with the BIOS disabled, you also need the NTBOOTDD.SYS file.

T A B L E 6.3 Boot File Failure Messages	**Boot File**	**Error If File Is Missing or Corrupt**
	NTLDR	`Boot: Couldn't find NTLDR. Please insert another disk.`
	BOOT.INI	`Windows NT could not start because the following file is missing or corrupt: <nt_root>\system32 \ntoskrnl.exe Please re-install a copy of the above file.`
	BOOTSECT.DOS	`I\O Error accessing boot sector file multi(0)disk(0)rdisk(0) partition(1): \bootsect.dos`

TABLE 6.3 *(cont.)* Boot File Failure Messages	Boot File	Error If File Is Missing or Corrupt
	NTDETECT.COM	NTDETECT v1.0 Checking Hardware… NTDETECT v1.0 Checking Hardware…
	NTOSKRNL.EXE	Windows NT could not start because the following file is missing or corrupt: <nt_root>\system32\ntoskrnl.exe Please re-install a copy of the above file.

If you have used Disk Administrator and your system fails to boot, suspect the BOOT.INI file first. By adding logical partitions, you can cause the ARC name to change. When using Disk Administrator, pay careful attention to the exit messages because you will be warned if the BOOT.INI needs to be edited (and if so, what the edits should be). Users frequently ignore this message.

Recovery of NT Boot Files

If any of your boot files are missing or corrupt, you can repair the failure through the emergency repair disk (ERD). To repair your boot files, you will need the three NT setup disks and the ERD.

- If you do not already have the setup disks, you can create them from the Windows NT Server CD by typing WINNT /ox.

- To create the ERD, type RDISK from a command prompt on the computer for which the ERD is being created.

The steps to recover your boot files are:

1. Boot with the NT Setup Boot disks. Start with insert Disk 1, and insert Disk 2 when prompted.

2. When prompted, choose R for Repair.

3. Insert Setup Disk 3 when prompted.

4. As requested, insert the ERD.

5. Select the "Verify Windows NT system files" option.

6. Select the components you want to restore.

At this point, your NT boot files should be properly restored.

In the next section, you'll learn how to troubleshoot configuration errors.

Troubleshooting Configuration Errors

Configuration errors come in many sizes and shapes. NT has a variety of utilities that can be used to identify and correct configuration errors. These utilities include:

- Server Manager
- Windows NT Diagnostics
- Last Known Good Option
- Emergency Repair Disk (ERD)
- Control Panel
- Registry Editor

These options and using them for troubleshooting purposes are covered in the following subsections.

Troubleshooting Using Server Manager

The Server Manager utility can also be used to identify configuration errors. Through Server Manager, you can identify which NT computers are currently active in the domain. In addition, for each NT computer you can see:

- The services that are running
- The users who are attached to the computer
- The resources that are being accessed
- The configuration of directory replication

If a service does not start automatically, you can manually try to start the service. If the service still doesn't start, you may receive an error message that can then be used to help track the problem.

Another good source for tracking configuration problems is through the Windows NT Diagnostics.

Troubleshooting Using Windows NT Diagnostics

The Windows NT Diagnostics utility can be very useful in diagnosing configuration errors. To access this utility, select Start ≻ Programs ≻ Administrative Tools (Common) ≻ Windows NT Diagnostics. You will see a screen similar to Figure 6.1.

FIGURE 6.1

Windows NT Diagnostics Dialog Screen

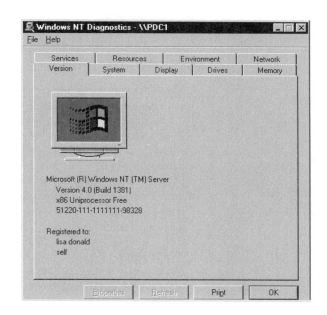

An overview of each tab within the Windows NT Diagnostics main dialog box is provided in Table 6.4.

TABLE 6.4: Windows NT Diagnostics Tabs

Windows NT Diagnostic Tab	Information Provided
Version	Version shows the build of NT that you are using, including version number and service packs, the platform that NT is installed on, and the registration information.

T A B L E 6.4: Windows NT Diagnostics Tabs *(continued)*

Windows NT Diagnostic Tab	Information Provided
System	Through the System tab, you can see the platform that NT is installed on, the HAL (hardware abstraction layer) that is being used, BIOS information, and the identification of the processor(s) installed in the computer.
Display	Displays verbose information on your video adapter and driver.
Drives	The Drives tab displays the drives that are currently detected. This includes floppy drives, local hard drives, networked drives, and CD-ROM drives. If you click on a drive, you can see more detailed information. For example, you can see the number of clusters, the clusters in use, and the file system attributes that are applied to the drive.
Memory	Shows verbose information on memory and memory usage. Includes information on physical RAM as well as the page file.
Services	This tab can provide a wealth of information. Two buttons allow you to select whether you want services or devices. If you click services, you can see all the services that are installed on your computer and the state of the service. If you click on a specific service, you see verbose information on the service, including general information and service flags, as well as any dependencies the service has. If you click Devices, you see similar information for all of the kernel drivers.
Resources	By clicking the Resources tab, you can see all of the resources that are in use on your computer. This is especially important when adding hardware because you can see what devices, IRQs, I/O ports, DMA, and Memory addresses are in use.
Environment	The Environment tab will show the environment variables that have been set for the system and the local user. You can see the variable and the value assigned to it.
Network	The Network tab shows general information, such as the access levels of users who are logged on and the domains and servers that have authenticated the users. In addition, there are buttons for Transports, Settings, and Statistics that allow you to see verbose information as the tabs relate to the network.

The next subsection describes the Last Known Good option and how it can be used to troubleshoot network configuration errors.

Troubleshooting the Last Known Good Option

Each time you successfully log on, the system saves your configuration in the registry under HKEY_LOCAL_MACHINE\SYSTEM\CurrentControlSet. You can boot back to this configuration by selecting the Last Known Good configuration during system boot.

You can use this option if you change your system's configuration, and it will no longer successfully boot.

If you are upgrading your SCSI driver and the new driver is incorrect, causing the NT boot to fail, you can revert to your previous configuration (with the driver that previously worked) by using the Last Known Good option.

The next subsection will overview the emergency repair disk.

During the boot process, you will see a screen asking if you want to use the Last Known Good Configuration. If the answer is Yes, hit the space bar when you see this prompt.

Emergency Repair Disk (ERD)

The ERD is a repair disk created for each individual NT computer. It contains that computer's specific configuration information and should be updated after any major system change. The ERD contents include:

- Portions of the registry, including startup environmental variables
- The computer's default profile and other configuration items
- The system configuration files for the computer

The following sections overview how to create the ERD and how to restore information from the ERD.

Creation of the ERD

To create the ERD, take the following steps on the computer for which the ERD is being created:

1. Select Start ➤ Run.
2. In the Run dialog box, type RDISK.
3. Select the Create Repair Disk option.
4. Insert the floppy disk and continue.

That's all it takes to create the ERD. To restore the data from the ERD, see the next subsection.

Restoring Information from the ERD

If you need to use your ERD, you will need the three NT Setup disks. The ERD itself is not bootable, and most of the files are stored in compressed format.

To restore the ERD, boot to the NT Setup Boot disks and choose the Repair option. You will be prompted for your unique ERD and will be asked to specify what information should be restored.

If you have misplaced your NT Setup Boot disks, you can create them by using the NT Server CD. From the I386 directory, type WINNT /ox (or WINNT32 /ox if you are on an NT platform).

Troubleshooting through the Control Panel

You can also troubleshoot some configurations through the various Control Panels. One of the most commonly used Control Panel applets is the Network applet. Configure your computer name and network identification, services, protocols, adapters, and bindings through Control Panel ➤ Network.

For each tab, you can view what is currently configured, and you can reconfigure options that are not correctly configured.

As you may have noticed, you almost always have to restart your NT computer after configuration changes are made.

NT Registry

The NT registry is a hierarchical database that stores all of the operating systems configuration information. Configuration information includes hardware configuration, device driver information, network and local service configuration, environmental variables, and protocol configuration.

The registry is made up of five main subtrees that include:

- HKEY_LOCAL_MACHINE
- HKEY_CURRENT_CONFIG

- HKEY_CURRENT_USER
- HKEY_USERS
- HKEY_CLASSES_ROOT

The function of each subtree is defined in Table 6.5.

TABLE 6.5 NT Registry Subtree Descriptions	Subtree	Description
	HKEY_LOCAL_MACHINE	Contains configuration information about the local computer. This subtree is most commonly used in troubleshooting. You can find configuration information on the computer's hardware, drivers, operating system configuration, and service configuration.
	HKEY_CURRENT_CONFIG	This subtree is an alias of HKEY_LOCAL_MACHINE\System\CurrentControlSet\HardwareProfiles\Current. All information about the current hardware profile is stored here.
	HKEY_CURRENT_USER	This subtree contains all of the configuration information about the user who is currently logged on. This includes things like desktop appearance and user environment variables.
	HKEY_USERS	HKEY_USERS is a parent to HKEY_CURRENT_USER and contains all active user profiles.
	HKEY_CLASSES_ROOT	Specifies all file-type association information.

The following sections overview how to back up the registry, how to edit the registry, and how to troubleshoot services through the registry.

Backing Up and Restoring the Registry

The same utilities are used to back up and restore the NT registry. The following methods can be used:

- Using the NT Backup Utility

- Backing up and restoring specific keys through the Registry Editor (although this is not 100% reliable)

- Creating or updating the ERD

> By default, the ERD will only back up part of the registry. If the registry is small enough, you can force the entire registry to be backed up by using the RDISK /s command line switch.

Editing the Registry

The registry can be edited through the REGEDT32 and the REGEDIT commands.

The REGEDT32 command is a 32-bit registry editor designed for NT. This is the preferred registry editor utility because it makes changes to the registry in a more controlled manner and provides better support for NT.

The REGEDIT command is from the Windows 95 operating system and is included with NT Server 4. REGEDIT has better search capabilities than REGEDT32. REGEDIT can search for keys and text. REGEDT32 can only search based on keys.

Troubleshooting Services through the Registry

Through the registry, you can see which services are defined on the computer. You can see this through HKEY_LOCAL_MACHINE\SYSTEM\CurrentControlSet\Services. Figure 6.2 shows an example using the Alerter service.

If your service is not loading correctly, the following keys can provide useful information:

- DependOnGroup

- DependOnService

The DependOnGroup key lists any program groups that must load successfully before this service can load.

The DependOnService key lists any other services that must be loaded before the specified service can load.

To see if a specific service is loaded or if a service failed due to a dependency failure, you can use utilities such as Event Viewer, NT Diagnostics, and Control Panel ➤ Services in conjunction with the Registry Editor.

FIGURE 6.2

Registry Editor Services Example

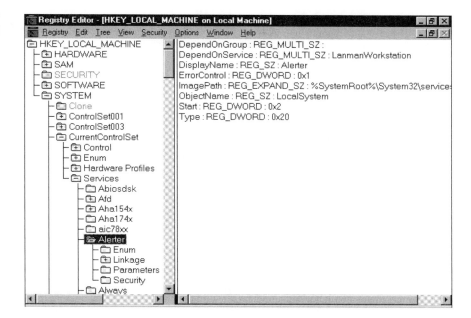

It goes without saying that the NT Registry is a complex and intricate topic. Whole volumes have been written on the subject. The important point is to be able to move around inside the Registry and investigate settings in the course of troubleshooting. Take great care when editing Registry values. A single error can result in the complete failure of the NT Operating System!

The next section will highlight common print errors.

Troubleshooting Printer Errors

Print errors have many causes. To troubleshoot a printer error, you should first try to isolate where the problem is occurring within the print process. The print process is composed of the following areas:

1. A shared printer is created on a print server by an Administrator or Print Operator.

2. A User makes a connection to the shared printer.

3. The client application generates a print job and sends it to the shared printer.

4. The print server receives the job spools, and may perform additional rendering (processing) on the spooled job.

5. The print server directs the job to the print device.

6. The print device prints the job.

Some common print errors you might encounter are listed in Table 6.6 (along with possible solutions).

	Error	Possible Solution
TABLE 6.6 Common Print Problems and Solutions	The print job is printed as garbage, or prints with strange characters or fonts.	Make sure the correct print driver is installed for the correct client.
	Hard disk is thrashing and print jobs are not being sent to the print device.	Make sure the disk has sufficient space. If not, move the spool file to another location.
	Jobs are reaching the server but aren't printing, or they aren't reaching the print server.	Stop and restart the spooler service.

If jobs have been submitted to a print device that is not functioning, you can create a new port on the print server and specify the UNC name of the failed printer. This allows the new print device to service existing jobs without requiring users to resubmit their print jobs or submit future jobs to a different printer.

To move the spooler file to another location, access the Advanced tab of the print server properties, and specify an alternate spool file location. Spool files are defined for the print server as opposed to specific printers.

In the next section, you will learn about general RAS troubleshooting.

Troubleshooting RAS Errors

RAS errors can be caused by many things. This section will identify some of the more common problems caused by RAS hardware and RAS setup.

RAS Hardware

The following list of questions helps identify issues related to RAS hardware:

- Is the communication hardware on the HCL (hardware compatibility list)?
- If the hardware connects to a COM port, is the COM port enabled through system BIOS?
- If the hardware connects to a COM port, is the port good?
- Is the device configured correctly?
- Does the device conflict with any other system device settings (COM port and IRQ)?
- Is the connection cable good and the proper type or configuration?
- Has the hardware been used on another computer and/or operating system?

If you suspect that a modem is not working properly, you can edit the registry entry HKEY_LOCAL_MACHINE\System\CurrentControlSet\Services\ RasMan\Parameters and change the Logging entry to 1. This will allow a log called DEVICE.LOG to be created in the \WINNT\SYSTEM32\RAS folder. This log can be used to diagnose modem connections.

Troubleshooting RAS Setup

If you know your hardware is good, then the next thing to check is the RAS configuration. You should try to narrow the problem to the RAS server or the RAS client. If other RAS clients can connect to the server or if the client can connect to other RAS servers, then you will have a clue as to whether the problem is on the client or on the server side. A direct RAS connection can be made which bypasses the communications hardware by hardwiring the suspect computer to a known, good computer using a null modem cable.

The following list identifies items to check in RAS setup:

- Make sure that the user has RAS dial-in permissions. These permissions can be assigned through:
  - Remote Access Admin
  - User Manager for Domains
- Verify that the client is using PPP to connect to the RAS server.
- Make sure that the client and server are using a common WAN protocol.
- Ensure that the client and server have common password and data encryption requirements.

To view the status of your RAS ports, you can use the Remote Access Admin utility.

The next section will help you identify connectivity problems.

Troubleshooting Connectivity Problems

Network connectivity problems can have many causes. Some network connectivity problems are related to hardware errors, while other problems are related to software. In this section, we'll address hardware problems first, then software related problems.

Hardware Connectivity Errors

Some connectivity errors relate to hardware. Common errors that occur are:

- The adapter cable may be loose or bad.
- Your network card may be configured incorrectly.
- You network card may be bad.
- You may have a problem with other hardware such as a hub.

Table 6.7 gives some possible solutions for each of these problems.

T A B L E 6.7:   Common Hardware Connectivity Problems and Solutions

Hardware Connectivity Error	Solution
Bad Cable	Test the connection with a known, good cable. Make sure that you have the proper cable for the adapter card you are using. For example, if you are using 100mbps Ethernet, make sure you have category 5 twisted-pair cable. Additionally, a cable tester will aid in isolating a cable break or wiring fault.
Incorrect Configuration on Network Card	Make sure the configuration on the NIC matches the configuration in NT. This is especially important for network cards that use a manual software configuration or setup. If you are using Ethernet with multiple connectors, make sure the cable type is set properly.
Bad Network Card	This seems obvious, but some general tips are to make sure you don't handle the cards improperly. You may damage your card though ESD (electrostatic discharge). If you suspect the card is bad, test the card by replacing it with a known, good card.
Other Hardware Errors	Reset hubs if possible. Try to connect to a port that is verified as working.

When you troubleshoot, you should change only one component at a time.

The next subsection will help you identify software related errors.

Software Connectivity Errors

Connectivity problems can also be related to software configuration errors. The first thing you should verify is that the computers are running a common protocol. Once that has been verified, you can use the information in the following sections to troubleshoot NWLink and TCP/IP. Given the simple nature of NetBEUI, connectivity problems with this network protocol are very rare.

NWLink Errors

One of NWLink's advantages is that it is a simple protocol to install and configure. The main configuration error that occurs with NWLink is in configuring the frame type. Frame type refers to how data is formatted into frames for transmission. If the sender and receiver do not have matching frame types, they will not be able to communicate. This is especially important in Ethernet environments where there are more than one of the four possible frame types in use. Different networking environments default to different frame types, as shown in Table 6.8.

	Frame Type	Environment Used In
TABLE 6.8 Common Frame Type Usage	Ethernet_802.2	This is the IEEE Ethernet standard. NT will try to default to this frame type if you choose the auto-detect frame type. NetWare 3.12 and NetWare 4.x environments default to the Ethernet_802.2 frame type.
	Ethernet_802.3	This is sometimes called Ethernet Raw because it does not use the 802.2 LLC header as does the Ethernet_802.2 frame type. This frame type was the default format used by NetWare 3.11 and earlier.
	Ethernet_II	This frame type used to be popular in UNIX environments using TCP/IP.
	Ethernet_SNAP	Apple developed a unique Ethernet frame format for Macintosh networks in the early days of networking. This frame type is used by Macintoshes using EtherTalk adapters.

As shown in Figure 6.3, when you select NWLink frame type, you can choose:

- Auto Frame Type Detection
- Manual Frame Type Detection

In this example, the NWLink protocols for this NIC have been set for the default network number (00000000) to accept either 802.2 or 802.3 Ethernet Frame types. Additionally, the NIC has been set up with a unique internal network ID to support File & Print Services for NetWare clients or for IPX Routing.

FIGURE 6.3

NWLink Configuration
Properties

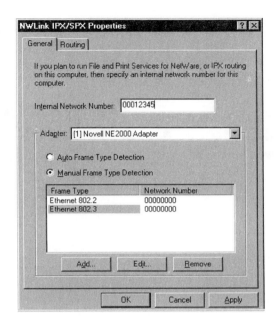

Table 6.9 defines how you determine if you will use auto-detect or manual configuration for frame type.

TABLE 6.9: NWLink Frame Type Configuration Options

Frame Type Option	When This Option Should Be Selected
Auto Frame Type Detection	Use auto-frame -type detection if you aren't sure what frame type is being used and you want NT to auto-detect what it finds on the cable. NT will listen to the cable, and prefer the Ethernet_802.2 frame type. If Ethernet_802.2 can't be detected, it will configure the first frame type it detects.
Manual Frame Type Detection	Mainly use manual-frame-type detection if you need to configure multiple frame types. (For example, when you need to connect to a computer using Ethernet_802.2 and another computer running Ethernet_802.3.) Also use this option if your network uses multiple frame types and you want to configure your computer for a frame type other than Ethernet_802.2.

TCP/IP Errors

TCP/IP requires more configuration than NWLink and is, therefore, subject to more configuration errors. As seen in Figure 6.4, you can specify that TCP/IP be configured automatically through a DHCP server or manually.

FIGURE 6.4

TCP/IP Configuration
Properties

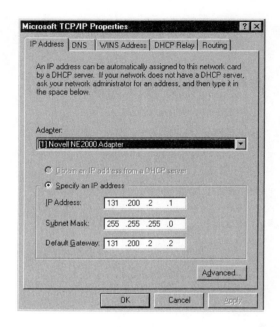

Automatic TCP/IP Configuration

You can specify automatic configuration by specifying that you want this NIC to be configured as a DHCP client from a DHCP server. If there are errors with this configuration, you should check:

- That the DHCP server is correctly configured. Configuration data that isn't provided by the DHCP server must still be manually configured for the network interface card. Remember, however, that manually configured data will override DHCP provided configurations.

- That the physical media is good between the DHCP client and the DHCP server.

Manual TCP/IP Configuration

If you choose not to use DHCP, you can manually configure your TCP/IP client. Make sure you properly configure the IP address, the subnet mask, and (if used) the default gateway. The next section defines additional utilities that can be used to troubleshoot TCP/IP.

Utilities Used to Identify TCP/IP Errors

TCP/IP comes with several utilities that can be used to troubleshoot TCP/IP. They are listed in Table 6.10.

T A B L E   6.10:   TCP/IP Diagnostic Utilities

TCP/IP Utility	Description
IPCONFIG	This is one of the most useful commands in diagnosing IP configuration errors. By using IPCONFIG, you will see your computer's IP address, subnet mask, and default gateway. IPCONFIG /all displays more verbose IP configuration information. If you are using DHCP, you can use IPCONFIG /release and IPCONFIG /renew to drop and renew your DHCP-supplied IP configuration.
PING	Used to test a connection between two hosts by sending an ICMP echo request and echo reply. You can help determine where an error is occurring by pinging the loop-back IP address (127.0.0.1), the IP address of the local host, the default gateway IP address, and the IP address of the remote host. If communications fail at any of these points, you have a better idea of where to look for the problem.
ARP	ARP is used to view the local ARP cache, a data table which defines mappings between IP addresses and local hardware or MAC addresses.
NETSTAT	Used to show TCP/IP statistics and any current connections.
ROUTE	This command is used to verify that all of the local IP routing tables are properly defined.
TRACERT	This diagnostic utility is used to trace the route of a packet across an internetwork to a remote IP address. TRACERT works by sending an ICMP packet using echo request and echo reply.

In the next section, you will learn how to troubleshoot resource access and permissions problems.

Troubleshooting Resource Access and Permission Problems

When you are having trouble accessing a resource, one common problem is that the account does not have the appropriate access permissions. The following subsections provide suggestions to help you troubleshoot access of local and network (or shared) resources.

Local Access

If you are accessing a resource locally, you should determine if the resource is on a FAT or NTFS partition.

- If the partition is FAT, then you know the problem does not relate to access permissions.

- If the partition is NTFS, the problem may be related to access permissions.

Figure 6.5 illustrates some common access problems.

- Mary is a member of Sales and Sales Temps. Because Sales Temps has been assigned No Access, Mary will have No Access regardless of the permissions she has been assigned through her membership in Sales.

- Michelle is a member of Sales. She tries to access E:\DATA\SUBDIR. When she tries to access the folder, she is denied. When the administrator set up the permissions, the Replace Permissions on Subdirectories box was not checked.

FIGURE 6.5

NTFS Permissions
Example

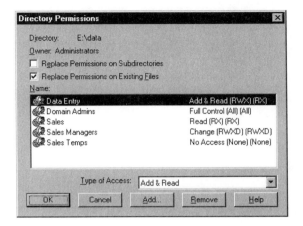

- Tom has been a member of the Sales group. He was recently promoted to a manager and added to the Sales Managers group. However, when he accesses the E:\DATA folder, he can only Read data. Tom needs to log out and log on again to have his access token updated with his new membership.

Network Access

With network access, you are governed by both share permissions and any NTFS permissions that may have been assigned. The more restrictive permission will be applied. The same issues that were involved with local access for groups and directories on NTFS volumes are also applied to all network share accesses.

Resolving Disk Failures in a Fault-Tolerant Environment

The main reason fault-tolerant disk strategies are implemented is so that mission-critical data isn't lost when failure occurs. In Unit 1, you learned how to select the appropriate fault-tolerance solution. In this section, you'll learn what to do when errors occur.

Tape Backup

No fault-tolerance solution takes the place of tape backup. Tape backups are typically done daily. In the event of any partial or total failure, you can always restore your data.

The most complete backup solution is to use the NT Backup utility. This utility is used to back up and restore your entire NT Server, including the registry.

You should test your restore operation to verify that your backups are good. This is part of any good, disaster-prevention strategy.

Mirroring and Duplexing

Mirroring and duplexing are used to copy data from one drive to another. This is the only fault-tolerance option available for the NT system and boot partition. You handle mirror and duplex failures in the same manner.

Recovery options are based on whether or not the failed drive contains the boot partition. The following subsections describe recovery options of data drives and the boot partition drive.

Mirror-Set Failure on a Data Drive

To recover from a mirror-set failure on a data drive, take the following steps:

1. Break the mirror set through Disk Administrator, and delete the failed partition.

2. Replace the failed hard drive.

3. Use the Disk Administrator to establish a new mirror with the free space on the new drive.

Mirror-Set Failure on the Boot Partition

If the boot partition is on a failed mirror set, you must determine if the primary drive failed, or if the secondary drive failed. If the secondary drive failed, you would take the steps listed for recovery of a data drive.

If the primary drive failed, then recovery becomes more complex because the ARC pathname to the system partition must be modified to allow the Operating System to complete a start up.

Prior to the failure, you should have created an NT boot floppy that contains an edited BOOT.INI file. This file should specify the ARC pathname of the secondary boot partition. (See Unit 1 for more information on ARC naming conventions.) Then you would take the following steps:

1. Boot with the NT boot disk you created prior to the failure.

2. Use Disk Administrator to break the mirror set and delete the failed partition.

3. Copy the BOOT.INI from the floppy disk to the system partition.

4. Replace the failed hardware.

5. Using the free space on the new drive, establish a new mirror set.

 Refer back to "Troubleshooting Boot Failures" to identify which files should be copied to your NT boot disk.

In the next subsection, you will learn how to recover from a disk failure if you are using a stripe set with parity.

Stripe Set with Parity

A stripe set with parity can contain 3–32 drives. If any one of these drives fails, the data will be reconstructed from the parity information that is stored on the other drives within the stripe set. The system overhead in calculating the data from parity is very high, and you will notice significant performance degradation.

To regenerate your stripe set, take the following steps:

1. Replace the failed drive.

2. Use Disk Administrator to regenerate the stripe set using the free space on the new drive.

Advanced Problem Resolution

Advanced problem resolution includes NT blue-screen resolution, memory dump configuration, the Kernel Debugger, and viewing event logs through the Event Viewer utility. These topics are covered in the following subsections.

NT Blue Screens

NT blue screens or stop screens are bad signs. A blue screen is generated when NT encounters a fatal system error and basically crashes.

Through the blue screen, you are able to get information which can be useful in troubleshooting the problem. Specifically, you can determine information as shown in Table 6.11.

Area of Screen	Information Generated
Top	Error code and parameters
Middle	All modules and drivers that have loaded and initialized successfully
Bottom	All modules and drivers that are waiting to be loaded

T A B L E 6.11

Information Generated Through Blue Screens

Memory Dump Configuration

You can configure NT to create a memory dump in the event a blue screen is generated. To create a memory dump, access Control Panel ➤ System ➤ Startup/Shutdown property tab as shown in Figure 6.6.

To configure NT to create the dump file, check the Write debugging information to: box. By default, the dump file will be created in `%SystemRoot%\Memory.dmp`.

To create a dump file, you must have a paging file on the boot partition that is at least 1MB larger than the amount of RAM installed on the NT Server.

Kernel Debugger

Advanced troubleshooting can be accomplished through a utility called the Kernel Debugger. This utility can be used when you are dealing with Microsoft Technical Support to help identify and resolve problems that are occurring on your NT server.

The most common way to connect to Microsoft is through RAS. Figure 6.7 illustrates how this would be configured.

FIGURE 6.6

Control Panel ➤
System ➤ Startup/
Shutdown Property
Tab Dialog Box

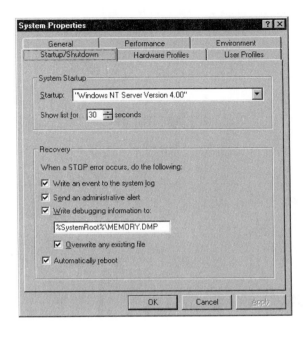

FIGURE 6.7

Kernel Debugger
Configuration

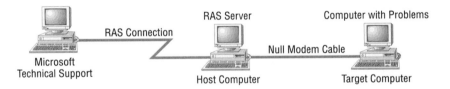

The following list specifies requirements for the Kernel Debugger:

- Both the Host and Target computer must be running the same version of NT.

- Symbol files (from the NT Server CD) must be copied to the host computer. Symbol files include extra code to be used for debugging purposes.

- The BOOT.INI file needs to be edited on the Target computer with the / debug or /crashdebug option.

- The Kernel Debugger is accessed through the i386kd.exe command.

- If dialing in to Microsoft as shown in Figure 6.7, the Host computer and the Microsoft computer must run the REMOTE command line utility.

Event Log Service through Event Viewer

The Event Viewer is used in NT to provide informational logs regarding your computer. Three different logs are kept which include:

- System
- Security
- Application

These logs are defined in Table 6.12.

	Log	Description
T A B L E 6.12 Event Viewer Log Options	System	This log is used to provide information about the NT operating system. You can see information such as hardware failures, software configuration errors, and the general well-being of your computer.
	Security	Contains information related to auditing. If you choose to enable auditing, you will see success or failure events related to auditing. This log can be viewed only by Administrators or users who have the Manage auditing and security log user right.
	Application	The application log contains errors from applications that are running on your server. For example, SQL errors would be logged here.

Within each log, events are recorded into one of five event types. These include:

- Error
- Information
- Warning
- Success Audit
- Failure Audit

To access Event Viewer, select Start ➢ Programs ➢ Administrative Tools (Common) ➢ Event Viewer. Figure 6.8 shows an example of this screen.

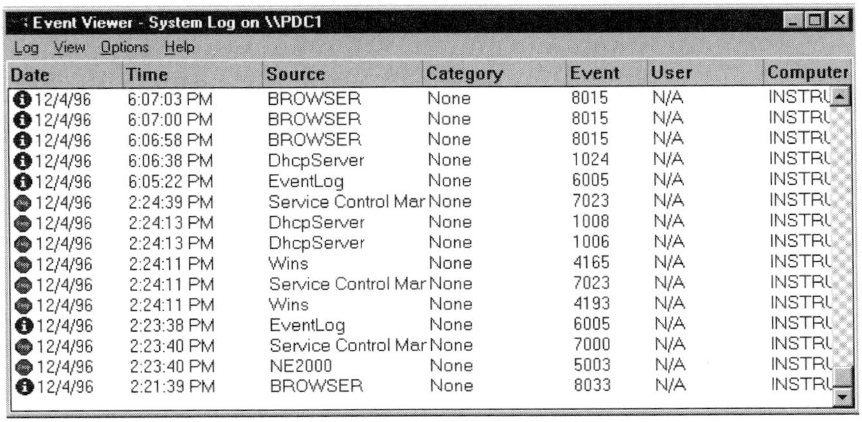

FIGURE 6.8

Event Viewer
System Log

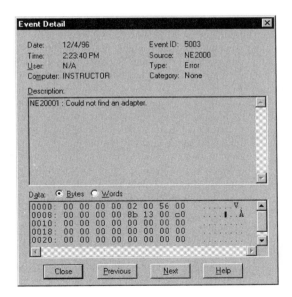

By default, the oldest events will be at the bottom of the list and the newest events will be recorded at the top of the list. In the case of Figure 6.8, the bottom Stop message is related to NE2000. If you click this entry, you will see more detailed information as shown in Figure 6.9.

FIGURE 6.9

Event Detail Within
Event Viewer

In this case, the reported error specifies that the NE2000 adapter could not be found. It is important to identify the first error, because subsequent errors are often dependencies that will be corrected when you correct the initial problem.

In this example, the NE2000 card has been configured incorrectly or possibly the card has suffered a hardware failure. To correct the problem, verify the NT settings though Control Panel ➢ Network ➢ Adapters ➢ Properties with the actual configuration on your network card.

This concludes the troubleshooting overview. Now it's time to test your knowledge.

Troubleshooting Installation Errors

1. True or False. If you install all of your hardware prior to installing NT, NT will correctly identify all devices and their configuration.

2. True or False. You should verify that all of your hardware is on the NT Hardware List before you install NT.

3. True or False. You can select a domain to join during NT Server installation by selecting from available domains from the drop-down box that is displayed.

4. True or False. Incorrect hardware configuration can cause the NT installation to fail.

Troubleshooting Boot Failures

5. The _____ file builds the menu choices that are seen during the NT boot process.

6. The _____ file is used to detect any hardware that is installed during the boot process.

7. The _____ file is the NT kernel file that is loaded during the boot process.

8. The _____ file controls the NT boot process.

9. The _____ file is used in the NT boot process if you have an SCSI controller with the BIOS disabled.

10. You make changes to your disk configuration through Disk Administrator. When you reboot the server, you get the following error message:

Windows NT could not start because the following file is missing or corrupt: <win_root> \system32\ntoskrnl.exe.

Please re-install a copy of the above file.

What boot file should be edited to correct the problem?

_____

11. The _____ file is used to load an alternate operating system during the NT boot process.

12. If NT boot files are missing, what is the quickest way to recover the files?

_____

13. When booting your NT Server, you get the following error message:

Boot: Couldn't find NTLDR.

Please insert another disk.

What boot file is missing or corrupt?

_____

14. When booting your NT Server, you get the following error message:

NTDETECT v1.0 Checking Hardware...
NTDETECT v1.0 Checking Hardware...

What boot file is missing or corrupt?

_____

15. When booting your NT Server, you get the following error message:

I\0 Error accessing boot sector file

multi(0)disk(0)rdisk(0)partition(1):\bootsect.dos

What boot file is missing or corrupt?

_____

16. What command is used to create the ERD that can be used to restore missing or corrupt boot files?

_____

Troubleshooting Configuration Errors

17. List the five subtrees that make up the NT registry.

_____

_____

_____

_____

_____

18. True or False. When you use the RDISK command to create an emergency repair disk, the entire registry is stored on the ERD by default.

19. What is the first course of action you should take if you make changes to your NT Server's configuration, and during the next reboot, your server blue screens?

_____

20. True or False. The ERD is a bootable disk.

21. What command do you use to create the three NT Boot Setup disks from a computer running DOS?

_____

22. What command do you use to create the three NT Boot Setup disks from a computer running NT?

_____

23. You are given an NT Workstation that is part of an NT domain called CORP. What utility can be used to see what network users have attached to the NT Workstation and what resources they currently have open?

_____

24. You are installing a new piece of hardware on your NT Server and want to see what memory addresses and IRQs are available. What NT utility will provide you with this information?

_____

25. How do you access the "Last Known Good" option during the NT boot process?

_____

26. What utility is used to configure your NT Server's services, protocols, adapters, and network bindings?

_____

27. The _____ utility is the most reliable utility for guaranteeing that your registry is always backed up in a complete and reliable manner.

28. The _____ command is the 32-bit registry editor that is native to NT.

29. The _____ command can be used to edit the NT registry. It is the Windows 95 registry editor and it provides better search capabilities than the native registry editor.

30. If a specific service is not loading properly, you can look at the _____ key in the registry to see if there are any service dependencies.

31. If a specific service is not loading properly, you can look at the _____ key in the registry to see if there are any group dependencies.

32. List three utilities that can be used to see if a specific service is running or not.

_____

_____

_____

33. The _____ registry subtree contains all of the configuration information about the local computer, and it is very useful in troubleshooting.

34. The _____ registry subtree contains all of the configuration information for the user who is currently logged on.

35. You can force the entire registry to be backed up to the ERD by using this command.

_____

Troubleshooting Printer Errors

36. What is the most likely print error if the print job prints garbage or is printing with strange characters or fonts?

_____

37. What course of action should you take first if print jobs reach the print server, but are not printing?

_____

38. How do you specify an alternate print spool file location?

_____

39. True or False. The print spool file can be set for each printer.

40. You have a print device that has failed. How can you redirect the print jobs to another print device without requiring the users to resubmit their print jobs that are still queued?

_____

41. What is the most likely problem if your hard disk is thrashing and print jobs are not being sent to the print device?

_____

42. What part of the print process is responsible for directing the print job from the spool file to the print device?

_____

Troubleshooting RAS Errors

43. Which utilities can be used to determine whether or not a user has RAS permissions?

_____

_____

44. If you are having RAS connection problems, and suspect that the problem may be due to encryption settings, what encryption setting should you choose?

_____

45. True or False. A RAS client can use SLIP or PPP to dial in to an NT RAS server.

46. What utility can be used to view the status of your RAS server's RAS ports?

_____

47. You suspect that one of the modems attached to your RAS server is not functioning properly. What utility do you use to enable the DEVICE.LOG file so that you can start logging all information on the problem?

_____

Troubleshooting Connectivity Problems

48. The _____ diagnostic utility can be used to display information about your IP configuration.

49. The _____ diagnostic utility can be used to test an IP connection between two hosts by sending an ICMP echo request and waiting for an ICMP echo reply.

50. How do you configure an NT Server using NWLink so that it uses the Ethernet_802.2 and the Ethernet_802.3 frame types?

_____

51. NWLink configuration errors are most likely caused by:

_____

52. If you choose NWLink Auto Frame Type Detection, which frame type will be preferred?

_____

53. By using the _____ service on an NT Server, you can minimize IP configuration errors on your Microsoft clients.

54. The _____ IP diagnostic utility can be used to verify that all local routing tables are properly defined.

55. When manually configuring IP clients, you should make sure that the following options are set correctly:

_____

_____

_____

Troubleshooting Resource Access and Permission Problems

56. John is a member of the SALES TEMPS, SALES, and EVERYONE groups. John is trying to access the E:\DATA folder that has the following permissions assigned:

> EVERYONE   No Access
>
> SALES TEMPS   Read
>
> SALES   Change
>
> SALES MANAGERS   Full Control

What are John's effective rights to this folder?

57. John is a member of the SALES TEMPS, SALES, and SALES MANAGERS groups. John is trying to access the E:\DATA folder that has the following permissions assigned:

> SALES TEMPS   Read
>
> SALES   Change
>
> SALES MANAGERS   Full Control

What are John's effective rights to this folder?

58. Rick is a member of the SALES group. He is trying to access a share called \\SALES\SALESDB. The share has the following permissions assigned:

> SALES   Change
>
> SALES MANAGERS   Full Control

Rick is promoted to manager and added to the SALES MANAGERS group. When he tries to access the \\SALES\SALESDB share, he still has only Change permission. What is the most likely problem?

59. Bonnie is a member of the SALES TEMPS, SALES, and SALES MANAGERS groups. Bonnie is trying to access the E:\DATA folder that has the following permissions assigned:

> SALES TEMPS   No Access
>
> SALES   Change
>
> SALES MANAGERS   Full Control

Bonnie tries to access the E:\DATA folder and is unable to gain access. What needs to be done so that Bonnie can access the E:\DATA folder?

_____

60. True or False. If a folder has NTFS and share permissions applied, the NTFS permissions will override the share permissions.

61. True or False. NTFS permissions assigned to a folder are assigned to any subfolders by default.

62. What are the default permissions applied to a newly created share?

_____

Resolving Disk Failures in a Fault-Tolerant Environment

63. What utility ships with NT Server to create system backups?

_____

64. What fault-tolerance method supports the system and boot partition?

_____

65. You are using disk duplexing on drive C:\ which contains the system and boot partition. The secondary drive fails. What do you need to do to recover?

_____

66. You are using disk duplexing on drive C:\ which contains the system and boot partition. The primary drive fails. What do you need to do to recover?

_____

67. You are using disk striping with parity over four drives. One of the drives in the set fails. What do you need to do to recover?

_____

68. You are using disk striping over four drives. One of the drives in the set fails. What do you need to do to recover?

_____

69. You are using disk striping with parity over four drives. Two of the drives in the set fail. What do you need to do to recover?

_____

Advanced Problem Resolution

70. What information can be extrapolated from an NT blue screen?

_____

_____

_____

71. How do you configure NT Server so that when a blue screen occurs, the contents of memory are sent to a dump file?

_____

72. What are the three logs generated through Event Viewer?

_____

_____

_____

73. List the five event types that can be recorded through Event Viewer.

_____

_____

_____

_____

_____

74. When viewing a series of errors through Event Viewer, what is usually the most significant error, the oldest or the newest error?

_____

75. The (host or target) _____ is the computer being debugged using the Kernel Debugger.

76. The _____ command line utility is used to execute the Kernel Debugger on an Intel computer.

77. What program provides support for remote computers using the Kernel Debugger?

_____

6-1   When booting your NT Server, you receive the following error message:

```
Windows NT could not start because the following file is missing or corrupt:
winnt\system32\ntoskrnl.exe.
Please re-install a copy of the above file.
```

What do you do?

   A. Boot with the NT Setup disks, use the repair option, and when prompted use ERD to restore the missing file.

   B. Use the `WINNT` command with the /r switch to replace the missing file.

   C. Replace the missing file from your last tape backup.

   D. Boot the system with the ERD and replace the missing file.

6-2   You are about to edit the registry with some entries that are supposed to enhance performance. You are slightly worried because of the warnings that specify dire consequences if the registry is improperly edited. You want to create a backup of the registry before any changes are made. Your registry is fairly small. What is the quickest way to back up and restore the registry in the event that problems occur from the edited registry?

   A. Use the command line utility `RDISK /s` to create an emergency repair disk that has the entire registry backed up.

   B. Back up the registry through the NT Backup utility.

   C. Back up the registry through Windows NT Diagnostics ➢ Tools ➢ Backup Registry option.

   D. Use the command line utility `ERD /s` to create an emergency repair disk that has the entire registry backed up.

┌───────────────┤ **S A M P L E   T E S T** ├───────────────┐

6-3   Your NT Server is configured as shown:

Drive 0   Drive 1
System and   Data Partition
Boot Partition

Drive 0 fails. What do you do?

A. Boot with the NT Setup disk and then restore your last tape backup.

B. Just reinstall NT Server.

C. Reinstall the NT Server, then restore your last tape backup.

D. Boot with the NT Setup disk, reinstall NT Server, use the ERD, and then restore your last tape backup.

6-4   Your NT Server is configured as shown:

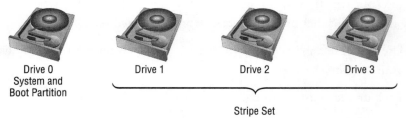

Drive 0   Drive 1   Drive 2   Drive 3
System and
Boot Partition

Stripe Set

Drive 3 fails. What do you do?

A. Replace the failed drive, re-create the stripe set, and restore the data from tape backup.

B. Replace the failed drive, and use Disk Administrator to regenerate the stripe set.

C. Replace the failed drive. NT will automatically regenerate the stripe set.

D. Replace the failed drive, and use the ERD to regenerate the stripe set.

SAMPLE TEST

6-5 Your NT Server is configured as shown:

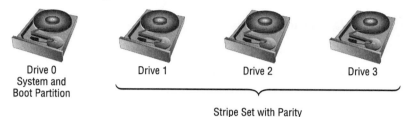

Drive 0
System and
Boot Partition

Drive 1   Drive 2   Drive 3

Stripe Set with Parity

Drive 3 fails. What do you do?

A. Replace the failed drive, re-create the stripe set, and restore the data from tape backup.

B. Replace the failed drive, and use Disk Administrator to regenerate the stripe set with parity.

C. Replace the failed drive. NT will automatically regenerate the stripe set with parity.

D. Replace the failed drive, and use the ERD to regenerate the stripe set with parity.

6-6 Your NT Server is configured as shown:

C:\   C:\

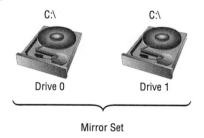

Drive 0   Drive 1

Mirror Set

Drive 0 (Primary) and 1 (Secondary) contain the system
and boot partition as well as data.

Drive 1 fails. What do you do?

A. Break the mirror set, replace the failed drive, and use Disk Administrator to regenerate the mirror set.

B. Break the mirror set, replace the failed drive, and use Disk Administrator to establish a new mirror set.

C. Just replace the failed drive, then use Disk Administrator to regenerate the mirror set.

D. Just replace the failed drive in the same position as the failed drive. NT will automatically re-create the mirror set.

6-7 You are having problems. Your NT Server crashes on an intermittent basis. You call Microsoft for support and they direct you to send in a memory dump. How do you configure NT to create a memory dump when the system crashes?

A. Through Dr. Watson

B. Through the Windows NT Diagnostics utility

C. Though Control Panel ➤ System

D. Through Event Viewer ➤ Tools

6-8 When booting your NT Server, you get an error message stating that one or more services did not start and that you should check Event Viewer. When you look at the Event Viewer System log, you see the following screen. What is the most likely problem?

Date	Time	Source	Category	Event	User	Computer
12/4/96	6:07:03 PM	BROWSER	None	8015	N/A	INSTRU
12/4/96	6:07:00 PM	BROWSER	None	8015	N/A	INSTRU
12/4/96	6:06:58 PM	BROWSER	None	8015	N/A	INSTRU
12/4/96	6:06:38 PM	DhcpServer	None	1024	N/A	INSTRU
12/4/96	6:05:22 PM	EventLog	None	6005	N/A	INSTRU
12/4/96	2:24:39 PM	Service Control Mar	None	7023	N/A	INSTRU
12/4/96	2:24:13 PM	DhcpServer	None	1008	N/A	INSTRU
12/4/96	2:24:13 PM	DhcpServer	None	1006	N/A	INSTRU
12/4/96	2:24:11 PM	Wins	None	4165	N/A	INSTRU
12/4/96	2:24:11 PM	Service Control Mar	None	7023	N/A	INSTRU
12/4/96	2:24:11 PM	Wins	None	4193	N/A	INSTRU
12/4/96	2:23:38 PM	EventLog	None	6005	N/A	INSTRU
12/4/96	2:23:40 PM	Service Control Mar	None	7000	N/A	INSTRU
12/4/96	2:23:40 PM	NE2000	None	5003	N/A	INSTRU
12/4/96	2:21:39 PM	BROWSER	None	8033	N/A	INSTRU

Event Viewer - System Log on \\PDC1 — Log View Options Help

A. Service Control Manager

B. DhcpServer

SAMPLE TEST

C. WINS

D. NE2000

6-9   When booting your NT Server, you get an error message stating that one or more services did not start and that you should check Event Viewer. When you look at the Event Viewer System log, you see the following screen. What errors are most likely caused by a dependency error? Choose all that apply.

Event Viewer - System Log on \\PDC1						_ □ ×
Log View Options Help						
Date	Time	Source	Category	Event	User	Computer
12/4/96	6:07:03 PM	BROWSER	None	8015	N/A	INSTRU
12/4/96	6:07:00 PM	BROWSER	None	8015	N/A	INSTRU
12/4/96	6:06:58 PM	BROWSER	None	8015	N/A	INSTRU
12/4/96	6:06:38 PM	DhcpServer	None	1024	N/A	INSTRU
12/4/96	6:05:22 PM	EventLog	None	6005	N/A	INSTRU
12/4/96	2:24:39 PM	Service Control Mar	None	7023	N/A	INSTRU
12/4/96	2:24:13 PM	DhcpServer	None	1008	N/A	INSTRU
12/4/96	2:24:13 PM	DhcpServer	None	1006	N/A	INSTRU
12/4/96	2:24:11 PM	Wins	None	4165	N/A	INSTRU
12/4/96	2:24:11 PM	Service Control Mar	None	7023	N/A	INSTRU
12/4/96	2:24:11 PM	Wins	None	4193	N/A	INSTRU
12/4/96	2:23:38 PM	EventLog	None	6005	N/A	INSTRU
12/4/96	2:23:40 PM	Service Control Mar	None	7000	N/A	INSTRU
12/4/96	2:23:40 PM	NE2000	None	5003	N/A	INSTRU
12/4/96	2:21:39 PM	BROWSER	None	8033	N/A	INSTRU

A. Service Control Manager

B. DhcpServer

C. WINS

D. NE2000

┌─────────────────────────────────┐
│ **S A M P L E   T E S T** │
└─────────────────────────────────┘

6-10   Your NT Server is configured as shown:

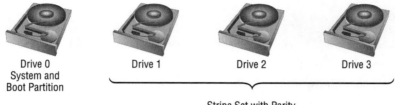

Drives 1 and 3 fail. What do you do?

     A. Replace the failed drives, re-create the stripe set with parity, and restore the data from tape backup.

     B. Replace the failed drives, and use Disk Administrator to regenerate the stripe set with parity.

     C. Replace the failed drives. NT will automatically regenerate the stripe set with parity.

     D. Replace the failed drives, and use the ERD to regenerate the stripe set with parity.

6-11   In order to optimize your NT Server, you make some changes to the registry. The next time you restart your computer, you get a blue screen. What is your first course of action?

     A. Boot with the ERD that was created when you installed the server.

     B. Reboot the server, using the Last Known Good option when prompted.

     C. Boot the server with the NT boot disk, use REGEDT32 to undo the changes you made, and then reboot the NT Server again.

     D. Use you last tape backup to restore the server.

6-12   One of your users, Ron, calls you and says that his NT computer will not boot. He reports that he is getting the following error message:

```
Windows NT could not start because the following file is missing or corrupt:
winnt\system32\ntoskrnl.exe.
```

```
Please re-install a copy of the above file.
```

The only change that has been made is the addition of a new drive. What is the most likely problem?

    A. The `ntoskrnl.exe` file was corrupted.

    B. The `ntoskrnl.exe` file needs to be edited.

    C. The `boot.ini` file was corrupted.

    D. The `boot.ini` file needs to be edited.

6-13 Your NT Server was attacked by a virus and some of the boot files need to be replaced. You decide to use your ERD, but realize that you cannot find your NT Setup disks. You sit at an NT Workstation and have the NT Server CD. What is your best option?

    A. Run `SETUP /ox`

    B. Run `WINNT /b`

    C. Run `WINNT32 /ox`

    D. Run `MAKEFLOP /ox`

6-14 After booting your NT Server, you realize that the Alerter service did not load properly. You want to check to see if there are any services that must be loaded as prerequisites before the Alerter service will load. What do you check?

    A. Through the registry editor, check the ServicePrerequisite key under HKEY_LOCAL_MACHINE\SYSTEM\CurrentControlSet\Services\Alerter.

    B. Through the registry editor, check the DependOnService key under HKEY_LOCAL_MACHINE\SYSTEM\CurrentControlSet\Services\Alerter.

    C. Through the registry editor, check the GroupPrerequisite key under HKEY_LOCAL_MACHINE\SYSTEM\CurrentControlSet\Services\Alerter.

    D. Through the registry editor, check the DependOnGroup key under HKEY_LOCAL_MACHINE\SYSTEM\CurrentControlSet\Services\Alerter.

6-15 You are using NWLink as your transport protocol. You know that all the computers on the network also use the NWLink protocol. You notice that you can access some computers, but not others. What is the most likely problem?

    A. The network addresses have not been properly configured on all computers.

    B. The subnet masks have not been properly configured on all computers.

    C. The default gateways have not been properly configured on all computers.

    D. The computers do not use a common frame type.

6-16 Kathy is a member of the CORP domain. She belongs to the Accounting Users and Accounting Managers groups. These are the only groups that should have access to this folder. The following permissions have been applied to E:\ACCT.

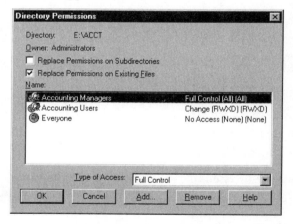

When Kathy tries to locally access the E:\ACCT folder, she is denied access. What needs to be done so that Kathy can access the folder?

    A. Assign the EVERYONE group the Read permission.

    B. Remove the EVERYONE group from the Access Control List.

    C. Check the share permissions to determine that they are not restricting Kathy's access.

    D. Remove Kathy from the EVERYONE group.

SAMPLE TEST

6-17 When booting your NT Server, you get a blue screen. What information can be viewed from this screen? Choose all that apply.

    A. Error code and parameters

    B. A description of the error code that was generated

    C. A suggested course of action to recover from the specified error

    D. A list of all modules and drivers that were successfully loaded

    E. A list of all of the modules that were waiting to be loaded

6-18 Your NT Server has been crashing about once a week on an intermittent basis. You are working with Microsoft Technical Support to try to resolve the problem. Technical support asks you to send a memory dump. You configure your NT Server to create a dump file. Where will this file be stored by default?

    A. \WINNT\Memory.dmp

    B. \WINNT\System32\Memory.dmp

    C. \WINNT\Mem.dmp

    D. \WINNT\System32\Mem.dmp

6-19 You are using the Kernel Debugger to try to debug a problem on your NT Server. What file executes the Kernel Debugger utility on an Intel platform?

    A. REMOTE

    B. i386KD

    C. NTDEBUG

    D. DEBUG

6-20 You are working with Microsoft Technical Support to try to determine why your NT Server keeps blue screening. You use the Kernel Debugger over RAS to try and resolve the problem. What file is required on the NT Server to support remote access of the Kernel Debugger?

    A. REMOTE

    B. i386KD

    C. NTDEBUG

    D. DEBUG

6-21 You are configuring your NT Server so that the boot and system partition are mirrored. To prepare for recovery in the event of primary drive failure, you create an NT boot floppy. What file needs to be edited to reflect the configuration of the secondary partition?

    A. NTLDR

    B. BOOT.INI

    C. BOOTSECT.DOS

    D. NTOSKRNL.EXE

6-22 Your NT Server is configured to dual-boot between DOS and NT Server. This has worked in the past, but now when you try to boot to DOS, the boot is not successful. What boot file is most likely to cause the error?

    A. NTLDR

    B. BOOT.INI

    C. BOOTSECT.DOS

    D. NTOSKRNL.EXE

6-23   Your NT Server has been suffering from intermittent problems that you suspect are caused by your SCSI adapter. You call the vendor for the SCSI adapter and are told to disable the BIOS on the SCSI adapter. When you reboot the NT Server, it does not boot successfully. What action(s) are required to fix the problem?

    A. You need to edit the BOOT.INI file.

    B. You need to edit the registry to reflect the new configuration.

    C. You need to cold boot the server one more time, so that NTDETECT can recognize the configuration change.

    D. You need to add the NTBOOTDD.SYS file to your system partition.

6-24   You are adding a new piece of hardware to your NT Server. The hardware is configured through a software setup program and you must configure the IRQ and Base I/O address for the hardware. What is the best utility to use to determine what resources are in use and what resources are still available?

    A. Control Panel

    B. Windows NT Diagnostics

    C. REGEDT32

    D. Server Manager

6-25   Which of the following are contained in the ERD if you create it through the RDISK command with no switches? Choose all that apply.

    A. The entire registry

    B. The default profile

    C. The configuration files for the computer

    D. The SAM database

6-26 When sending print jobs to the printer, you notice that the hard disk is thrashing and print jobs are not being printed. What is the most likely problem?

    A. The spool file is full.

    B. The printer is not correctly configured.

    C. The printer is not using the correct print driver.

    D. The spooler service needs to be stopped and restarted.

6-27 When sending print jobs to the printer, you notice that the jobs are reaching the printer, but they are not being sent to the print device. What is the most likely problem?

    A. The spool file is full.

    B. The printer is not correctly configured.

    C. The printer is not using the correct print driver.

    D. The spooler service is hung and needs to be stopped and restarted.

UNIT

7

Final Review

FINAL REVIEW

Think you're ready for the exam yet? Here's a good way to find out. Grab your watch and make note of the time. The real exam will have about 55 questions and a 90-minute time limit. You'll have to score about 75% or better to pass. These 55 questions are representative of what you'll see. Good Luck!

1. You have two domains: the EAST domain and the WEST domain. The EAST domain contains a printer, called LASER, on an NT Server, called FS-EAST, to which users in the WEST domain need access. The FS-EAST computer contains a local group called PRINT USERS. The PDC in the WEST domain also contains a global group called PRINT USERS. What should you configure? Choose all that apply.

A. Create a one-way trust where the EAST domain trusts the WEST domain.

B. Create a one-way trust where the WEST domain trusts the EAST domain.

C. Add the WEST\DOMAIN USERS global group to the FS-EAST\PRINT USERS local group.

D. Create a WEST\PRINT USERS local group and add it to the FS-EAST\PRINT USERS local group.

2. Kathy is a user in the NORTH domain who needs Full Control permission to the \\ACCT\DATA share that exists in the SOUTH domain on an NT server. Currently no trust relationship exists. How do you grant Kathy permission? Choose all that apply.

A. Create a one way-trust where the NORTH domain trusts the SOUTH domain.

B. Create a one-way trust where the SOUTH domain trusts the NORTH domain.

C. Create a local group on the ACCT computer that has Full Control permission to the \\ACCT\DATA share. Add Kathy to this group.

D. Create a global group on the ACCT computer that has Full Control permission to the \\ACCT\DATA share. Add Kathy to this group.

3.   You are designing your NT network and have decided to use TCP/IP as your network protocol. You want to simplify administration as much as possible. You decide to use DHCP, WINS, and DNS. Which of the following benefits will you receive? Choose all that apply.

   A. DNS and WINS will help resolve IP addresses to each computer's hardware address.

   B. DHCP will be used to automatically configure IP information.

   C. DHCP will be used to broadcast client NetBIOS names across the network.

   D. DNS and WINS will help resolve host names or NetBIOS names to IP addresses.

4.   Your company uses the single domain model with a domain called CORP. Within this domain you have an NT member server called ACCT. You are creating a template account that will be used to create members of the accounting department. You want all of the users' home directories for the accounting users to be located on the ACCT server in a share called HOME. How do you configure this?

   A. Specify Connect To in the template account's Profile box and specify a drive letter. Then add \\CORP\ACCT\%LogonName%.

   B. Specify Connect To in the template account's Profile box and specify a drive letter. Then add \\ACCT\%HomeDirectory%.

   C. Specify Connect To in the template account's Profile box and specify a drive letter. Then add \\ACCT\%UserName%.

   D. Specify Connect To in the template account's Profile box and specify a drive letter. Then add \\ACCT\%LogonName%.

5.   You have just received a network printer that you must configure. The printer will be used by NT and UNIX clients. You configure the print server to support the LPD service. What configuration information must be provided for this printer? Choose all that apply.

   A. The IP address of the network printer

   B. The IP address of the print server with which the network printer is associated

    C. The NetBIOS name of the network printer

    D. The fully qualified domain name of the network printer

    E. The hardware address of the network printer

6. You have just received a network printer that you must configure. The printer will use the DLC protocol. What must you configure? Choose all that apply.

    A. The DLC protocol must be added to the printer's print server.

    B. The DLC protocol must be installed on all network clients that will use the printer.

    C. The DLC address of the network printer must be specified in the printer's configuration.

    D. The fully qualified domain name of the network printer must be specified in the printer's configuration.

    E. The hardware address of the network printer must be specified in the printer's configuration.

7. You have two domains: US and ASIA. You want the users with Administrative rights in the US domain to be able to manage user and group accounts in the ASIA domain. What do you do?

    A. Add the US\Domain Admins global group to the ASIA\Server Operators local group.

    B. Add the US\Domain Admins global group to the ASIA\Account Operators local group.

    C. Add the US\Administrators local group to the ASIA\Administrators local group.

    D. Add the US\Administrators local group to the ASIA\Account Operators local group.

8. You are logged on to the domain from your Windows NT Workstation computer that has the NT administrative tools installed. You log on as a member of the Domain Admins group. You want to create a share on the APPS server for the D:\EMAIL folder. What utility do you use at your desktop?

    A. Windows Explorer

B. WinFile

C. The NET SHARE command line utility

D. Server Manager

9. Your NT Server is configured as a BDC. The BDC supports logon authentication for about 1,000 computers. The primary function of the server is logon authentication and providing clients with logon scripts. How should the server service be configured for maximum optimization?

A. Balance

B. Maximize Throughput for Domain Controllers

C. Maximize Throughput for File Sharing

D. Maximize Throughput for Network Applications

10. Your network is configured as shown:

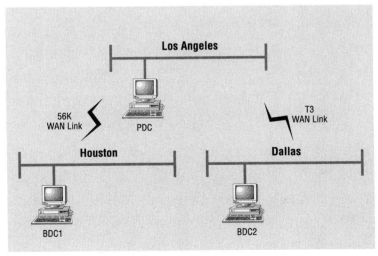

FINAL REVIEW

Because the WAN link between Houston and Los Angeles is very slow, you want to limit domain synchronization, so that synchronization occurs only 50% of the time. The other WAN links have sufficient bandwidth, and you are not concerned with domain synchronization over these links. What do you do?

    A. Adjust the Pulse registry parameter on the PDC.

    B. Adjust the Pulse registry value on the BDC in Houston.

    C. Adjust the Synchronization registry value on the BDC in Houston.

    D. Adjust the ReplicationGovernor value on the BDC in Houston.

11.   Your department has a high-speed laser printer. Because of the high volume of traffic, there is often a delay when sending print jobs. You install a second printer that is reserved for the MANAGERS group. How do you configure the printer?

    A. When creating the printer, add a $ behind the name so that it is a hidden printer. Tell the MANAGERS the share name so that they can connect to the printer.

    B. Remove EVERYONE from the printer's permission list and add only the MANAGERS group with Print permissions.

    C. Change the group EVERYONE's print permission from Print to No Access. Then add only the MANAGERS group with Print permissions.

    D. Add the MANAGERS group to the Print Operators group and remove group EVERYONE from the printer's permissions list.

12.   You have decided to use directory replication to copy the system policy from the PDC to all BDCs within the domain. You configure the directory replicator service. The PDC will be the export computer. Where do you place the system policy file on the PDC so that it will be replicated properly?

    A. \WINNT\SYSTEM32\REPL\IMPORT

    B. \WINNT\SYSTEM32\REPL\EXPORT

C. \WINNT\SYSTEM32\REPL\IMPORT\SCRIPTS

D. \WINNT\SYSTEM32\REPL\EXPORT\SCRIPTS

13. Your company is a Microsoft Solutions Provider. You have been asked to install a computer as a BDC for your client's domain called ACME. You have no connection to your client's network. When attempting to configure the server as a BDC for domain ACME, you receive an error message stating that the PDC for the ACME domain cannot be located. What do you do?

   A. Install the server as a member server, when the server is connected to the ACME domain, use Control Panel ➤ Network ➤ Identification tab to specify that the computer should join domain ACME. Use Server Manager to specify that the computer should be configured as a BDC.

   B. Install the server as a PDC, define the domain as ACME. When the final connection is made, demote the computer to BDC through Server Manager.

   C. Choose the Ignore option when the PDC cannot be contacted. When the final connection is made, the BDC will automatically get the needed configuration information from the PDC.

   D. You cannot install the BDC in this case. You must wait until the computer is connected to the ACME domain.

14. Your company is a Microsoft Solutions Provider. You have been asked to install a computer as a member server for your client's domain called ACME. You have no connection to your client's network. When attempting to add the member server to domain ACME, you receive an error message stating that the PDC for the ACME domain cannot be located. What do you do?

   A. Install the server as a member server, and specify that the computer is a part of a workgroup. When the server is connected to the ACME domain, use Control Panel ➤ Network ➤ Identification tab to specify that the computer should join domain ACME. You will need to supply an administrator's name and password.

   B. Install the server as a member server, specify that the computer be installed into a workgroup. When the final connection is made, you will only need to add the computer to the domain through Server Manager.

C. Choose the Ignore option when the PDC cannot be contacted. When the final connection is made, the member server will automatically get the needed configuration information from the PDC.

D. You cannot install the member server in this case. You must wait until the computer is connected to the ACME domain.

15. You are using Network Monitor to analyze all of the network traffic that is generated to or from your NT Server. You start a capture during the morning, and capture traffic over a one hour period. At the end of the capture, you have about 10,000 frames. You want to isolate all traffic related to the Browser service. How should you configure the data filter?

A. Service==Browser

B. Protocol==Browser

C. Service==SMB

D. Protocol==SMB

16. You are using TCP/IP as your network transport protocol. You have an NT server that routes packets between two subnets as shown in the following graphic:

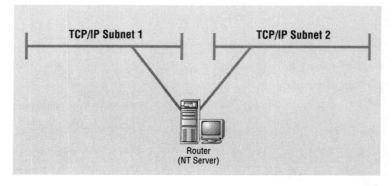

You want to use dynamic routing between the two subnets. What needs to be done? Choose all that apply.

A. Install the IP SAP agent as a service.

B. Install RIP for IP as a service.

C. Install RIP for NWLink IPX/SPX as a service.

D. Enable IP routing in the TCP/IP protocol properties.

E. Enable NetBIOS broadcast propagation (broadcast of type 20 packets).

17. Your network has primarily consisted of NetWare servers in a NetWare network. You have been introducing NT servers using an NT domain model. Some of the users have user accounts on the NetWare and the NT servers. Other users have only NetWare accounts. You want to migrate all of the NetWare users to the NT domain. You want to make sure that the NT accounts are not modified in any way during the migration process. You also want the NetWare account names to conform to your NT naming convention as the names are transferred. How should you configure the Migration Tool for NetWare?

A. Choose the Overwrite option in the Duplicate Names tab of the Migration Tool for NetWare utility.

B. Choose the Customize option on the Duplicate Names tab of Migration Tool for NetWare.

C. Choose the Mapping File option when configuring Migration Tool for NetWare.

D. Specify that all user names should be transferred. After the transfer is complete, use User Manager for Domains to rename accounts with the NT naming convention.

18. You have an NT Server that is running the BackOffice applications SMS and SQL server. You are concerned because the server is running very slowly. You configure Performance Monitor to collect a baseline. The following statistics are recorded:

Object	Counter Value	Value
Processor	%Processor Time	85
Processor	Interrupts Per Second	2,990
System	Processor Queue Length	1
Memory	Pages Per Second	16
Logical Disk	Average Disk Queue Length	1
Logical Disk	%Disk Time	35

Based on the stated values, what component is the most likely bottleneck?

A. Memory

B. Processor

C. Disk subsystem

D. No bottleneck is indicated.

19. You are very concerned about network security, so you design and implement a security policy for your NT domain. To minimize the risk of intruders breaking into your network, you configure the Account Policy for your domain so that Account Lockout will lockout an account forever if three bad attempts are made within a 30-minute period. One of your users, Michael, changed his password on Friday. On Monday, Michael could not remember what he had changed his password to, and he ended up locking his account out. What do you do?

A. While logged on as an Administrator, delete Michael's account and re-create it. Assign a password to him and check the User Must Change Password at Next Logon option.

B. While logged on as an Administrator, uncheck the Account Disabled option. Assign a new password to him and check the User Must Change Password at Next Logon option.

C. While logged on as an Administrator, uncheck the Account Locked Out option. Assign a new password to him and check the User Must Change Password at Next Logon option.

D. While logged on as an Administrator, uncheck the Account Locked and Disabled option. Assign a new password to him and check the User Must Change Password at Next Logon option.

20.   You have just configured the NT Server so that only Administrators can log on at the NT domain controllers. You have also configured the user account EMService so that it has the "log on as a service" right. What auditing option would allow you to track these kinds of events?

A. Configure auditing in User Manager for Domains to track Success or Failure of Use of User Rights.

B. Configure auditing in User Manager for Domains to track Success or Failure of User and Group Management.

C. Configure auditing in User Manager for Domains to track Success or Failure of Security Policy Changes.

D. Configure auditing in User Manager for Domains to track Success or Failure of User Rights Security Policy Changes.

21. You are in the process of designing your network architecture. Your company has three main divisions. Each division has 500 employees. The main goal of your network architecture is to have all user management centralized. However, all divisions require complete control of their resources, so resource management must be decentralized. Which domain model should you use?

    A. Single domain model

    B. Master domain model

    C. Multiple master domain model

    D. Complete trust domain model

22. You are configuring your RAS server. You want to specify that all passwords and data be encrypted for users who connect to the server. How do you configure this?

    A. Configure the RAS server to Require Microsoft Encrypted Authentication. Check the Require Data Encryption option.

    B. Through the Remote Access Admin utility, specify that each user is required to use Microsoft Encrypted Authentication. Check the Require Data Encryption option.

    C. Configure the RAS server to Accept Only C2-E2 Encrypted Passwords and Data.

    D. Through the Remote Access Admin utility, specify that each user is required to use Only Microsoft Encrypted Passwords and Data.

23. You have configured your backup software so that the NT servers are backed up between 2:00 A.M. and 6:00 A.M. You do not want any users to be logged on during this time period. What do you do?

    A. Configure the logon hours for the domain through Account Policies.

    B. Configure the logon hours for the EVERYONE group.

    C. Configure the logon hours for the Domain Users group.

    D. Configure logon hours for each individual user account.

24. Your network uses TCP/IP as the network transport protocol. The network is configured as shown:

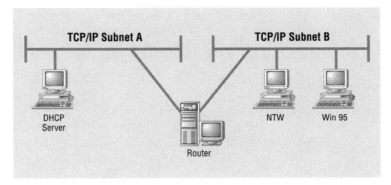

You have a DHCP server on Subnet A. What do you configure so that clients on Subnet B can have their IP configuration automatically defined?

   A. Install the DHCP Relay Agent on the DHCP Server.

   B. Install the DHCP Forwarding Service on the router.

   C. Install the DHCP Relay Agent on the router.

   D. Configure each client on Subnet B with the address of the DHCP server on Subnet A.

25. You have installed the LPD service on your NT Server that is configured as a print server. How will UNIX clients submit print jobs?

   A. Through the lpd command

   B. Through the lpr command

   C. Through the lpq command

   D. Through the NetBIOS name of the printer

26. You have an NT Server that is running the BackOffice applications SMS and SQL server. You are concerned because the server is running very slowly. You configure Performance Monitor to collect a baseline. The following statistics are recorded:

Object	Counter Value	Value
Processor	%Processor Time	40
Processor	Interrupts Per Second	1,200
System	Processor Queue Length	1
Memory	Pages Per Second	16
Logical Disk	Average Disk Queue Length	1
Logical Disk	%Disk Time	85

Based on the stated values, what component is the most likely bottleneck?

A. Memory

B. Processor

C. Disk subsystem

D. No bottleneck is indicated.

27.   You have an NT Server that is running the BackOffice applications SMS and SQL server. You are concerned because the server is running very slowly. You configure Performance Monitor to collect a baseline. The following statistics are recorded:

Object	Counter Value	Value
Processor	%Processor Time	85
Processor	Interrupts Per Second	2,990
System	Processor Queue Length	1
Memory	Pages Per Second	16
Logical Disk	Average Disk Queue Length	0
Logical Disk	%Disk Time	0

Why are the disk counters flat?

A. The DiskPerf service has not been started.

B. The DiskMon service has not been started.

C. You must run DISKPERF -y at the command prompt and restart the computer.

D. You must run DISKMON -y at the command prompt and restart the computer.

28.   You have just purchased 100 computers that will be installed as NT Workstations into the CORP domain. Brad has volunteered to help you install the computers. During installation, each computer should be able to join the NT domain. What are the minimum rights Brad can be assigned to complete this task?

A. Assign Brad's User Account to the Add Workstations to the Domain User Right.

B. Add Brad's User Account to the Administrators group.

C. Add Brad's User Account to the Server Operators group.

D. Add Brad's User Account to the Account Operators group.

29. You have 20 clients using Microsoft client software that currently connect to an NT Server called NTSERVER. These clients now need to access a NetWare server called NWSERVER. You want to install GSNW. What configuration is required? Choose two answers.

    A. Install NWLink IPX/SPX Compatible Transport protocol on NTSERVER.

    B. Install NWLink IPX/SPX Compatible Transport protocol on NTSERVER and all of the client computers.

    C. Create a service account called NTGATEWAY on NTSERVER.

    D. Create a group on NWSERVER called NWGATEWAY.

    E. Create a group on NWSERVER called NTGATEWAY.

30. Your company uses three domains: CORP, EAST, and WEST. Each domain contains users and resources. Users in the CORP domain require access to resources in the EAST and WEST domains. Users in the WEST domain require access to resources in the EAST domain. What minimum trust relationships must be established? Choose two answers.

    A. Set up a one-way trust relationship where the CORP domain trusts the EAST and WEST domains.

    B. Set up one-way trust relationships where EAST and WEST domains trust the CORP domain.

    C. Set up a one-way trust relationship where the EAST domain trusts the WEST domain.

    D. Set up a one-way trust relationship where the WEST domain trusts the EAST domain.

31. You have created system policy files for the SALES and SALES MANAGERS groups through the System Policy Editor. Brett is a member of both groups. How do you determine which groups system policy file will be enforced?

    A. Specify which group is Brett's primary group through the Group Property of Brett's user account in User Manager for Domains.

    B. Specify group priority for each group through User Manager for Domains.

    C. Create multiple policy files for each group. Specify which policy file Brett will use in Brett's Profile property in User Manager for Domains.

    D. Specify group priority for each group through System Policy Editor.

32. Your company uses three domains: CORP, EAST, and WEST. You are using the Complete Trust Domain model. You want the CORP administrators to be able to manage the EAST and WEST domain controllers. What do you do?

    A. Add the CORP\Domain Admins group to the Administrators group on the PDC in the EAST and WEST domains.

    B. Add the CORP\Administrators group to the Administrators group on the PDC in the EAST and WEST domains.

    C. Add the CORP\Domain Admins group to the Domain Admins group on the PDC in the EAST and WEST domains.

    D. Add the CORP\Administrators group to the Domain Admins group on the PDC in the EAST and WEST domains.

33. Your network consists of NT Servers and NT Workstations. Several of your users log on from different computers. How do you specify that users should get their customized user profiles no matter which computer they use to log on?

    A. Specify that the users use a roaming profile through System Profile Editor.

    B. Specify that the users use a roaming profile through System Policy Editor.

    C. Specify a UNC path for the user's profile for each user in the user's User Manager for Domains Profile property. Then copy the user's local profile to the roaming directory by using the User Profiles tab in the System Control Panel.

    D. You don't have to configure anything. NT uses roaming profiles by default.

34. Your network consists of NT Server and NT Workstations. You configure a profile that will be used by all of the Sales department. What should you do so that no users of the Sales department are able to modify the profile?

    A. Rename the `NTUSER.DAT` file `NTUSER.MAN`.

    B. Place the `NTUSER.DAT` file on an NTFS partition and assign the SALES group Read permission.

    C. Configure the profile as Read-Only through the System Profile Editor.

    D. Configure the profile as mandatory through the System Policy Editor.

35. You have just changed your NT Registry and now your NT Server will not boot. Before changes were made, you updated the Emergency Repair Disk. You want to perform the repair process, but you do not have the NT Setup disks. You have a Windows 95 laptop that you can use. What do you do?

    A. Create the Setup disks from the NT Server CD by using the `WINNT /ox` command.

    B. Create the Setup disks from the NT Server CD by using the `WINNT /b` command.

    C. Create the Setup disks from the NT Server CD by using the `RDISK /ox` command.

    D. Create the Setup disks from the NT Server CD by using the `RDISK /b` command.

36. You have 25 NT Workstations that are configured in a workgroup. You now want to configure the computers to be part of the CORP domain. What two steps must be completed?

    A. Use the Server Manager utility to add the computers to the domain.

    B. Use User Manager for Domains to add the computers to the domain.

    C. At the PDC, specify that the computers are part of the domain through Control Panel ➤ Network.

    D. At each client computer, specify that the computer is part of the CORP domain through Control Panel ➤ Network.

37.   Your NT Server uses disk striping with parity over five drives. If one of the drives fails, what should you do to restore the disk fault tolerance?

   A. Replace the failed hardware and regenerate the stripe set with parity.

   B. Break the stripe set, replace the failed hardware, and reestablish the stripe set with parity.

   C. Replace the failed hardware and restore the stripe set with parity from tape backup.

   D. Replace the failed hardware, use the Emergency Repair Disk, and regenerate the stripe set with parity.

38.   Your NT Server uses disk striping with parity over five drives. If two of the drives fail, what should you do to restore the disk fault tolerance?

   A. Replace the failed hardware and regenerate the stripe set with parity.

   B. Break the stripe set, replace the failed hardware, and reestablish the stripe set with parity.

   C. Replace the failed hardware and restore the stripe set with parity from tape backup.

   D. Replace the failed hardware, use the Emergency Repair Disk, and regenerate the stripe set with parity.

39.   You are creating a system policy file that should be used by any users who authenticate to your NT domain controller. What should the system policy file be called and where should it be stored?

   A. \WINNT\SYSTEM32\REPL\IMPORT\SCRIPTS\NTCONFIG.DAT

   B. \WINNT\SYSTEM32\REPL\IMPORT\SCRIPTS\NTCONFIG.POL

   C. \WINNT\SYSTEM32\REPL\POLICIES \NTCONFIG.DAT

   D. \WINNT\SYSTEM32\REPL\POLICIES\NTCONFIG.POL

40. Your network consists of two domains, CORP and MIS. No trust relationship is defined. The CORP domain contains a printer called LASER. The CORP\Print Users local group has Print permission assigned to this printer. You move the LASER printer to the MIS domain. Once moved, you create a local group called MIS\Print Users that has Print permission on the print server that now hosts the LASER printer. What needs to be done so that the users in the CORP domain who used to access this printer can access the printer again? Choose two answers.

A. Define a one-way trust so that CORP trusts MIS.

B. Define a one-way trust so that MIS trusts CORP.

C. Add the CORP\Print Users local group to the MIS\Print Users local group.

D. Create a global group on the CORP domain called Domain Print Users, and add the users from the CORP domain who need to access the LASER printer. Add this global group to the MIS\Print Users local group.

41. Your company uses three domains: CORP, WEST, and EAST. The CORP domain contains a member server called DBSERVER with a share, called DB, to which all users in the EAST and WEST domain need Read access. What do you do? Choose all that apply.

A. Create one-way trusts so that the CORP domain trusts the WEST and EAST domains.

B. Create one-way trusts so that the WEST and EAST domains trust the CORP domain.

C. Create a global group on the CORP\DBSERVER computer called DB Users. Assign this group Read permission to the DB share. Add the WEST\Domain Users and the EAST\Domain Users global group to the group you just created.

D. Create a local group, called DB Users, on the CORP\DBSERVER computer. Assign this group Read permission to the DB share. Add the WEST\Domain Users and the EAST\Domain Users global group to the group you just created.

42.   You have hired an outside consultant, Ed, who will be responsible for designing an auditing policy to track all user and group management. What is the minimum assignment that must be made so that Ed can view and manage the auditing logs?

    A. Add Ed to the Administrators group on the PDC.

    B. Add Ed to the Server Operators group on the PDC.

    C. Add Ed to the Account Operators group on the PDC.

    D. Grant Ed the Manage Auditing and Security Log user right on the PDC.

43.   You have just hired a new user, Todd, who will be responsible for managing the NT domain controllers and the member servers within your domain. Todd's primary functions include backing up and restoring the computers, and managing all shared directories on the computers. What are the minimum permissions you can assign to Todd?

    A. Make Todd a member of the Administrators group on the PDC.

    B. Make Todd a member of the Server Operators group on the PDC.

    C. Grant Todd the Manage Servers user right on the PDC.

    D. Make Todd a member of the Administrators group on the PDC and on each member server.

    E. Make Todd a member of the Server Operators group on the PDC and on each member server.

    F. Grant Todd the Manage Servers user right on the PDC and on each member server.

44.   You have a share called \\ACCT\DATA that has the following permissions assigned:

ACCT TEMPS	No Access
ACCT USERS	Read
ACCT MANAGERS	Change
DOMAIN ADMINS	Full Control

This share points to a folder called C:\DATA that is on an NTFS partition. The NTFS permissions have been left at the default value, EVERYONE has Full Control. Monica is a member of ACCT USERS and ACCT MANAGERS. When accessing this share, what are Monica's effective permissions?

A. No Access

B. Read

C. Change

D. Full Control

45. You have a share called \\ACCT\DATA that has the following permissions assigned:

ACCT TEMPS	No Access
ACCT USERS	Read
ACCT MANAGERS	Change
DOMAIN ADMINS	Full Control

This share points to a folder called C:\DATA that is on an NTFS partition. The NTFS permissions have been left at the default value, EVERYONE has Full Control. Monica is a member of ACCT USERS and ACCT MANAGERS. Monica is accessing the resource locally. What are Monica's effective permissions?

A. No Access

B. Read

C. Change

D. Full Control

46. You are configuring auditing for the D:\PAYROLL folder on the ACCT server that is configured as a BDC. The D: drive is on an NTFS partition. What prerequisite must be met?

A. You must start the auditing service on the ACCT computer.

B. You must check the Enable Auditing on Partition option for the D:\ drive through Disk Administrator.

   C. You must check the Enable Auditing on Partition option for the D:\ drive through drive properties in My Computer.

   D. You must enable auditing in the Audit Policy of User Manager for Domains to audit success and failure of File and Object Access.

47. You have just reconfigured the virus scanner program that runs on all of your NT Workstations. In order for the changes to take effect, you must stop and restart the virus scanner service on all of the workstations. You are sitting at your NT Workstation that has the NT Administrative Tools installed. What utility do you use?

   A. Control Panel ➤ Services

   B. Server Manager

   C. Windows NT Diagnostics

   D. Control Panel ➤ Network ➤ Services

48. You are configuring the Directory Replicator service. To which two groups do you add the replicator service account?

   A. Account Operators

   B. Server Operators

   C. Backup Operators

   D. Replicator

49. You have an NT printer that services jobs from 25 Windows NT 4.0 Workstations and 25 Windows 95 clients. You just downloaded new drivers for the print device that will provide significant performance improvement. What do you do?

   A. Install the new print drivers on the print server for Windows NT 4.0 and Windows 95 that hosts the printer, and also install them on each NT Workstation and Windows 95 client.

B. Install the new print driver for Windows NT 4.0 on the print server that hosts the printer, and install the Windows 95 driver on each Windows 95 client.

C. Install the new print driver for Windows 95 on the print server that hosts the printer, and install the NT 4.0 drivers on each NT Workstation.

D. Install the new print drivers for Windows NT 4.0 and Windows 95 on the print server that hosts the printer, and do nothing else.

50. Your network has a mixture of NT and NetWare servers. You decide to migrate the NetWare users, groups, and data to an NT Server. What must be installed on the NT Server that will participate in the migration? Choose all that apply.

A. NWLink IPX/SPX Compatible Transport protocol

B. CSNW

C. GSNW

D. File and Print Services for NetWare

51. You have an NT domain that consists of a PDC, 3 BDCs, 3 member servers, and 50 NT Workstations. You want Max to be able to back up all computers within the domain. What configuration is required? Choose all that apply.

A. Max must be added to the Backup Operators group on the PDC.

B. Max must be added to the Backup Operators group on the BDCs.

C. Max must be added to the Backup Operators group on each member server.

D. Max must be added to the Backup Operators group on each NT Workstation.

52. You have noticed high broadcast traffic that is caused by clients attempting to resolve NetBIOS computer names to IP addresses. What service would reduce these broadcasts?

    A. DHCP

    B. WINS

    C. DNS

    D. LMHOSTS

53. You are configuring your IIS server so that it will appear to host two separate web servers. What needs to be done to configure IIS virtual servers? Choose all that apply.

    A. You will need a unique IP address for each virtual server.

    B. Specify that you will be using virtual servers through the Advanced tab of the WWW service. Each virtual server must have a unique name.

    C. You will need to create a home directory for each virtual server.

    D. Configure each virtual server so that the IP address is associated with the home directory that will be used by the virtual server.

    E. Configure each virtual server so that the unique virtual server name is associated with the home directory that will be used by the virtual server. Do this through the WWW service Advanced property tab.

54. Which area should you watch in Network Monitor to determine how much bandwidth is being used during a network capture?

    A. %Network Utilization

    B. %Bandwidth Utilization

    C. Frames per Second

    D. Packets per Second

55. You have an NT Server that blue screens every day between 4:00 P.M. and 5:00 P.M. You called Microsoft Technical Support and they directed you to use the Kernel Debugger and establish a remote session through RAS to the Technical Support department. Which of the following files must you use?

    A. I386KD.EXE

    B. REMOTE.EXE

    C. DEBUGGER.EXE

    D. DUMPEXAM.EXE

APPENDIX

Study Question and
Sample Test Answers

Unit 1

Study Questions

Planning Directory Services

1. Single domain model
    Master domain model
    Multiple master domain model
    Complete trust domain model

2.

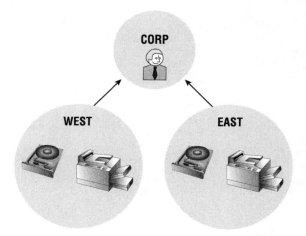

Explanation: In the master domain model, the accounts are in the master domain and the resources are in the resource domains. In this case, CORP is the master domain, EAST and WEST are the resource domains. The resource domains point to the domains they trust, so the trust arrow will go from the resource domains to the accounts domains.

3.

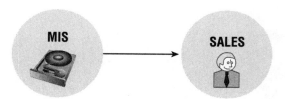

4. True (See Illustration A.)

5. False (See Illustration B.)

6. False (See Illustration C.)

7. True (See Illustration D.)

Explanation: When figuring out trust relationships, you should always draw the relationship to make the answer clear. The following diagrams represent the trust relationships that would be required to make each statement true. After establishing what the proper trust relationships should be, you can determine if the original diagram allows access or not.

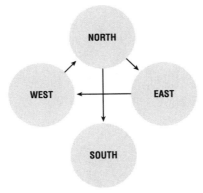

Trust relationships required for statements to be true

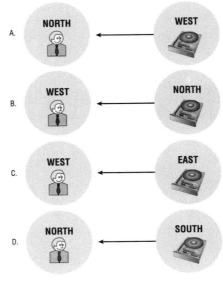

8. MARKETING, SALES

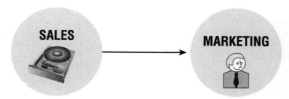

9. 20

   Explanation: To determine the number of trust relationships in the complete trust model, use the following formula $N*(N-1)$ where N is the number of domains. In this case, $5*(5-1)$ which equals 20 trust relationships.

10.

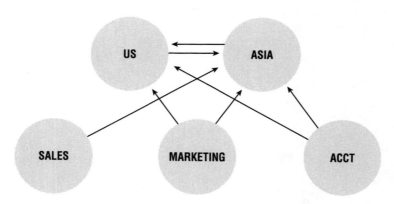

   Explanation: In the master domain model, the master domains have two-way trusts between the master or accounts domains. Each of the resource domains trusts each of the accounts domains.

11. No

   Explanation: In order for Michelle to access the resource, the trust arrow would have to point to her domain.

12.

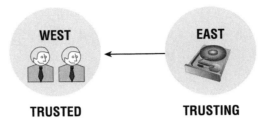

Explanation: The trusted domain contains the users. You point to the users you trust. The diagram shows the correct trust arrow and location of users and resources based on this scenario.

13. ONE

14. ONE, TWO

15. TWO, THREE

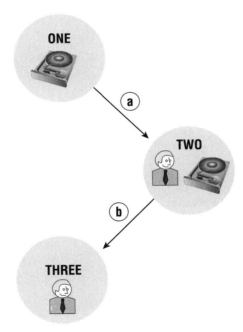

Explanation: To answer this question, look at each individual trust. The first trust relationship is defined as in the previous diagram. Domain TWO is trusted and domain ONE is trusting. Users in domain TWO can access resources in domain ONE. In the second trust relationship, domain TWO trusts domain THREE. Domain THREE is trusted and domain TWO is trusting. Users in domain THREE can access resources in domain TWO.

16. ONE, TWO

17. TWO, FOUR

18. ONE, TWO, THREE

19. ONE, THREE, FOUR

    Explanation: If you answered this question correctly, then it's safe to assume that you understand trust relationships. The easiest way to answer this question was to look at the arrows and see which domains pointed at you. If another domain had an arrow going to your domain, then you could potentially use that domain's resources through the trust relationship.

20. False

21. A BDC should be placed on each WAN link.

    Explanation: By placing a BDC on each WAN link, users can authenticate to the local BDC, therefore reducing WAN traffic caused by logon validation. This also provides fault tolerance because you have a local domain controller which can still be used for authentication in the event that the WAN link fails.

22. Place all BDCs on the SF segment.

    Explanation: Although this solution will reduce SAM synchronization traffic, it will increase logon validation traffic from the remote segments.

Planning Disk Drive Configurations

23. duplexing

24. mirroring

25. Disk mirroring (and duplexing)

26. disk space 2,000MB

    parity information 500MB

    Explanation: Disk striping with parity will use the sum of one drive from the stripe set with parity to store the parity information in stripes across the stripe set.

27. 1

28. 5

29. 2, 32

30. 3, 32

Protocol Selection

31. DHCP server

32. Connection to an IBM mainframe running 3270 applications

    HP network printers

    Explanation: DLC does not offer full data-link services, and it is not intended to be used to connect two computers together.

33. NWLink IPX/SPX Compatible Transport protocol

34. By installing Services for Macintosh

35. TCP/IP

36. TCP/IP

37. WINS

38. NWLink IPX/SPX Compatible Transport protocol

    TCP/IP

Sample Test

1-1 A

Explanation: Because you have a small number of accounts and you will be centralizing account and resource management, the single domain model is the best choice.

1-2 C

1-3 B

Explanation: You need one drive to set up a mirror on the system and boot partition and a minimum of three additional drives for the stripe set with parity.

1-4 B

Explanation: The master domain model will best meet this scenario. Each department has the necessary equipment to configure a PDC and at least one BDC for its domain. With this domain model, you can then centralize accounts management to the accounts domain, while allowing decentralized management of the resource (departmental) domains.

1-5 A

Explanation: Before you even look at the answers on a question like this, you should diagram the correct solution. Then based on the diagram, select the answer that matches. In this case, the required trust relationships would be:

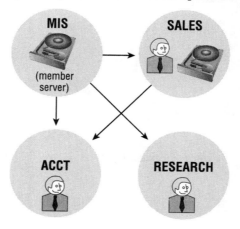

1-6 D

Explanation: Disk striping is not fault tolerant, but it does offer enhanced performance.

1-7 C

Explanation: DLC does not support communications between two PCs and it is not supported by the Microsoft redirector. Network clients sending jobs to network printers do not need to have DLC installed, but the print server that supports the network printer must use DLC.

1-8 B

Explanation: Draw the relationships out as shown in the following diagram to provide the answer to this question.

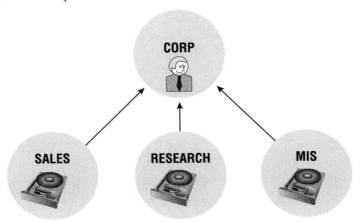

1-9 B

Explanation: Although disk mirroring is fault tolerant and it can be used for the system and boot partition, it will not increase performance.

1-10 B

1-11 D

1-12   B

> **Explanation:** Draw the relationships out as shown in the following diagram to provide the answer to this question.

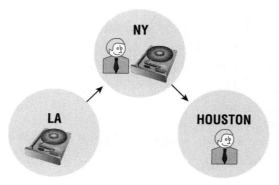

1-13   C

> **Explanation:** This scenario needs centralized accounts management, but decentralized resource management. This would point to the master domain model, but due to the large number of accounts, you would need to use the multiple master domain model.

1-14   B

> **Explanation:** Although disk striping with parity is fault tolerant and improves performance, it can't be used for the system and boot partition.

1-15   B, C

1-16   B

1-17   C

> **Explanation:** With disk duplexing, you have more fault tolerance because you are using two disk controllers.

1-18   D

> **Explanation:** The domains are already created, and now you need to provide access to resources in other domains. You would set up trust relationships which would then be the complete trust domain model.

1-19   A

Explanation: Draw this out as shown in the following diagram to provide the answer to this question. The D solution is not selected because you should have only one logon account for each user.

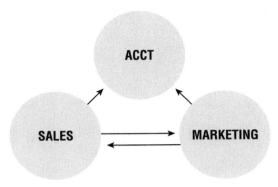

1-20   C

Explanation: Disk striping with parity will use the sum of one drive from the stripe set with parity to store the parity information in stripes across the stripe set.

1-21   A

Explanation: Disk striping does not store parity information, so the entire stripe set can be used for data.

1-22   B

Explanation: In order to meet both options, you would have had to use the master domain model so that resource management could be decentralized.

1-23   B

Explanation: In order to meet both options, you would have had to place a BDC from the master domain on each WAN link to minimize logon validation traffic.

1-24   A

Unit 2

Study Questions

NT Server Roles

1. PDC
   BDC
   Member server

2. False

   Explanation: In addition to other congfiguration differences, the registry configuration of domain controllers and member servers is significantly different which requires you to reinstall a member server if you want it to become a domain controller.

3. True

   Explanation: The preferred promotion method takes place when the PDC is up and running because this will reduce the likelihood of SAM database corruption, but a BDC could still be promoted even if the PDC were unavailable.

4. The BDC
   The ReplicationGovernor

5. Server Manager

6. False

   Explanation: When a BDC is installed into a domain, the PDC is required to be up and running.

7. False

   Explanation: When a BDC is installed into a domain, it gets a copy of the domain SID. The only way a BDC can change domains is through reinstallation.

8. True

    Explanation: Because a member server does not contain the domain SAM, it is not configured with a domain SID. This means member servers are free to change domains.

9. False

    Explanation: BDCs are not automatically promoted. You need to promote a BDC through Server Manager. The election process is associated with browsing.

10. False

    Explanation: Although you should have at least one BDC for fault tolerance, they are not required.

11. domain

12. local

13. 5

14. False

    Explanation: The PDC contains the only read-write copy of the SAM database. BDCs have read-only copies of the SAM database.

15. False

    Explanation: The PDC only partially synchronizes the SAM database with information that has changed since the last synchronization under normal circumstances.

Network Protocols and Bindings

16. By installing Services for Macintosh.

17. DHCP

18. WINS

19. False

    Explanation: When you install the DLC protocol, you don't configure anything.

20. frame type

21. scope

22. False

    Explanation: The whole point of using WINS is so that this mapping will occur dynamically.

23. default gateway

24. DHCP Manager

25. `lmhosts`

26. Top of the binding order

    Explanation: By placing the most commonly used protocols at the top of the binding order, you increase performance.

NT Server Core Services

27. Any NT Server (PDC, BDC, or member server)

28. Any NT Server or NT Workstation

29. The PDC

30. Backup Browsers

31. Windows NT Workstation 3.5

32. Replicator
    Backup Operators

33. `winnt\system32\repl\export`

34. Managing logon scripts between the PDC and BDCs
Managing system policy files between the PDC and BDCs

Hard Disk Configuration

35. Disk mirroring (and duplexing)
Disk striping with parity

36. Disk mirroring (and duplexing)

37. 3, 32

38. False

Explanation: Disk mirroring doesn't offer any write performance gains.

39. Disk Administrator

40. Disk stripe with parity

41. False

Explanation: You implement disk duplexing the same way you implement disk mirroring, by establishing a disk mirror.

42. CONVERT

Printer Configuration

43. They must all be able to share the same print driver.

44. TCP/IP Print service

45. lpr

46. lpq

47. The MAC address of the DLC printer network interface device

48. Create two printers. Assign each group to a printer. Assign the Managers group printer a higher priority.

49. The IP address

    The domain name the printer uses

50. Print

51. Create two printers. Use the scheduling option to specify that one printer is available only during specific hours of the day. Direct users to send large jobs to the printer with limited hours.

52. Windows NT 4.0 for all processors

    Window NT 3.5x for all processors

    Windows 95

53. Create a printer pool

NT Server Configuration for Client Support

54. Be a member of the Administrators group

    Be a member of the Account Operators group

    Have the "Add workstations to the domain" user right

55. Server Manager

56. Services for Macintosh

57. Upgrade the Macintosh clients to EtherTalk.

    Install a third-party router that connects LocalTalk to Ethernet.

    Install an LocalTalk card in your NT server so that is will act as a router.

58. False

    Explanation: Only NT computers are added to the domain.

Sample Test

2-1   D

2-2   C

2-3   A, C, D

2-4   A

2-5   A

2-6   B, C, D

2-7   B, C

2-8   C, D

2-9   B

Explanation: A stripe set with parity can't contain the system or boot partition. In addition, a stripe set with parity requires a minimum of three drives.

2-10   B

2-11   B

2-12   D

Explanation: When a BDC is installed into a domain, it gets a copy of the domain SID. The only way a BDC can change domains is through reinstallation.

2-13   B

Explanation: Because a member server does not contain the domain SAM, it does not get configured with a domain SID. This means member servers are free to change domains.

2-14   A

2-15   C

2-16   A

2-17   B

2-18   C

> **Explanation:** This question illustrates why you should read all of the answers before making a selection. A is also a good choice, but because C takes the solution one step further, it is a better solution.

2-19   B

Unit 3

Study Questions

User and Group Management

1. %username%

2. Check the Account Disabled box in the User properties of User Manager for Domains.

3. \WINNT\SYSTEM32\REPL\IMPORT\SCRIPTS

4. Administrators
   Server Operators

5. Account Operators

6. Server Operators

7. False

   Explanation: You can only define logon hours on a per-user basis.

8. False

   Explanation: NT doesn't offer a mechanism for limiting concurrent logons. The closest option is to specify from which computers a user can log on.

9. You would assign the user or group the "Back up files and directories" user right.

10. Assign the user the "Manage auditing and security log" user right.

11. In a multidomain environment, you assign permissions to EVERYONE when you want permissions to apply to users from within the domain and users from trusted domains. You assign permissions to Domain Users when you want only users from within your domain to access the resource.

12. If you want a user to have administrative rights to the local computer, add the user to the Administrators local group. If you add a user to the Administrators group on the PDC, this would include the BDCs because they share the domain SAM. If you add a user to the Domain Admins group, they will be added to the PDC's Administrators local group. In addition, the Domain Admins group is added to the Administrators local group of any computer that joins the domain.

13. global, local, global, local

14. True

15. False

    Explanation: Global groups exist only on NT domain controllers.

16. False

    Explanation: Global groups can contain only users from within the local domain SAM database.

17. Domain Admins

18. Directory Replication

19. User and Group Management

20. The Password Uniqueness account policy

21. Account Lockout

22. The Administrator must unlock the account.

23. File and Object Access

24. Security Policy Changes

25. Event Viewer

Profiles and Policies

26. \WINNT\PROFILES\%*username*%

27. NTUSER.DAT

28. By renaming the NTUSER.DAT file to NTUSER.MAN

29. NTCONFIG.POL

30. User Manager for Domains

Explanation: You create a roaming profile by specifying a UNC path in the Profiles user property of the user for whom you are defining the roaming profile. Existing profiles are then moved or copied by using the User Profiles tab of the System Control Panel.

31. Control Panel ➤ System ➤ User Profiles tab

32. The user won't be able to successfully complete the logon.

33. You can assign group priority in the System Policy Editor utility.

34. System Policy Editor

35. False

Explanation: You should only copy user profiles through Control Panel ➤ System ➤ User Profiles tab.

36. Users
Groups
Computers

37. registry

Remote Administration

38. Windows NT Workstation (also applies to NT member servers)
    Windows 95

39. Server Manager

40. From Options, select Low Speed Connection option.

41. False

    Explanation: You only get the DHCP Manager utility on NT computers that have the administrative tools installed.

42. Explorer, My Computer

43. Explorer

Disk Resource Management

44. Administrators
    Server Operator

    Explanation: NT workstations also contain a group called Power Users that can create network shares.

45. False

    Explanation: You can only audit file events on NTFS partitions.

46. Read

    Explanation: When accessing a network share, you are bound by the most restrictive of your share permissions or your NTFS permissions.

47. True

48. True

49. Full Control

    Explanation: Jill will receive the most permissive access in this case.

50. No Access

    Explanation: If a user has No Access permission through user or group membership, then it does not matter what other access permissions have been assigned.

51. Audit Execute on the file for group Everyone.

52. Audit Success or Failures of any Read or Write events within the folder.

53. List

Managing Events in an Enterprise Environment

54. SALES, ACCT

55. global

56. local

57. Account DB Users (or local)

58. Sales Managers user (or global)

59. The PDC in the SALES domain.

60. ACCTSERVER (or member server)

61. Sales Managers (or global), Account DB Users (or local)

62. The SALES and ACCT domains will have to trust the CORP domain.

63. No default global group exists to manage backups.

    Explanation: A default local group, Backup Operators, manages backup and restore operations.

64. The global group you create needs to be added to the CORP\Backup Operators group, the SALES\Backup Operators group, and the ACCT\Backup Operators group on each domain's PDC.

65. The global group they belong to would have to be added to the Backup Operators group on each member server because each member server stores its own unique copy of the SAM database.

66. The global group they belong to would have to be added to the Backup Operators group on each NT workstation because each NT workstation stores its own unique local copy of the SAM database.

67. False

    Explanation: By default Dustin has no administrative rights to the ASIA domain. In order for Dustin to have administrative rights, he needs to be added to the ASIA\Administrators local group.

68. Add the global group, US\Domain Admins to the local group Administrators on the PDC in the ASIA domain.

69. Read

    Explanation: The ASIA Domain Users are part of the Everyone group.

70. The Asia Domain User group has not been assigned any permissions to this share.

71. Ryan is not a member of any group that has been granted any access to this share.

72. Read

    Explanation: Ryan has the Read right because he is a part of group Everyone.

Sample Test

3-1 B

3-2 D

3-3 D

    Explanation: In this question, you know that you are using the master domain model. This requires one-way trust relationships with the EAST and WEST domains trusting the CORP domain. To assign permissions, you logically group users and place them in a global group in their home domain (in this case CORP). You would create a local group at the resource they require access to, then add the global group to the local group.

3-4   A

3-5   D

Explanation: You can define logon hours only on a per-user basis.

3-6   C

3-7   B, C

Explanation: To create a roaming profile, specify a UNC name in the users profile properties. Profiles can be copied only through Control Panel ➤ System ➤ User Profiles tab.

3-8   B

Explanation: You can only add global groups to local groups.

3-9   B, D

Explanation: This is one of those questions where you'll want to sketch the problem before you attempt to answer it. In this case, the users are in the EAST domain and the resource is in the WEST domain. This means tthe WEST domain must trust the EAST domain. In the EAST domain, you'll need to create a global group that will then be added to the local group WEST\Data Users. You can't use the existing local group because you can't add a local group to a local group.

3-10   D

Explanation: Because Rhonda is a member of Sales Temps, and Sales Temps has No Access, Rhonda will have No Access. If you remove her from this group, then the access permissions will be cumulative and become 'Change.'

3-11   D

3-12   C

3-13   B

3-14   C

3-15   C

3-16   D

3-17   B

3-18   C

3-19   A

Explanation: Sketch this problem before attempting to answer the question. Because there are users in the NORTH domain, you'll need to create a global group in the NORTH domain. In the SOUTH domain, create a local group on the resource. Add the global group to the local group.

3-20   B

Explanation: You'll need a global group in the domain where Brad exists, the SOUTH domain. This global group needs to be added to the Server Operators group in the NORTH and SOUTH domains.

3-21   D

3-22   B

Explanation: Because the server is installed as a member server, it will have its own unique local SAM database. You can then remove the Domain Admins global group from the Administrators local group and assign only the users you want to manage the server.

3-23   B

3-24   B, C

3-25   B

Unit 4

Study Questions

NetWare Connectivity

1.   NWLink IPX/SPX Compatible Transport protocol

2. GSNW

3. Migration Tool for NetWare

4. NWLink IPX/SPX Compatible Transport

5. NTGATEWAY, NetWare

6. Mapping file

7. NWLink IPX/SPX Compatible Transport, GSNW

8. In the main screen of the GSNW configuration box, you can specify print options for the gateway users. One option is whether or not banner pages will be printed.

9. True

10. False

    Explanation: You only need to create a user on the NetWare server to act as a gateway account. This user must be part of the NTGATEWAY group that is also created on the NetWare server.

11. In the Username tab of Migration Tool for NetWare, you would specify the Overwrite with new Info option for duplicate usernames.

12. In the Username tab of Migration Tool for NetWare, you would specify the Ignore option for duplicate usernames.

13. The mapping file

14. The Defaults tab allows you to specify whether or not NetWare supervisor equivalents are added to the Administrators group through the Add Supervisors to the Administrators group option. This selection is not a default action.

15. File and Print Services for NetWare

16. Client Services for NetWare (CSNW)

17. False

    Explanation: You only need to create a user on the NetWare server to act as a gateway account. This user must be a part of the NTGATEWAY group that is also created on the NetWare server.

18. False

    Explanation: GSNW can only be installed on NT Servers.

19. True

20. True

21. The destination NT drive must be NTFS.

    Explanation: Because FAT does not offer local security, NTFS is required.

22. False

23. False

24. True

25. False

26. True

    Explanation: The destination drive must be NTFS.

27. The Account Defaults tab allows you to specify whether or not NetWare account restrictions will be enforced through the Use Supervisor Defaults option.

28. Selecting the Pop-Up Errors logging option

29. Selecting the Verbose User/Group logging option

30. Use the Trial migration.

MultiProtocol Routing

31. Routing Information Protocol (RIP) for Internet Protocol (IP)
    DHCP Relay Agent
    RIP for NWLink IPX/SPX Compatible Transport protocol

32. DHCP Relay Agent

33. Routing Information Protocol (RIP) for Internet Protocol (IP)

34. RIP for NWLink IPX/SPX Compatible Transport protocol

35. Different

36. ROUTE

37. IPXROUTE

38. SAP

39. NetBIOS Broadcast Propagation (broadcast of type 20 packets)

40. The router that connects the two segments

Internet Information Server and Internet Services

41. DNS

42. FTP

43. WWW

44. Intranet refers to private networks, whereas Internet refers to the world-wide, public network.

45. You must have an IP address for each virtual server you will support. The server's network card must be configured so that it supports each IP address. Through the Internet Service Manager, you must assign a unique IP address to each WWW virtual server's folder.

46. A virtual directory does not exist on the same computer that hosts the IIS server. (Although to users who connect to the IIS server, it appears as if it is local.)

47. In the WWW Service Properties, you can define whether or not Anonymous Logon is allowed.

48. IUSR_*computername*

49. Internet Service Manager

50. Windows NT Challenge/ Response (MS-CHAP)

51. By specifying which IP addresses can access the FTP service

52. False

    Explanation: You can configure logging, but not auditing.

53. Through the Directories tab of the WWW service, select the Enable Default Document option and specify that `welcome.htm` is the default document.

54. Specify grant access to the IP addresses of the users who should be able to access the WWW service in the Advanced tab of the WWW service.

55. `\WINNT\System32\LogFiles`

56. Allow Anonymous.

57. False

    Explanation: The DNS entries are managed manually.

Remote Access Server

58. Require Microsoft encrypted authentication

59. User Manager for Domains
    Remote Access Admin

60. No Call Back
Set By Caller

61. The Use Static Address Pool option

62. The Use DHCP to assign remote TCP/IP client addresses option

63. On the RAS server, you would select the Allow remote clients to request a predetermined IP address in the RAS TCP/IP configuration properties. On the RAS client, you would specify the IP address that the RAS client would use.

64. NetBEUI
IPX
TCP/IP

65. Allow any authentication including clear text.

66. Allow any authentication including clear text.

Explanation: This option is required because SLIP does not support encrypted passwords.

67. PPP

Explanation: SLIP can be used as a dial-out protocol, but NT RAS only supports PPP for dial-in connections.

68. PPTP

69. Preset To:

70. Require encrypted authentication

71. PSTN

72. False

Explanation: SLIP can be used as a dial-out protocol, but NT RAS only supports PPP for dial-in connections.

73. True

74. IPX

Sample Test

4-1   C

4-2   D

4-3   C

4-4   A, E

4-5   A

4-6   A, D

4-7   D

4-8   C

4-9   B

4-10 A

4-11 A

4-12 C

4-13 B

4-14 A

4-15 C, E, F

4-16 C, E

4-17 D, F, G

4-18 B

4-19 A

4-20 A, D, E

4-21 B

4-22 A, B, C

4-23   D

4-24   B, C

4-25   C

Unit 5

Study Questions

Baseline Measurement of System Performance

1. Performance Monitor
   Network Monitor

2. True

3. True

4. False

   Explanation: You should take your baselines during representative hours so you know how your system is performing during normal working hours. Performance Monitor does not create a significant drain on system resources.

Using Performance Monitor

5. DISKPERF -y at the command line, then restart the computer.

6. Chart
   Alert
   Log
   Report

7. Processor
   Memory
   Disk Subsystem
   Network Subsystem

8. Memory (insufficient RAM)

9. 50%

10. 3, processor

11. False

    Explanation: The processor is only considered a bottleneck if the %Processor Time value is above 80%.

12. 2

13. Chart

14. Log

15. 20

16. False

    Explanation: You should have 20% or 4MB of available memory, whichever is greater.

17. Alert

18. True

Network Monitor

19. False

    Explanation: You can monitor only network traffic that is sent or received by the server, or any network broadcasts from an NT Server running Network Monitor. To view all network traffic, use the version of Network Monitor that ships with SMS.

20. By viewing the % Network Utilization bar graph.

21. True

22. Protocol
    Specific MAC address
    Protocol property

23. By looking at Station statistics generated during the capture period from the main screen of Network Monitor.

24. Through Control Panel ➤ Network ➤ Services ➤ Add... ➤ Network Monitor Tools and Agent

25. By setting a display filter that specifies: Protocol==DHCP

26. True

27. False

    Explanation: It does not display the name of the logged-on user.

Performance Optimization

28. Through Control Panel ➤ Network ➤ Services ➤ Server ➤ Properties

29. Maximize throughput for network applications

30. Minimize memory used

31. Maximize throughput for file sharing

32. Minimize memory used
    Balance
    Maximize throughput for file sharing
    Maximize throughput for network applications

33. 64

Sample Test

5-1   A

5-2   A

Explanation: DHCP is used to dynamically assign IP addresses and configuration.

5-3   A

5-4   C

5-5   B

5-6   C

Explanation: Filtering by MAC addresses ensures that all frames going to CLIENT1's network interface card will be captured, regardless of protocol.

5-7   B

Explanation: Processor queue length should be below 4.

5-8   B

Explanation: % Processor Time should be below 80%.

5-9   D

5-10   C

Explanation: % Disk Time should be below 50%.

5-11   A

Explanation: Pages per second should be below 20.

5-12   C

5-13   C

5-14   D

Unit 6

Study Questions

Troubleshooting Installation Errors

1. False

   Explanation: NT will try to identify your hardware and configuration, but this is not guaranteed.

2. False

   Explanation: You should check the Hardware Compatibility List (HCL).

3. False

   Explanation: You must select the domain by entering the domain name. You do not see a drop-down box.

4. True

Troubleshooting Boot Failures

5. BOOT.INI

6. NTDETECT.COM

7. NTOSKRNL.EXE

8. NTLDR

9. NTBOOTDD.SYS

10. BOOT.INI

11. BOOTSECT.DOS

12. Use the Emergency Repair Disk (ERD).

13. NTLDR

14. NTDETECT.COM

15. BOOTSECT.DOS

16. RDISK

Troubleshooting Configuration Errors

17. HKEY_LOCAL_MACHINE
HKEY_CURRENT_CONFIG
HKEY_CURRENT_USER
HKEY_USERS
HKEY_CLASSES_ROOT

18. False

Explanation: Only portions of the registry are backed up unless you use the RISK /s command.

19. First reboot and then try the Last Known Good option.

20. False

Explanation: In order to use the ERD, you must use the NT Setup disks.

21. WINNT /ox

22. WINNT32 /ox

23. Server Manager

24. Windows NT Diagnostics

25. By hitting the space bar when prompted during the boot process

26. Network Control Panel applet

27. NT Backup

28. REGEDT32

29. REGEDIT

30. DependOnService

31. DependOnGroup

32. Control Panel ➤ Services
    Server Manager
    Windows NT Diagnostics

33. HKEY_LOCAL_MACHINE

34. HKEY_CURRENT_USER

35. RDISK /s

Troubleshooting Printer Errors

36. You are using the wrong print driver.

37. Stop and restart the spooler service.

38. Through the Advanced tab of the print servers properties

39. False

    Explanation: The print spool file is set per print server.

40. Create a new port on the print server and specify the UNC path of the failed printer.

41. Your print spool file may be full.

42. The print server

Troubleshooting RAS Errors

43. Remote Access Admin

User Manager for Domains

44. Allow any authentication including clear text

45. False

Explanation: RAS only supports PPP for dial-in connections.

46. Remote Access Admin

47. The registry editor

Explanation: You make a change to HKEY_LOCAL_MACHINE\System\Current ControlSet\Services\RasMan\Parameters.

Troubleshooting Connectivity Problems

48. IPCONFIG

49. PING

50. Use Manual Frame Type Detection and specify both frame types.

51. Incorrect frame type

52. Ethernet_802.2

53. DHCP

54. ROUTE

55. IP address

Subnet Mask

Default Gateway (only required if routing is needed)

Troubleshooting Resource Access and Permission Problems

56. No Access

Explanation: By default all users are members of EVERYONE. You should never assign No Access to group EVERYONE.

57. Full Control

58. He needs to log off and log on again to update his access token.

59. Bonnie needs to be removed from the SALES TEMPS group, or the SALES TEMP group needs to be removed from the Access Control List (ACL). She then needs to log on again and create a new Access Token.

60. False

Explanation: Whichever permission is the more restrictive will apply.

61. False

Explanation: Only files within the folder receive the access permissions assigned by default.

62. The Everyone group is granted Full Control.

Resolving Disk Failures in a Fault-Tolerant Environment

63. NT Backup

64. Disk mirroring (duplexing)

65. Break the mirror set and delete the failed partition, replace the failed drive, and establish a new mirror set.

66. Boot with the NT boot disk that has BOOT.INI edited to point to the boot partition on the secondary drive, break the mirror set and delete the failed partition, copy the BOOT.INI file to the secondary drives system partition, replace the failed drive, and establish a new mirror set.

67. Replace the failed drive, and regenerate the stripe set through Disk Administrator.

Explanation: Remember, you do not have any fault tolerance if you just use disk striping.

68. Replace the failed drive, re-create the stripe set through Disk Administrator, and restore the data from tape backup.

Explanation: You do not have any fault tolerance because you are using only disk striping.

69. Replace the failed drives, re-create the stripe set with parity, and restore the data from your tape backup.

Explanation: You do not have any fault tolerance if more that one drive fails in your stripe set with parity.

Advanced Problem Resolution

70. Error code and parameters

All modules and drivers that have loaded and initialized successfully

All modules and drivers that are waiting to be loaded

71. By going to Control Panel ➤ System ➤ Startup/Shutdown property tab and checking the Write Debugging Information To: box.

72. System

Security

Application

73. Error

Information

Warning

Success Audit

Success Failure

74. The oldest

Explanation: The oldest error may be a dependency that is causing the other errors to occur.

75. Target

76. i386kd.exe

77. REMOTE.EXE

Sample Test

6-1 A

6-2 A

6-3 C

6-4 A

6-5 B

6-6 B

6-7 C

6-8 D

6-9 A, B, C

6-10 A

6-11 B

6-12 D

6-13 C

6-14 B

6-15 D

6-16 B

6-17 A, D, E

6-18 A

6-19 B

6-20   A

6-21   B

6-22   C

6-23   A, D

Explanation: You need to edit the BOOT.INI file because with the SCSI disabled, you will need to change the ARC name from MULTI to SCSI. You will also need the NTBOOTDD.SYS file because it supports SCSI adapters that do not use the SCSI BIOS.

6-24   B

6-25   B, C, D

6-26   A

6-27   D

Unit 7

Final Review

1. A, C

2. B, C

3. B, D

4. C

5. A, D

6. A, E

7. B

8. D

9. C

10. D

11. B

12. D

13. D

14. A

15. A

16. B, D

17. C

18. B

19. C

20. C

21. B

22. A

23. D

24. C

25. B

26. C

27. C

28. A

29. A, E

30. B, C

31. D

32. A

33. C

34. A

35. A

36. A, D

37. A

38. C

39. B

40. B, D

41. A, D

42. D

43. E

44. C

45. D

46. D

47. B

48. C, D

49. D

50. A, C

51. A, C, D

52. B

53. A, C, D

54. A

55. A, B

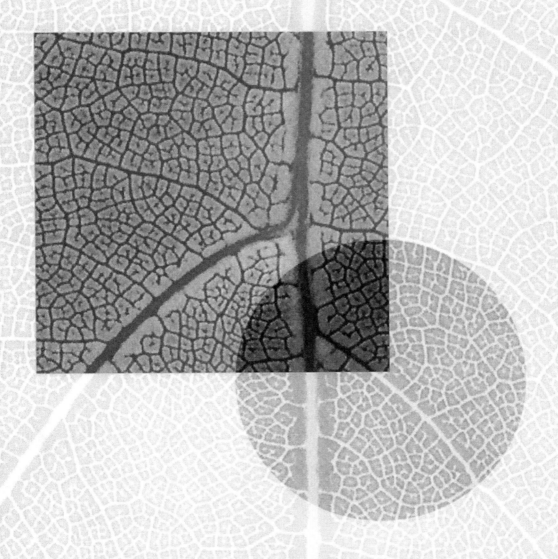

Glossary

Access Control Entries (ACE) Each Access Control List (ACL) has an associated ACE which lists the permissions that have been granted or denied to the users and groups listed in the ACL. See *Access Control List.*

Access Control List (ACL) Lists of security identifiers contained by objects that allow only certain processes—those identified in the list as having the appropriate permission—to activate the services of that object. See *Object, Security Identifier, Permissions.*

Access Tokens Objects containing the security identifier of a running process. A process started by another process inherits the starting process' access token. The access token is checked against each object's ACL to determine whether or not appropriate permissions are granted to perform any requested service. See *Access Control List, Access Control Entries, Permissions, Object, Security Identifier, Process.*

Account Lockout Used to specify how many invalid logon attempts should be tolerated before a user account is locked out. Account lockout is set through User Manager for Domains. See *Security, User Manager for Domains.*

Account Policies Account policies are used to determine password and logon requirements. Account policies are set through User Manager for Domains. See *User Manager for Domains.*

Accounts Containers for security identifiers, passwords, permissions, group associations, and preferences for each user of a system. The User Manager for Domains utility is used to administer accounts. See *Security Identifier, Preferences, Permissions, Passwords, Groups.*

ACE See *Access Control Entries.*

ACL See *Access Control List.*

Adapter Any hardware device that allows communications to occur through physically dissimilar systems. This term usually refers to peripheral cards that are permanently mounted inside computers and provide an interface from the computer's bus to another media such as a hard disk or a network. See *Network Interface Card, SCSI.*

Address Resolution Protocol (ARP) An Internet protocol for resolving an IP address into a Physical layer address (such as an Ethernet media access controller address). See *Physical Layer, Internet Protocol.*

Administrative Tools   A program group on NT domain controllers that contains utilities such as User Manager for Domains, Server Manager, Disk Administrator, Performance Monitor, and Network Monitor. See *User Manager for Domains, Server Manager, Disk Administrator, Performance Monitor, Network Monitor.*

ADMINISTRATOR Account   A special account in Windows NT that has the ultimate set of security permissions and can assign any permission to any user or group. The ADMINISTRATOR account is used to correct security problems. See *Permissions.*

Administrators   Users who are part of the ADMINISTRATORS group. This group has the ultimate set of security permissions. See *Administrator Account, Permissions, Groups.*

Advanced Projects Agency Network (ARPANET)   Predecessor to the Internet that was developed by the Department of Defense in the late 1960's.

AppleTalk   The built-in (to firmware) suite of network protocols used by Macintosh computers. Windows NT Server uses AppleTalk to service Macintosh clients by simulating an Apple server. See *Macintosh, Network Protocol.*

Applications   Large software packages that perform a specific function, such as word processing, Web browsing, or database management. Applications typically consist of more than one program. See *Programs.*

Application Layer   The layer of the OSI model that interfaces with User mode programs called applications by providing high-level network services based on lower-level network layers. Network file systems like named pipes are an example of Application-layer software. See *Named Pipes, OSI Model, Application.*

ARP   See *Address Resolution Protocol.*

ARPANET   See *Advanced Research Projects Agency Network.*

Asymmetrical Multiprocessing   A multiple processor architecture in which certain processors are designated to run certain threads or in which scheduling is not done on a fair-share basis. Asymmetrical multiprocessing is easier to implement than symmetrical multiprocessing, but it does not scale well as processors are added. See *Microprocessor, Symmetrical Multiprocessing.*

Asynchronous Transfer Mode (ATM)   A wide area transport protocol that runs at many different speeds and supports real-time, guaranteed packet delivery in hardware, as well as lower-quality levels of service on a bandwidth-available basis. ATM will eventually replace all other wide area protocols, as most worldwide PTSN providers have declared their support for the international standard. See *Public Switched Telephone Network, Wide Area Network*.

ATM   See *Asynchronous Transfer Mode.*

Audit Policy   Audit policy determines which user events you want to track for security reasons. Audit policy can track the success or failure of specified security events; it is set in the User Manager for Domains. See *Security, User Manager for Domains*.

Back Up   The process of writing all the data contained in online mass storage devices to offline mass storage devices for the purpose of safe keeping. Backups are usually performed from hard disk drives to tape drives. Also referred to as archiving. See *Hard Disk Drive*.

Backup Browser   A computer on a Microsoft network that maintains a list of computers and services available on the network. The Master Browser supplies this list. The backup browser distributes the browsing service load to a workgroup or domain. See *Master Browser*.

Backup Domain Controllers   Servers that contain accurate replications of the security and user databases; these servers can authenticate workstations in the absence of a primary domain controller (PDC). See *Primary Domain Controller*.

Baseline   A snapshot record of your computer's current performance statistics that can be used for analysis and planning purposes.

Basic Input/Output System (BIOS)   A set of routines in firmware that provides the most basic software interface drivers for hardware attached to the computer. The BIOS contains the bootstrap routine. See *Boot, Driver, Firmware*.

Bindery   A NetWare structure that contains user accounts and permissions. It is similar to the Security Accounts Manager in Windows NT. See *Security Accounts Manager*.

Binding   The process of linking network services to network service providers. The binding facility allows users to define exactly how network services operate in order to optimize the performance of the system. By default, Windows enables all possible bindings. The Network control panel is used to change bindings. See *Network Layer, Data Link Layer*.

BIOS   See *Basic Input/Output System*.

Bit   A binary digit. A numeral having only two possible values, 0 or 1. Computers represent these two values as a high (voltage present) or a low (no voltage present) state on a control line. Bits are accumulated in sets of certain sizes to represent higher values. See *Byte*.

Boot   The process of loading a computer's operating system. Booting usually occurs in multiple phases, each successively more complex until the entire operating system and all its services are running. Also called bootstrap. The computer's BIOS must contain the first level of booting. See *Basic Input/Output System*.

Boot Partition   The boot partition is the partition that contains the system files. The system files are located in **C:\WINNT** by default. See *Partition, System Partition*.

BOOTP   See *Bootstrap Protocol*.

Bootstrap Protocol (BOOTP)   Predecessor to the DHCP protocol. BOOTP was used to assign IP addresses to diskless workstations. See *Dynamic Host Configuration Protocol*.

Bottlenecks   Components operating at their peak capacity that restrict the flow of information through a system. Used singularly, the term indicates the single, most restrictive component in a system.

Bridge   A device that connects two networks of the same Data Link protocol by forwarding those packets destined for computers on the other side of the bridge. See *Router, Data Link Layer*.

Browser   A computer on a Microsoft network that maintains a list of computers and services available on the network.

Browsing   The process of requesting the list of computers and services on a network from a browser.

Caching   A speed optimization technique that keeps a copy of the most recently used data in a fast, high-cost, low-capacity storage device rather than in the device on which the actual data resides. Caching assumes that recently used data is likely to be used again. Fetching data from the cache is faster than fetching data from the slower, larger storage device. Most caching algorithms also copy next-most-likely to be used data and perform write caching to further increase speed gains. See *Write-Back Caching, Write-Through Caching.*

CD-ROM   See *Compact Disk-Read Only Memory.*

Central Processing Unit (CPU)   The central processing unit of a computer. In microcomputers such as IBM PC compatible machines, the CPU is the micro-processor. See *Microprocessor.*

Client   A computer on a network that subscribes to the services provided by a server. See *Server.*

Client Services for NetWare (CSNW)   A service provided with Windows NT that connects an NT client to NetWare file servers. See *NetWare, Client Services for NetWare.*

Client/Server   A network architecture that dedicates certain computers called servers to act as service providers to computers called clients, which users operate to perform work. Servers can be dedicated to providing one or more network services such as file storage, shared printing, communications, e-mail service, and Web response. See *Share, Peer.*

Client/Server Applications   Applications that split large applications into two components: computer-intensive processes that run on application servers and user interfaces that run on clients. Client/server applications communicate over the network through interprocess communication mechanisms. See *Client, Server, Interprocess Communications.*

Code   Synonymous with software but used when the software is the object of discussion, rather than the utility it provides. See *Software.*

COM Port   Communications port. A serial hardware interface conforming to the RS-232 standard for low-speed serial communications. See *Modem, Serial.*

Compact Disk-Read Only Memory (CD-ROM)   A media for storing extremely large software packages on optical read-only discs. CD-ROM is an adaptation of the CD medium used for distributing digitized music. CD-ROM discs can hold up to 650MB of information and cost very little to produce in mass quantity. See *Hard Disk Drive.*

Components Interchangeable elements of a complex software or hardware system. See *Module*.

Compression A space optimization scheme that reduces the size (length) of a data set by exploiting the fact that most useful data contains a great deal of redundancy. Compression reduces redundancy by creating symbols smaller than the data they represent and an index that defines the value of the symbols for each compressed set of data.

Computer A device capable of performing automatic calculations based on lists of instructions called programs. The computer feeds the results of these calculations (output) to peripheral devices that can represent them in useful ways, such as graphics on a screen or ink on paper. See *Microprocessor*.

Computer Name A 1–15 character NetBIOS name used to uniquely identify a computer on the network. See *Network Basic Input/Output System*.

Control Panel A software utility that controls the function of specific operating system services by allowing users to change default settings for the service to match their preferences. The Registry contains the Control Panel settings on a system and/or per-user basis. See *Registry, Account*.

Cooperative Multitasking A multitasking scheme in which each process must voluntarily return time to a central scheduling route. If any single process fails to return to the central scheduler, the computer will lock up. Both Windows and the Macintosh operating system use this scheme. See *Preemptive Multitasking, Windows for Workgroups 3.11*.

CPU See *Microprocessor*.

CSNW See *Client Services for NetWare*.

Data Link Control (DLC) An obsolete network transport protocol that allows PCs to connects to older IBM mainframes and HP printers. See *TCP/IP*.

Data Link Layer In the OSI model, the layer that provides the digital interconnection of network devices and the software that directly operates these devices, such as network interface adapters. See *Physical Layer, Network Layer, OSI Model*.

Database A related set of data organized by type and purpose. The term also can include the application software that manipulates the data. The Windows NT Registry (a database itself) contains a number of utility databases such as user account and security information. See *Registry*.

DDE   See *Dynamic Data Exchange.*

Default Shares   Resources shared by default when Windows NT is installed. See *Share, Resource.*

Desktop   A directory that the background of the Windows Explorer shell represents. By default the desktop contains objects that contain the local storage devices and available network shares. Also a key operating part of the Windows GUI. See *Explorer, Shell.*

DHCP   See *Dynamic Host Configuration Protocol.*

Dial-Up Connections   Data Link-layer digital connections made via modems over regular telephone lines. The term *dial-up* refers to temporary digital connections, as opposed to leased telephone lines, which provide permanent connections. See *Data Link Layer, Public Switched Telephone Network, Modem.*

Directories   In a file system directories are containers that store files or other directories. Mass storage devices have a root directory that contains all other directories, therefore creating a hierarchy of directories sometimes referred to as a *directory tree.* See *File, File System.*

Directory Replication   The process of copying a directory structure from an import computer to an export computer(s). Anytime changes are made to the export computer, the import computer(s) is automatically updated with the changes.

Disk Administrator   Graphical utility used to manage disks.

Disk Duplexing   Disk duplexing is similar to disk mirroring, but in addition to the features of disk mirroring, also uses two separate controllers for better performance and reliability. See *Disk Mirroring.*

Disk Mirroring   The process of keeping an exact duplicate of data on two different partitions located on different physical drives. Used for fault tolerance. See *Disk Duplexing.*

Disk Striping   Data that is stored across partitions of identical size on different drives. Also referred to as RAID 0. See *Redundant Array of Inexpensive Disks.*

Disk Striping with Parity   Disk striping with parity distributed across the stripe set for fault tolerance features. Also referred to as RAID 5. See *Stripe Set, Redundant Array of Inexpensive Disks.*

DLC See *Data Link Control.*

DNS See *Domain Name Service.*

Domain In Microsoft networks, a domain is an arrangement of client and server computers referenced by a specific name that share a single, security-permissions database. On the Internet, a domain is a named collection of hosts and subdomains, registered with a unique name by the InterNIC. See *Workgroup, InterNIC.*

Domain Controllers Servers that authenticate workstation network logon requests by comparing a username and password against account information stored in the user accounts database. A user cannot access a domain without authentication from a domain controller. See *Primary Domain Controller, Backup Domain Controller, Domain.*

Domain Name The textual identifier of a specific Internet Host. Domain names are in the form of **server.organization.type** (**www.microsoft.com**) and are resolved to Internet addresses by Domain Name Servers. See *Domain Name Server.*

Domain Name Server An Internet host dedicated to the function of translating fully qualified domain names into IP addresses. See *Domain Name.*

Domain Name Service (DNS) The TCP/IP network service that translates textual Internet network addresses into numerical Internet network addresses. See *TCP/IP, Internet.*

Drive See *Hard Disk Drive.*

Drive Letters Single letters assigned as abbreviations to the mass storage volumes available to a computer. See *Volumes.*

Driver A program that provides a software interface to a hardware device. Drivers are written for the specific device they control, but they present a common software interface to the computer's operating system, allowing all devices (of a similar type) to be controlled as if they were the same. See *Data Link Layer, Operating System.*

Dynamic Data Exchange (DDE) A method of interprocess communication within the Microsoft Windows operating systems.

Dynamic Host Configuration Protocol (DHCP) DHCP is a method of automatically assigning IP addresses to client computers on a network.

Electronic Mail (E-Mail)   A type of client/server application that provides a routed, stored-message service between any two user e-mail accounts. E-mail accounts are not the same as user accounts, but a one-to-one relationship usually exists between them. Because all modern computers can attach to the Internet, users can send e-mail over the Internet to any location that has telephone or wireless digital service. See *Internet*.

Emergency Repair Disk   A disk containing the critical system files (such as portions of the Registry, the **autoexec.bat** file, and the **config.sys** file) necessary to recover your NT machine in some cases.

Encryption   The process of obscuring information by modifying it according to a mathematical function known only to the intended recipient. Encryption secures information being transmitted over nonsecure or untrusted media. See *Security*.

Enterprise Network   A complex network consisting of multiple servers and multiple domains over a large geographic area.

Environment Variables   Variables, such as the search path, that contain information available to programs and batch files about the current operating system environment.

ERD   See *Emergency Repair Disk*.

Ethernet   The most popular Data Link-layer standard for local area networking. Ethernet implements the carrier sense multiple access with collision detection (CSMA/CD) method of arbitrating multiple computer access to the same network. This standard supports the use of Ethernet over any type of media including wireless broadcast. Standard Ethernet operates as 10 megabits per second. Fast Ethernet operates at 100 megabits per second. See *Data Link Layer*.

Exchange   Microsoft's messaging application. Exchange implements Microsoft's mail application programming interface (MAPI) as well as other messaging protocols such as POP, SNMP, and faxing to provide a flexible message composition and reception service. See *Electronic Mail, Fax Modem*.

Explorer   The default shell for Windows 95 and Windows NT 4.0. Explorer implements the more flexible desktop objects paradigm rather than the Program Manager paradigm used in earlier versions of Windows. See *Desktop*.

FAT   See *File Allocation Table*.

Fault Tolerance   Any method that prevents system failure by tolerating single faults, usually through hardware redundancy.

Fax Modems   Special modems that include hardware to allow the transmission and reception of facsimiles. See *Modem, Exchange.*

FDDI   See *Fiber Distributed Data Interface.*

Fiber Distributed Data Interface (FDDI)   A Data Link layer that implements two counter-rotating token rings at 100 megabits per second. FDDI was a popular standard for interconnecting campus and metropolitan area networks because it allows distant digital connections at high speed, but ATM is replacing FDDI in many sites. See *Asynchronous Transfer Mode, Data Link Layer.*

File Allocation Table (FAT)   The file system used by MS-DOS and available to other operating systems such as Windows (all versions), OS/2, and the Macintosh. FAT has become something of a mass storage compatibility standard because of its simplicity and wide availability. FAT has few fault tolerance features and can become corrupted through normal use over time. See *File System.*

File Attributes   Bits stored along with the name and location of a file in a directory entry that show the status of a file, such as archived, hidden, read-only, etc. Different operating systems use different file attributes to implement such services as sharing, compression, and security.

File System   A software component that manages the storage of files on a mass storage device by providing services that can create, read, write, and delete files. File systems impose an ordered database of files on the mass storage device, called volumes, that use hierarchies of directories to organize files. See *Mass Storage Device, Files, Database, Volumes, Directories.*

File Transfer Protocol (FTP)   A simple Internet protocol that transfers complete files from an FTP server to a client running the FTP client. FTP provides a simple no-overhead method of transferring files between computers but cannot perform browsing functions. You must know the URL of the FTP server to which you want to attach. See *Internet, Uniform Resource Locator.*

Files   A set of data stored on a mass storage device identified by a directory entry containing a name, file attributes, and the physical location of the file in the volume. See *Volume, Mass Storage Device, Directory, File Attributes.*

Firmware   Software stored permanently in nonvolatile memory and built into a computer to provide its BIOS and a bootstrap routine. Simple computers may have their entire operating system built into firmware. See *BIOS, Boot, Software*.

Format   The process of preparing a mass storage device for use with a file system. There are actually two levels of formatting. Low-level formatting writes a structure of sectors and tracks to the disk with bits used by the mass storage controller hardware. The controller hardware requires this format, and it is independent of the file system. High-level formatting creates file system structures such as an allocation table and a root directory in a partition, therefore creating a volume. See *Mass Storage Device, Volume*.

Frame   A data structure that network hardware devices use to transmit data between computers. Frames consist of the addresses of the sending and receiving computers, size information, and a check sum. Frames are envelopes around packets of data that allow the packets to be addressed to specific computers on a shared media network. See *Ethernet, FDDI, Token Ring*.

FTP   See *File Transfer Protocol*.

Gateway   A computer that serves as a router, a format translator, or a security filter for an entire network.

Gateway Services for NetWare (GSNW)   An NT Server service that is used to connect NT Servers and NT clients to NetWare resources via the gateway software. See *Gateway, NetWare, Client Services for NetWare*.

GDI   See *Graphical Device Interface*.

Global Group   A special group that only exists on NT Server domain controllers. A global group can only contain members from within its domain. See *Local Group*.

Gopher   Serves text and links to other Gopher sites. Gopher predates HTTP by about a year, but has been made obsolete by the richer format provided by HTTP. See *Hypertext Transfer Protocol*.

Graphical Device Interface (GDI)   The programming interface and graphical services provided to Win32 for programs to interact with graphical devices such as the screen and printer. See *Programming Interface, Win32*.

Graphical User Interface (GUI)   A computer shell program that represents mass storage devices, directories, and files as graphical objects on a screen. A cursor driven by a pointing device such as a mouse manipulates the objects. See *Shell, Explorer.*

Group Identifiers   Security identifiers that contain the set of permissions given to a group. When a user account is part of a group, the group identifier is appended to that user's security identifier, therefore granting the individual user all the permissions assigned to that group. See *Security Identifier, Accounts, Permissions.*

Groups   Security entities to which users can be assigned membership for the purpose of applying the broad set of group permissions to the user. By managing permissions for groups and assigning users to groups, rather than assigning permissions to users, security administrators can keep coherent control of very large security environments. See *Permissions, Accounts, Security, Local Group, Global Group.*

GSNW   See *Gateway Services for NetWare.*

GUI   See *Graphical User Interface.*

HAL   See *Hardware Abstraction Layer.*

Hard Disk   See *Hard Disk Drives.*

Hard Disk Drives   Mass storage devices that read and write digital information magnetically on disks that spin under moving heads. Hard disk drives are precisely aligned and cannot normally be removed. Hard disk drives are an inexpensive way to store gigabytes of computer data permanently. Hard disk drives also store the installed software of a computer. See *Mass Storage Device.*

Hardware Abstraction Layer (HAL)   A Windows NT service that provides basic input/output services such as timers, interrupts, and multiprocessor management for computer hardware. The HAL is a device driver for the motherboard circuitry that allows different families of computers to be treated the same by the Windows NT operating system. See *Driver, Service, Interrupt Request.*

Hardware Compatibility List (HCL)   The listing of all hardware devices supported by Windows NT. Hardware on the HCL has been tested and verified as being compatible with NT. You can view the current HCL at http://microsoft.com/ntserver/hcl.

Hardware Profiles Used to manage portable computers which have different configurations based on their location.

HCL See *Hardware Compatibility List*.

High Performance File System (HPFS) The file system native to OS/2 that performs many of the same functions of NTFS when run under OS/2. See *File System, New Technology File System*.

Home Directory A directory used to store users' personal files and programs.

Home Page The default page returned by an HTTP server when a URL containing no specific document is requested. See *Hypertext Transfer Protocol, Uniform Resource Locator*.

Host An Internet Server. Hosts are constantly connected to the Internet. See *Internet*.

HPFS See *High Performance File System*.

HTML See *Hypertext Markup Language*.

HTTP See *Hypertext Transfer Protocol*.

Hyperlink A link embedded in text or graphics that has a Web address embedded in it. By clicking the link, you jump to another Web address. You can identify a hyperlink because it is a different color from the rest of the Web page. See *World Wide Web*.

Hypertext Markup Language (HTML) A textual data format that identifies such sections of a document as headers, lists, hypertext links, etc. HTML is the data format used on the World Wide Web for the publication of Web pages. See *Hypertext Transfer Protocol, World Wide Web*.

Hypertext Transfer Protocol (HTTP) Hypertext transfer protocol is an Internet protocol that transfers HTML documents over the Internet and responds to context changes that happen when a user clicks on a hypertext link. See *Hypertext Markup Language, World Wide Web*.

Icon A graphical representation of a resource (in a graphical user interface) that usually takes the form of a small (32 × 32) bitmap. See *Graphical User Interface*.

IDE   A simple mass storage device interconnection bus that operates at 5Mbps and can handle no more than two attached devices. IDE devices are similar to but less expensive than SCSI devices. See *Small Computer Systems Interface, Mass Storage Device*.

IIS   See *Internet Information Server*.

Industry Standard Architecture (ISA)   The design standard for 16-bit Intel compatible motherboards and peripheral buses. The 32/64-bit PCI bus standard is replacing the ISA standard. Adapters and interface cards must conform to the bus standard(s) used by the motherboard in order to be used with a computer.

Integrated Services Digital Network (ISDN)   A direct, digital dial-up PSTN Data Link-layer connection that operates at 64K per channel over regular twisted-pair cable between a subscriber site and a PSTN central office. ISDN provides twice the data rate of the fastest modems per channel. Up to 24 channels can be multiplexed over two twisted pairs. See *Public Switched Telephone Network, Data Link Layer, Modem*.

Intel Architecture   A family of microprocessors descended from the Intel 8086, itself descended from the first microprocessor, the Intel 4004. The Intel architecture is the dominant microprocessor family. It was used in the original IBM PC microcomputer adopted by the business market and later adapted for home use.

Interactive User   A user who physically logs on to the computer where the user account resides is considered interactive, as opposed to a user who logs in over the network. See *Network User*.

Internet   A voluntarily interconnected global network of computers based on the TCP/IP protocol suite. TCP/IP was originally developed by the U.S. Department of Defense's Advanced Research Projects Agency to facilitate the interconnection of military networks and was provided free to universities. The obvious utility of worldwide digital network connectivity and the availability of free complex networking software developed at universities doing military research attracted other universities, research institutions, private organizations, businesses, and finally the individual home user. The Internet is now available to all current commercial computing platforms. See *FTP, Telnet, World Wide Web, TCP/IP*.

Internet Explorer   A World Wide Web browser produced by Microsoft and included free with Windows 95 and Windows NT 4.0. See *World Wide Web, Internet.*

Internet Information Server (IIS)   Serves Internet higher-level protocols like HTTP and FTP to clients using Web browsers. See *Hypertext Transfer Protocol, File Transfer Protocol, and World Wide Web.*

Internet Protocol (IP)   The Network layer protocol upon which the Internet is based. IP provides a simple connectionless packet exchange. Other protocols such as UDP or TCP use IP to perform their connection-oriented or guaranteed delivery services. See *TCP/IP, Internet.*

Internet Service Provider (ISP)   A company that provides dial-up connections to the Internet. See *Internet.*

Internetwork Packet eXchange (IPX)   The Network and Transport layer protocol developed by Novell for its NetWare product. IPX is a routable, connection-oriented protocol similar to TCP/IP but much easier to manage and with lower communication overhead. See *IP, NetWare, NWLink.*

InterNIC   The agency that is responsible for assigning IP addresses. See *Internet Protocol, IP Address.*

Interprocess Communications (IPC)   A generic term describing any manner of client/server communication protocol, specifically those operating in the application layer. Interprocess communications mechanisms provide a method for the client and server to trade information. See *Named Pipes, Remote Procedure Call, NetBIOS, Mailslots, NetDDE, Local Procedure Call.*

Interrupt Request (IRQ)   A hardware signal from a peripheral device to the microcomputer indicating that it has I/O traffic to send. If the microprocessor is not running a more important service, it will interrupt its current activity and handle the interrupt request. IBM PCs have 16 levels of interrupt request lines. Under Windows NT each device must have a unique interrupt request line. See *Microprocessor, Driver, Peripheral.*

Intranet   A privately owned network based on the TCP/IP protocol suite. See *Transmission Control Protocol/Internet Protocol.*

IP   See *Internet Protocol.*

IP Address   A 4-byte number that uniquely identifies a computer on an IP internetwork. InterNIC assigns the first bytes of Internet IP addresses and administers them in hierarchies. Huge organizations like the government or top-level ISPs have class A addresses, large organizations and most ISPs have class B addresses, and small companies have class C addresses. In a class A address, InterNIC assigns the first byte, and the owning organization assigns the remaining three bytes. In a class B address, InterNIC or the higher level ISP assigns the first two bytes, and the organization assigns the remaining two bytes. In a class C address, InterNIC or the higher level ISP assigns the first three bytes, and the organization assigns the remaining byte. Organizations not attached to the Internet are free to assign IP addresses as they please. See *IP, Internet, InterNIC.*

IPC   See *Interprocess Communications.*

IPX   See *Internetwork Packet eXchange.*

IRQ   See *Interrupt Request.*

ISA   See *Industry Standard Architecture.*

ISDN   See *Integrated Services Digital Network.*

ISP   See *Internet Service Provider.*

Kernel   The core process of a preemptive operating system, consisting of a multitasking scheduler and the basic security services. Depending upon the operating system, other services such as virtual memory drivers may be built into the Kernel. The Kernel is responsible for managing the scheduling of threads and processes. See *Operating System, Drivers.*

LAN   See *Local Area Network.*

LAN Manager   The Microsoft brand of a network product jointly developed by IBM and Microsoft that provided an early client/server environment. LAN Manager/Server was eclipsed by NetWare, but was the genesis of many important protocols and IPC mechanisms used today, such as NetBIOS, named pipes, and NetBEUI. Portions of this product exist today in OS/2 Warp Server. See *OS/2, Interprocess Communications.*

LAN Server   The IBM brand of a network product jointly developed by IBM and Microsoft. See *LAN Manager.*

Local Area Network (LAN)   A network of computers operating on the same high-speed, shared media network Data Link layer. The size of a local area network is defined by the limitations of high-speed, shared media networks to generally less than 1 kilometer in overall span. Some LAN backbone Data Link-layer protocols such as FDDI can create larger LANs called metropolitan or medium area networks (MANs). See *Wide Area Network, Data Link Layer.*

Local Group   A group that exists in an NT computer's local accounts database. Local groups can reside on NT Workstations or NT Servers and can contain users or global groups. See *Global Group.*

Local Printer   A local printer is a printer that uses a physical port and that has not been shared. If a printer is defined as local, the only users who can use the printer are the local users of the computer to which the printer is attached. See *Printer, Printing Device, Network Printer.*

Local Procedure Call (LPC)   A mechanism that loops remote procedure calls without the presence of a network so that the client and server portion of an application can reside on the same machine. Local procedure calls look like remote procedure calls (RPCs) to the client and server sides of a distributed application. See *Remote Procedure Call.*

Local Security   Security that governs a local or interactive user. Local security can be set through NTFS partitions. See *Security, Interactive User, New Technology File System, Network Security.*

LocalTalk   A Data Link-layer standard for local area networking used by Macintosh computers. LocalTalk is available on all Macintosh computers. The drawback of LocalTalk is that is only transmits at 230.4 kilobits per second (as opposed to Ethernet which can transmit at 10 megabits per second). See *Data Link Layer, Macintosh.*

Logging   The process of recording information about activities and errors in the operating system.

Logical Port   Printers can be attached to a network through a logical port. A logical port uses a direct connection to gain access to the network. This is done by installing a network card on the printer. The advantages to using logical ports are that they are much faster than physical ports and that you are not limited to the cabling limitations imposed by parallel and serial cable distances allowed when connecting a printer to a PC's parallel or serial ports. See *Printer, Printing Device.*

Logoff   The process of closing an open session with a server. See *Logon*.

Logon   The process of opening a network session by providing a valid authentication consisting of a user account name and a password to a domain controller. After logon, network resources are available to the user according to the user's assigned permissions. See *Domain Controller, Logoff*.

Logon Script   Command files that automate the logon process by performing utility functions such as attaching to additional server resources or automatically running different programs based on the user account that established the logon. See *Logon*.

Long Filename (LFN)   A filename longer than the eight characters plus a three-character extension allowed by MS-DOS. In Windows NT and Windows 95, long filenames may be up to 255 characters.

LPC   See *Local Procedure Call*.

Macintosh   A brand of computer manufactured by Apple Computers, Inc. Macintosh is the only successful line of computers neither based upon the original IBM PC nor running the UNIX operating system. Windows NT Server supports Apple computers despite their use of proprietary network protocols.

MacOS   The operating system that runs on an Apple Macintosh computer. See *Macintosh*.

Mailslots   A connectionless messaging IPC mechanism that Windows NT uses for browse request and logon authentication. See *Interprocess Communications*.

Mandatory User Profile   A profile created by an administrator and saved with a special extension (**.man**) so that the user cannot modify the profile in any way. Mandatory user profiles can be assigned to a single user or a group of users. See *User Profile*.

Mass Storage Device   Any device capable of storing many megabytes of information permanently, but especially those capable of random access to any portion of the information, such as hard disk drives and CD-ROM drives. See *SCSI, IDE, Hard Disk Drive, CD-ROM Drive*.

Master Browser   A network computer that keeps a list of computers and services available on the network and distributes the list to other browsers. The Master Browser may also promote potential browsers to be browsers. See *Browser, Browsing, Potential Browser, Backup Browser.*

Member Server   An NT server that has been installed as a nondomain controller. This allows the server to operate as a file, print and application server without the overhead of accounts administration.

Memory   Any device capable of storing information. This term is usually used to indicate volatile random access semiconductor memory (RAM) capable of high-speed access to any portion of the memory space, but incapable of storing information without power. See *Random Access Memory, Mass Storage Device.*

Microprocessor   An integrated semiconductor circuit designed to automatically perform lists of logical and arithmetic operations. Modern microprocessors independently manage memory pools and support multiple instruction lists called threads. Microprocessors are also capable of responding to interrupt requests from peripherals and include onboard support for complex floating point arithmetic. Microprocessors must have instructions when they are first powered on. These instructions are contained in nonvolatile firmware called a BIOS. See *BIOS, Operating System.*

Microsoft Disk Operating System (MS-DOS)   A 16-bit operating system designed for the 8086 chip that was used in the original IBM PC. MS-DOS is a simple program loader and file system that turns over complete control of the computer to the running program and provides very little service beyond file system support and that provided by the BIOS.

Migration Tool for NetWare   A utility used to migrate NetWare users, groups, file structures, and security to an NT domain. See *NetWare.*

Modem   Modulator/demodulator. A Data Link layer device used to create an analog signal suitable for transmission over telephone lines from a digital data stream. Modern modems also include a command set for negotiating connections and data rates with remote modems and for setting their default behavior. The fastest modems run at about 33Kbps. See *Data Link Layer.*

Module   A software component of a modular operating system that provides a certain defined service. Modules can be installed or removed depending upon the service requirements of the software running on the computer. Modules allow operating systems and applications to be customized to fit the needs of the user.

MPR   See *MultiProtocol Router.*

MS-DOS   See *Microsoft Disk Operating System.*

Multilink   A capability of RAS to combine multiple data streams into one network connection for the purpose of using more than one modem or ISDN channel in a single connection. This feature is new to Windows NT 4.0. See *Remote Access Service.*

Multiprocessing   Using two or more processors simultaneously to perform a computing task. Depending on the operating system, processing may be done asymmetrically, wherein certain processors are assigned certain threads independent of the load they create, or symmetrically, wherein threads are dynamically assigned to processors according to an equitable scheduling scheme. The term usually describes a multiprocessing capacity built into the computer at a hardware level in that the computer itself supports more than one processor. However, *multiprocessing* can also be applied to network computing applications achieved through interprocess communication mechanisms. Client/server applications are, in fact, examples of multiprocessing. See *Asymmetrical Multiprocessing, Symmetrical Multiprocessing, Interprocess Communications.*

MultiProtocol Router (MPR)   Services included with NT Server that allow you to route traffic between IPX and TCP/IP subnets. MPR also allows you to facilitate DHCP requests and forward BOOTP relay agents. See *Internetwork Packet Exchange, Transmission Control Protocol/Internet Protocol, Dynamic Host Configuration Protocol, Bootstrap Protocol.*

Multitasking   The capacity of an operating system to switch rapidly among threads of execution. Multitasking divides processor time among threads as if each thread ran on its own slower processor. Multitasking operating systems allow two or more applications to run at the same time and can provide a greater degree of service to applications than single-tasking operating systems like MS-DOS. See *Multiprocessing, Multithreading.*

Named Pipes   An interprocess communication mechanism implemented as a file system service, allowing programs to be modified to run on it without using a proprietary application programming interface. Named pipes were developed to support more robust client/server communications than those allowed by the simpler NetBIOS. See *OS/2, File Systems, Interprocess Communications.*

NDIS   See *Network Driver Interface Specification.*

NDS   See *NetWare Directory Services.*

NetBEUI   See *NetBIOS Extended User Interface.*

NetBIOS   See *Network Basic Input/Output System.*

NetBIOS Extended User Interface (NetBEUI)   A simple Network layer transport protocol developed to support NetBIOS installations. NetBEUI is not routable, and so it is not appropriate for larger networks. NetBEUI is the fastest transport protocol available for Windows NT.

NetBIOS Gateway   A service provided by RAS that allows NetBIOS requests to be forwarded independent of transport protocol. For example, NetBIOS requests from a remote computer connected via NetBEUI can be sent over the network via NWLink. See *Network Basic Input/Output System, NWLink, Net-BIOS over TCP/IP, NetBEUI.*

NetBIOS over TCP/IP (NetBT)   A network service that implements the Net-BIOS IPC over the TCP/IP protocol stack. See *NetBIOS, Interprocess Communications, TCP/IP.*

NetBT   See *NetBIOS over TCP/IP.*

NetDDE   See *Network Dynamic Data Exchange.*

NetWare   A popular network operating system developed by Novell in the early 1980s. NetWare is a cooperative, multitasking, highly optimized, dedicated-server network operating system that has client support for most major operating systems. Recent versions of NetWare include graphical client tools for management from client stations. At one time, NetWare accounted for more than 70 percent of the network operating system market. See *Windows NT, Client Services for Net-Ware, Gateway Services for NetWare, NWLink.*

NetWare Directory Services (NDS)   In NetWare a distributed hierarchy of network services such as servers, shared volumes, and printers. NetWare implements NDS as a directory structure having elaborate security and administration mechanisms. The CSNW provided in Windows NT 4.0 supports the NDS tree. See *NetWare, Client Services for NetWare, Gateway Services for NetWare*.

NetWare Link (NWLink)   A Windows NT transport protocol that implements Novell's IPX. NWLink is useful as a general purpose transport for Windows NT and for connecting to NetWare file servers through CSNW. See *Internetwork Packet eXchange, Client Services for NetWare, Gateway Services for NetWare*.

NetWare NetBIOS Link (NWNBLink)   NetBIOS implemented over NWLink. See *NetBIOS, NWLink, NetBT*.

Network   A group of computers connected via some digital medium for the purpose of exchanging information. Networks can be based on many types of media, such as twisted pair telephone-style cable, optical fiber, coaxial cable, radio, or infrared light. Certain computers are usually configured as service providers called *servers*. Computers that perform user tasks directly and that utilize the services of servers are called *clients*. See *Client/Server, Server, Network Operating System*.

Network Basic Input/Output System (NetBIOS)   A client/server interprocess communication service developed by IBM in the early 1980s. NetBIOS presents a relatively primitive mechanism for communication in client server/ applications, but its widespread acceptance and availability across most operating systems makes it a logical choice for simple network applications. Many of the network IPC mechanisms in Windows NT are implemented over NetBIOS. See *Interprocess Communication, Client/Server*.

Network Client Administrator   A utility within the Administrative Tools group that can be used to make installation startup disks, make installation disk sets, copy client-based administration tools, and view remoteboot information.

Network Driver Interface Specification (NDIS)   A Microsoft specification to which network adapter drivers must conform in order to work with Microsoft network operating systems. NDIS provides a many-to-many binding between network adapter drivers and transport protocols. See *Transport Protocol*.

Network Dynamic Data Exchange (NetDDE) An interprocess communication mechanism developed by Microsoft to support the distribution of DDE applications over a network. See *Interprocess Communication, DDE*.

Network Interface Card (NIC) A Physical layer adapter device that allows a computer to connect to and communicate over a local area network. See *Ethernet, Token Ring, Adapter*.

Network Layer The layer of the OSI model that creates a communication path between two computers via routed packets. Transport protocols implement both the Network layer and the Transport layer of the OSI stack. IP is a Network layer service. See *Internet Protocol, Transport Protocol, Open Systems Interconnect Model*.

Network Monitor A utility used to capture and display network traffic.

Network Operating System A computer operating system specifically designed to optimize a computer's ability to respond to service requests. Servers run network operating systems. Windows NT Server and NetWare are both network operating systems. See *Windows NT, Server, NetWare*.

Network Printer A network printer can use physical or logical ports. By defining a printer as a network printer, you make the printer available to local and network users. See *Printer, Printing Device, Local Printer*.

Network Security Security that governs a network. See *Security, Network User, Local Security*.

Network User A user who logs on to the network using the SAM from a remote domain controller. See *Interactive User*.

New Technology File System (NTFS) A secure, transaction-oriented file system developed for Windows NT that incorporates the Windows NT security model for assigning permissions and shares. NTFS is optimized for hard drives larger than 500MB and requires too much overhead to be used on hard disk drives smaller than 50MB.

Nonbrowser A computer on a network that will not maintain a list of other computers and services on the network. See *Browser, Browsing*.

NT Directory Services The synchronized SAM database that exists between the PDC and the BDCs within a domain. Directory Services also controls the trust relationships that exist between domains. See *Security Accounts Manager, Primary Domain Controller, Backup Domain Controller, Trust Relationship*.

NTFS   See *New Technology File System.*

NWLink   See *NetWare Link, Internetwork Packet eXchange.*

NWNBLink   See *NetWare NetBIOS Link.*

Object   A software service provider that encapsulates both the algorithm and the data structures necessary to provide a service. Usually, objects can inherit data and functionality from their parent objects, therefore allowing complex services to be constructed from simpler objects. The term *object oriented* implies a tight relationship between algorithms and data structures. See *Module.*

Object Counters   Containers built into each service object in Windows NT that store a count of the number of times an object performs its service or to what degree. You can use performance monitors to access object counters and measure how the different objects in Windows NT are operating. See *Object.*

Open Graphics Language (OpenGL)   A standard interface for the presentation of two- and three-dimensional visual data.

Open Systems Interconnect Model (OSI Model)   A model for network component interoperability developed by the International Standards Organization to promote cross-vendor compatibility of hardware and software network systems. The OSI model splits the process of networking into seven distinct services. Each layer uses the services of the layer below to provide its service to the layer above. See *Physical Layer, Data Link Layer, Network Layer, Transport Layer, Session Layer, Presentation Layer, Application Layer.*

OpenGL   See *Open Graphics Language.*

Operating System   A collection of services that form a foundation upon which applications run. Operating systems may be simple I/O service providers with a command shell, such as MS-DOS, or they may be sophisticated, preemptive, multitasking, multiprocessing applications platforms like Windows NT. See *Network Operating System, Preemptive Multitasking, Kernel.*

Operating System 2 (OS/2)   A 16-bit (and later, 32-bit) operating system developed jointly by Microsoft and IBM as a successor to MS-DOS. Microsoft bowed out of the 32-bit development effort and produced its own product, Windows NT, as a competitor to OS/2. OS/2 is now a preemptive, multitasking 32-bit operating system with strong support for networking and the ability to run MS-DOS and Win16 applications, but IBM has been unable to entice a large number of developers to produce software that runs native under OS/2. See *Operating System, Preemptive Multitasking.*

Optimization   Any effort to reduce the workload on a hardware component by eliminating, obviating, or reducing the amount of work required of the hardware component through any means. For instance, file caching is an optimization that reduces the workload of a hard disk drive.

OS/2   See *Operating System 2*.

OSI Model   See *Open Systems Interconnect Model*.

Owner   Used in conjunction with NTFS volumes. All NTFS files and directories have an associated owner who is able to control access and grant permissions to other users. See *New Technology File System*.

Page File   See *Swap File*.

Partition   A section of a hard disk that can contain an independent file system volume. Partitions can be used to keep multiple operating systems and file systems on the same hard disk. See *Volume, Hard Disk Drive*.

Password   A secret code used to validate the identity of a user of a secure system. Passwords are used in tandem with account names to log on to most computer systems.

PC   See *Personal Computer*.

PCI   See *Peripheral Connection Interface*.

PDC   See *Primary Domain Controller*.

Peer   A networked computer that both shares resources with other computers and accesses the shared resources of other computers. A nondedicated server. See *Server, Client*.

Performance Monitor   A utility provided with NT that provides graphical statistics that can be used to measure performance on your computer.

Peripheral   An input/output device attached to a computer. Peripherals can be printers, hard disk drives, monitors, and so on.

Peripheral Connection Interface (PCI)   A high-speed 32/64-bit bus interface developed by Intel and widely accepted as the successor to the 16-bit ISA interface. PCI devices support I/O throughput about 40 times faster than the ISA bus.

Permissions   Security constructs used to regulate access to resources by user name or group affiliation. Permissions can be assigned by administrators to allow any level of access, such as read-only, read/write, delete, etc., by controlling the ability of users to initiate object services. Security is implemented by checking the user's security identifier against each object's access control list. See *Security Identifier, Access Control List.*

Personal Computer (PC)   A microcomputer used by one person at a time (not a multiuser computer). PCs are generally clients or peers in a networked environment. High-speed PCs are called workstations. Networks of PCs are called local area networks. The term PC is often used to refer to computers compatible with the IBM PC.

Physical Layer   The cables, connectors, and connection ports of a network. The passive physical components required to create a network. See *OSI Model.*

Physical Port   Printers can be connected directly to a computer through a serial (COM) or parallel (LPT) port. If a printer is connected in this manner, it is using a physical port. See *Printer, Print Device.*

Point-to-Point Protocol (PPP)   A Network-layer transport that performs over point-to-point network connections such as serial or modem lines. PPP can negotiate any transport protocol used by both systems involved in the link and can automatically assign IP, DNS, and gateway addresses when used with TCP/IP. See *Internet Protocol, Domain Name Service, Gateway.*

Point-to-Point Tunneling Protocol (PPTP)   Protocol used to connect to corporate networks through the Internet or an ISP. See *Internet, Internet Service Provider.*

Policies   General controls that enhance the security of an operating environment. In Windows NT, policies affect restrictions on password use and rights assignment and determine which events will be recorded in the Security log.

Potential Browser   A computer on a network that may maintain a list of other computers and services on the network if requested to do so by a Master Browser. See *Browser, Master Browser.*

PowerPC   A microprocessor family developed by IBM to compete with the Intel family of microprocessors. The PowerPC is a RISC-architecture microprocessor with many advanced features that emulate other microprocessors. PowerPCs are currently used in a line of IBM computers and in the Apple Power Macintosh. Windows NT is available for the PowerPC.

PPP   See *Point-to-Point Protocol.*

PPTP   See *Point-to-Point Tunneling Protocol.*

Preemptive Multitasking   A multitasking implementation in which an interrupt routine in the Kernel manages the scheduling of processor time among running threads. The threads themselves do not need to support multitasking in any way because the microprocessor will preempt the thread with an interrupt, save its state, update all thread priorities according to its scheduling algorithm, and pass control to the highest priority thread awaiting execution. Because of the preemptive nature of the implementation, a thread that crashes will not affect the operation of other executing threads. See *Kernel, Thread, Operating System, Process.*

Preferences   Characteristics of user accounts, such as password, profile location, home directory and logon script.

Presentation Layer   The layer of the OSI model that converts and translates (if necessary) information between the Session and Application layers. See *OSI Model.*

Primary Domain Controller (PDC)   The domain server that contains the master copy of the security, computer, and user accounts databases and that can authenticate workstations. The PDC can replicate its databases to one or more backup domain controllers. The PDC is usually also the Master Browser for the domain. See *Backup Domain Controller, Domain, Master Browser.*

Print Device   A print device is the actual physical printer or hardware device to which you will print. See *Printer.*

Print Driver   Each printing device has its own command set. The print driver is the specific software that understands your print device. Each print device has an associated print driver. See *Print Device.*

Print Processor   Once a print job has been sent to the spooler, the print processor looks at the print job and determines whether or not the job needs further processing. The processing (also called rendering) is used to format the print job so that it can print correctly at the print device. See *Print Spooler.*

Print Server   Print servers are the computers on which the printers have been defined. When you send a job to a network printer, you are actually sending it to the print server first. See *Printer, Print Device.*

Print Spooler (Print Queue)   The print spooler is a directory or folder on the Print Server that actually stores the print jobs until they can be printed. It's very important that your Print Server and Print Spooler have enough hard disk space to hold all of the print jobs that could be pending at any given time. See *Print Server*.

Printer   In NT terminology, a printer is the software interface between the physical printer (see print device) and the operating system. You can create printers through the Printers folder. See *Print Device*.

Printing Pool   Printing pools are created when you have more than one printing device associated with a single printer. Printing pools can be used when you have printers that all use the same print driver that are in the same location. By using printing pools, you are then able to send your print job to the first available printer. See *Printer, Print Device*.

Priority   A level of execution importance assigned to a thread. In combination with other factors, the priority level determines how often that thread will get computer time according to a scheduling algorithm. See *Preemptive Multitasking*.

Process   A running program containing one or more threads. A process encapsulates the protected memory and environment for its threads.

Processor   A circuit designed to automatically perform lists of logical and arithmetic operations. Unlike a microprocessor, a processor may be designed from discrete components rather than be a monolithic integrated circuit. See *Microprocessor*.

Program   A list of processor instructions designed to perform a certain function. A running program is called a process. A package of one or more programs and attendant data designed to meet a certain application is called software. See *Software, Application, Process, Microprocessor*.

Programming Interfaces   Interprocess communications mechanisms that provide certain high-level services to running processes. Programming interfaces may provide network communication, graphical presentation, or any other type of software service. See *Interprocess Communication*.

Protocol   An established rule of communication adhered to by the parties operating under it. Protocols provide a context in which to interpret communicated information. Computer protocols are rules used by communicating devices and software services to format data in a way that all participants understand. See *Transport Protocol*.

PSTN   See *Public Switched Telephone Network*.

Public Switched Telephone Network (PSTN)   A global network of interconnected digital and analog communication links originally designed to support voice communication between any two points in the world, but quickly adapted to handle digital data traffic when the computer revolution occurred. In addition to its traditional voice support role, the PSTN now functions as the Physical layer of the Internet by providing dial-up and leased lines for the interconnections. See *Internet, Modem, Physical Layer*.

RAID   See *Redundant Array of Inexpensive Disks*.

RAID Controllers   Hard disk drive controllers that implement RAID in hardware. See *Redundant Array of Inexpensive Disks*.

RAM   See *Random Access Memory*.

Random Access Memory (RAM)   Integrated circuits that store digital bits in massive arrays of logical gates or capacitors. RAM is the primary memory store for modern computers, storing all running software processes and contextual data. See *Microprocessor*.

RARP   See *Reverse Address Resolution Protocol*.

RAS   See *Remote Access Service*.

Real-Time Application   A process that must respond to external events at least as fast as those events can occur. Real-time threads must run at very high priorities to ensure their ability to respond in real time. See *Process*.

Redirector   A software service that redirects user file I/O requests over the network. Novell implements the Workstation service and Client services for NetWare as redirectors. Redirectors allow servers to be used as mass storage devices that appear local to the user. See *Client Services for NetWare, File System*.

Reduced Instruction Set Computer (RISC)   A microprocessor technology that implements fewer and more primitive instructions than typical microprocessors and can, therefore, be implemented quickly with the most-modern semiconductor technology and speeds. Programs written for RISC microprocessors require more instructions (longer programs) to perform the same task as a normal microprocessor but are capable of a greater degree of optimization and therefore usually run faster. See *Microprocessor*.

Redundant Array of Inexpensive Disks (RAID)   A group of hard disk drives, coordinated by a special controller, that appears as one physical disk to a computer but stores its data across all the disks to take advantage of the speed and/or fault tolerance afforded by using more than one disk. RAID disk storage has several levels, including 0 (striping), 1 (mirroring), and 5 (striping with parity). RAID systems are typically used for very large storage volumes or to provide fault-tolerance features such as hot swapping of failed disks or automatically backing up data onto replacement disks.

Registry   A database of settings required and maintained by Windows NT and its components. The Registry contains all of the configuration information used by the computer. It is stored as a hierarchical structure and is made up of keys, hives, and value entries. You can use the Registry Editor (REGEDT32 command) to change these settings.

Remote Access Service (RAS)   A service that allows network connections to be established over PSTN lines with modems. The computer initiating the connection is called the RAS client; the answering computer is called the RAS host. See *Modem, Public Switched Telephone Network*.

Remote Procedure Calls (RPC)   A network interprocess communication mechanism that allows an application to be distributed among many computers on the same network. See *Local Procedure Call, Interprocess Communications*.

Remoteboot   The remoteboot service is used to start diskless workstations over the network.

Requests for Comments (RFCs)   The set of standards defining the Internet protocols as determined by the Internet Engineering Task Force and available in the public domain on the Internet. RFCs define the functions and services provided by each of the many Internet protocols. Compliance with the RFCs guarantees cross-vendor compatibility. See *Internet*.

Resource   Any useful service, such as a shared network directory or a printer. See *Share*.

Reverse Address Resolution Protocol (RARP)   The TCP/IP protocol which allows a computer that has a Physical-layer address (such as an Ethernet address), but does not have an IP address to request a numeric IP address from another computer on the network. See *TCP/IP*.

RFC   See *Request For Comments*.

RIP   See *Routing Information Protocol*.

RISC   See *Reduced Instruction Set Computer*.

Roaming User Profile   A user profile that is stored and configured to be downloaded from a server. The purpose of roaming user profiles is to allow a user to access his or her profile from any location on the network. See *User Profile*.

Router   A Network layer device that moves packets between networks. Routers provide internetwork connectivity. See *Network Layer*.

Routing Information Protocol (RIP)   A protocol within the TCP/IP protocol suite that allows routers to exchange routing information with other routers. See *Transmission Control Protocol/Internet Protocol*.

RPC   See *Remote Procedure Calls*.

SAM   See *Security Accounts Manager*.

Scheduling   The process of determining which threads should be executed according to their priority and other factors. See *Preemptive Multitasking*.

SCSI   See *Small Computer Systems Interface*.

Search Engine   Web sites dedicated to responding to requests for specific information, searching massive locally stored databases of Web pages, and responding with the URLs of pages that fit the search phrase. See *World Wide Web, Universal Resource Locator*.

Security   The measures taken to secure a system against accidental or intentional loss, usually in the form of accountability procedures and use restriction. See *Security Identifiers, Security Accounts Manager*.

Security Accounts Manager (SAM)   The module of the Windows NT executive that authenticates a username and password against a database of accounts, generating an access token that includes the user's permissions. See *Security, Security Identifier, Access Token.*

Security Identifiers (SID)   Unique codes that identify a specific user or group to the Windows NT security system. Security identifiers contain a complete set of permissions for that user or group.

Serial   A method of communication that transfers data across a medium one bit at a time, usually adding stop, start, and check bits to ensure quality transfer. See *COM Port, Modem.*

Serial Line Internet Protocol (SLIP)   An implementation of the IP protocol over serial lines. SLIP has been obviated by PPP. See *Point-to-Point Protocol, Internet Protocol.*

Server   A computer dedicated to servicing requests for resources from other computers on a network. Servers typically run network operating systems such as Windows NT Server or NetWare. See *Windows NT, NetWare, Client/ Server.*

Server Manager   Utility in the Administrative Tools group used to manage domains and computers.

Service   A process dedicated to implementing a specific function for another process. Most Windows NT components are services used by User-level applications.

Services for Macintosh   A service available through NT Server that allows Macintosh users to take advantage of NT file and print services. See *Macintosh.*

Session Layer   The layer of the OSI model dedicated to maintaining a bidirectional communication connection between two computers. The Session layer uses the services of the Transport layer to provide this service. See *OSI Model, Transport Layer.*

Share   A resource (e.g., directory, printer) shared by a server or a peer on a network. See *Resource, Server, Peer.*

Shell   The user interface of an operating system; the shell launches applications and manages file systems.

SID   See *Security Identifier*.

Simple Mail Transfer Protocol (SMTP)   An Internet protocol for transferring mail between Internet Hosts. SMTP is often used to upload mail directly from the client to an Intermediate host, but can only be used to receive mail by computers constantly connected to the Internet. See *Internet*.

Simple Network Management Protocol (SNMP)   An Internet protocol that manages network hardware such as routers, switches, servers, and clients from a single client on the network. See *Internet Protocol*.

Site   A related collection of HTML documents at the same Internet address, usually oriented toward some specific information or purpose. See *Hypertext Markup Language, Internet*.

SLIP   See *Serial Line Internet Protocol*.

Small Computer Systems Interface (SCSI)   A high-speed, parallel-bus interface that connects hard disk drives, CD-ROM drives, tape drives, and many other peripherals to a computer. SCSI is the mass storage connection standard among all computers except IBM compatibles, which use SCSI or IDE.

SMTP   See *Simple Mail Transfer Protocol*.

SNMP   See *Simple Network Management Protocol*.

Software   A suite of programs sold as a unit and dedicated to a specific application. See *Program, Application, Process*.

Spooler   A service that buffers output to a low-speed device such as a printer so the software outputting to the device is not tied up waiting for it.

Stripe Set   A single volume created across multiple hard disk drives and accessed in parallel for the purpose of optimizing disk access time. NTFS can create stripe sets. See *NTFS, Volume, File System*.

Subdirectory   A directory contained in another directory. See *Directory*.

Subnet Mask   A number mathematically applied to Internet protocol addresses to determine which IP addresses are a part of the same subnetwork as the computer applying the subnet mask.

Surf   To browse the Web randomly looking for interesting information. See *World Wide Web*.

Swap File The virtual memory file on a hard disk containing the memory pages that have been moved out to disk to increase available RAM. See *Virtual Memory*.

Symmetrical Multiprocessing A multiprocessing methodology wherein processes are assigned to processors on a fair share basis. This balances the processing load among processors and ensures that no processor will become a bottleneck. Symmetrical Multiprocessing is more difficult to implement than Asymmetrical multiprocessing as certain hardware functions such as interrupt handling must be shared between processors. See *Asymmetrical Multiprocessing, Multiprocessing*.

System Partition The system partition is the active partition on an Intel based computer that contains the hardware specific files used to load the NT operating system. See *Partition, Boot Partition*.

System Policy A policy used to control what a user can do and the user's environment. System policies can be applied to a specific user, group, a computer, or all users. System policies work by overwriting current settings in the Registry with the system policy settings. System policies are created through the System Policy Editor. See *Registry, System Policy Editor*.

System Policy Editor A utility found within the Administrative Tools group used to create system policies. See *System Policies*.

Task Manager An application that manually views and closes running processes. Task Manager can also be used to view CPU and memory statistics. Press Ctrl+Alt+Del to launch the Task Manager.

TCP See *Transmission Control Protocol*.

TCP/IP See *Transmission Control Protocol/Internet Protocol*.

TDI See *Transport Driver Interface*.

Telnet A terminal application that allows a user to log into a multiuser UNIX computer from any computer connected to the Internet. See *Internet*.

Thread A list of instructions running in a computer to perform a certain task. Each thread runs in the context of a process, which embodies the protected memory space and the environment of the threads. Multithreaded processes can perform more than one task at the same time. See *Process, Preemptive Multitasking, Program*.

Throughput   The measure of information flow through a system in a specific time frame, usually one second. For instance, 28.8Kbps is the throughput of a modem: 28.8 kilobits per second can be transmitted.

Token Ring   The second most popular Data Link-layer standard for local area networking. Token Ring implements the token passing method of arbitrating multiple-computer access to the same network. Token Ring operates at either 4 or 16Mbps. FDDI is similar to Token Ring and operates at 100Mbps. See *Data Link Layer*.

Transmission Control Protocol (TCP)   A Transport-layer protocol that implements guaranteed packet delivery using the Internet Protocol (IP). See *TCP/IP, Internet Protocol*.

Transmission Control Protocol/Internet Protocol (TCP/IP)   A suite of Internet protocols upon which the global Internet is based. TCP/IP is a general term that can refer either to the TCP and IP protocols used together or to the complete set of Internet protocols. TCP/IP is the default protocol for Windows NT.

Transport Driver Interface (TDI)   A specification to which all Windows NT transport protocols must be written in order to be used by higher-level services such as programming interfaces, file systems, and interprocess communications mechanisms. See *Transport Protocol*.

Transport Layer   The OSI model layer responsible for the guaranteed serial delivery of packets between two computers over an internetwork. TCP is the Transport-layer protocol for the TCP/IP transport protocol.

Transport Protocol   A service that delivers discreet packets of information between any two computers in a network. Higher level connection-oriented services are built upon transport protocols. See *TCP/IP, NWLink, NetBEUI, Transport Layer, IP, TCP, Internet*.

Trust Relationship   An administrative link that joins two or more domains. With a trust relationship, users can access resources in another domain if they have rights, even if they do not have a user account in the resource domain.

UDP   See *User Datagram Protocol*.

UNC   See *Universal Naming Convention*.

Uniform Resource Locator (URL)   An Internet standard naming convention for identifying resources available via various TCP/IP application protocols. For example, http://www.microsoft.com is the URL for Microsoft's World Wide Web server site, while ftp://gateway.dec.com is a popular FTP site. A URL allows easy hypertext references to a particular resource from within a document or mail message. See *HTTP, World Wide Web.*

Universal Naming Convention (UNC)   A multivendor, multiplatform convention for identifying shared resources on a network.

UNIX   A multitasking, kernel-based operating system developed at AT&T in the early 1970s and provided (originally) free to universities as a research operating system. Because of its availability and ability to scale down to microprocessor-based computers, UNIX became the standard operating system of the Internet and its attendant network protocols and is the closest approximation to a universal operating system that exists. Most computers can run some variant of the UNIX operating system. See *Multitasking, Internet.*

User Datagram Protocol (UDP)   A nonguaranteed network packet protocol implemented on IP that is far faster than TCP because of its lack of flow-control overhead. UDP can be implemented as a reliable transport when some higher-level protocol (such as NetBIOS) exists to make sure that required data will eventually be retransmitted in local area environments. At the Transport layer of the OSI model, UDP is connectionless service and TCP is connection-oriented service. See *Transmission Control Protocol.*

User Manager for Domains   A Windows NT application that administers user accounts, groups, and security policies at the domain level.

User Profile   Used to save each user's desktop configuration. See *Roaming Profile, Mandatory Profile.*

User Rights Policies   Used to determine what rights users and groups have when trying to accomplish network tasks. User Rights Policies are set through User Manager for Domains. See *User Manager for Domains.*

Username   A user's account name in a logon-authenticated system. See *Security.*

VDM   See *Virtual DOS Machine.*

Virtual DOS Machine (VDM)   The DOS environment created by Windows NT for the execution of DOS and Win16 applications. See *MS-DOS, Win16*.

Virtual Memory   A kernel service that stores memory pages not currently in use on a mass storage device to free up the memory occupied for other uses. Virtual memory hides the memory swapping process from applications and higher level services. See *Swap File, Kernel*.

Volume   A collection of data indexed by directories containing files and referred to by a drive letter. Volumes are normally contained in a single partition, but volume sets and stripe sets extend a single volume across multiple partitions.

WAN   See *Wide Area Network*.

Web Browser   An application that makes HTTP requests and formats the resultant HTML documents for the users. The preeminent Internet Client, most Web browsers understand all standard Internet protocols. See *Hypertext Transfer Protocol, Hypertext Markup Language, Internet*.

Web Page   Any HTML document on an HTTP server. See *Hypertext Transfer Protocol, Hypertext Markup Language, Internet*.

Wide Area Network (WAN)   A geographically dispersed network of networks, connected by routers and communication links. The Internet is the largest WAN. See *Internet, Local Area Network*.

Win16   The set of application services provided by the 16-bit versions of Microsoft Windows: Windows 3.1 and Windows for Workgroups 3.11.

Win32   The set of application services provided by the 32-bit versions of Microsoft Windows: Windows 95 and Windows NT.

Windows 3.11 for Workgroups   The current 16-bit version of Windows for less-powerful, Intel-based personal computers; this system includes peer networking services.

Windows 95   The current 32-bit version of Microsoft Windows for medium-range, Intel-based personal computers; this system includes peer networking services, Internet support, and strong support for older DOS applications and peripherals.

Windows Internet Name Service (WINS)   A network service for Microsoft networks that provides Windows computers with Internet numbers for specified NetBIOS names, facilitating browsing and intercommunication over TCP/IP networks.

Windows NT   The current 32-bit version of Microsoft Windows for powerful Intel, Alpha, PowerPC, or MIPS-based computers; the system includes peer networking services, server networking services, Internet client and server services, and a broad range of utilities.

Windows Sockets   An interprocess communications protocol that delivers connection-oriented data streams used by Internet software and software ported from UNIX environments. See *Interprocess Communications*.

WINS   See *Windows Internet Name Service*.

Workgroup   In Microsoft networks, a collection of related computers, such as a department, that don't require the uniform security and coordination of a domain. Workgroups are characterized by decentralized management as opposed to the centralized management that domains use. See *Domain*.

Workstation   A powerful personal computer, usually running a preemptive, multitasking operating system like UNIX or Windows NT.

World Wide Web (WWW)   A collection of Internet servers providing hypertext formatted documents for Internet clients running Web browsers. The World Wide Web provided the first easy-to-use graphical interface for the Internet and is largely responsible for the Internet's explosive growth.

Write-Back Caching   A caching optimization wherein data written to the slow store is cached until the cache is full or until a subsequent write operation overwrites the cached data. Write-back caching can significantly reduce the write operations to a slow store because many write operations are subsequently obviated by new information. Data in the write-back cache is also available for subsequent reads. If something happens to prevent the cache from writing data to the slow store, the cache data will be lost. See *Caching*, *Write-Through Caching*.

Write-Through Caching   A caching optimization wherein data written to a slow store is kept in a cache for subsequent re-reading. Unlike write-back caching, write-through caching immediately writes the data to the slow store and is, therefore, less optimal but more secure.

WWW   See World Wide Web.

X.25   A standard that defines packet-switching networks.

Index

Note to the Reader: Throughout this index **boldfaced** page numbers indicate primary discussions of a topic. *Italicized* page numbers indicate illustrations.

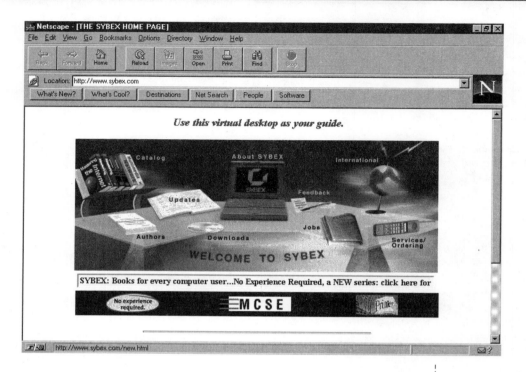